BATTALION

A British Infantry Unit's actions from El Alamein to the Elbe. 1942–1945

The 5th Battalion The Seaforth Highlanders

BATTALI

A British Infantry Unit's actions from El Alamein to the Elbe. 1942–1945

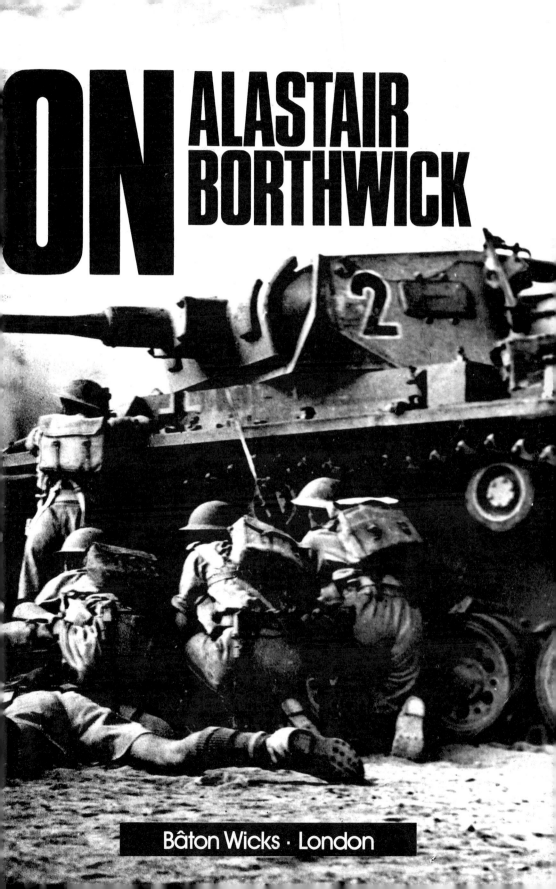

ON ALASTAIR BORTHWICK

Bâton Wicks · London

TO

LIEUTENANT COLONEL JACK WALFORD D.S.O.

First published as *Sans Peur* in 1946 by Eneas Mackay, Stirling

First published as *Battalion* in 1994 by Bâton Wicks Publications, London

All trade enquiries to: Cordee, 3a DeMontfort Street, Leicester

Cover illustration: The 5th Seaforths in Bremervörde in 1945.
Title page illustration: Infantrymen sheltering behind a knocked-out German tank at El Alamein − probably a staged publicity photo that nevertheless conveys some of the atmosphere during the battle. Photos: Imperial War Museum.

British Library Cataloguing in Publication Data:
Borthwick, Alastair
  Battalion: A British Infantry Unit's
  Actions from El Alamein to the Elbe,
  1942 − 1945. − 2Rev. ed
  I. Title
  940.54

ISBN 1-898573-00-X

Printed and bound in Great Britain by Butler and Tanner, Frome, Somerset

Contents

Maps and Diagrams in the Text

ACKNOWLEDGEMENTS   I could not have prepared this new edition without the help of Lt.Colonel A.A.Fairrie, who gave me the run of the Regimental Archive and helped in many other ways. Brigadier G.L.W.Andrews, who carried a camera in action, still had his negetives and made me free of them. The Imperial War Museum provided official photographs and the Museum's Ms Jane Carmichael gave me valuable support. I must also thank Major H.Barker M.B.E. of the Seaforth Highlanders' Regimental Association for his help.

   I acknowledge my debt to those who allowed their written material to be quoted, notably Major J.H.Davidson, Major Richard Fleming, Captain A.Grant Murray, Captain P.D.Nairne (who also contributed the sketch on page 98), Corporal G.S.Parkinson and Captain J.F.Watt. Others are quoted verbally (and named in the text) and are not listed here, but I acknowledge the debt I owe them all.

   Finally I should thank those who have assisted my publisher with advice in preparing this new volume: notably Major General James Moulton, Colonel John Peacock, Richard Hale, Iain Carmichael, James Gunn Henderson, Major Hugh Robertson, Lauchlan Gordon Duff, Mrs May Gardiner and Max Hastings, who allowed his favourable comments about the book to be used for publicity.

   A full list of photo credits follows: Imperial War Museum – 2/3, 8/9, 20/21, 29(2), 34/35, 46(2), 76/77, 114/115, 138/139, 154/155, 166/167, 182/183, 194/195, 196, 205(lower), 208/209, 210(2), 226/227, 244/245, 246, 258;   Regimental Archive – 13(3), 46(tr), 106/107, 126/127, 136(2), 156, 174, 184, 205(2), 228;   Brigadier G.L.W.Andrews – 33, 44/45, 51, 56/57, 58, 62, 66/67, 68, 70, 73, 74/75, 78, 84/85, 94/95, 96, 103, 104(2), 258(inset);   Major L.G.Begg 257.

INTRODUCTION

AN INFANTRY BATTALION in the Second World War had nine hundred or so men in it, nearly all of them civilians in uniform; and their battalion was their home. Everyone knew everyone else. Everyone had his place. Everything was familiar. Generals might think in terms of divisions or brigades but the infantryman's war was fought by battalions.

This book tells the story of one of them, the 5th Seaforths, starting at Alamein and ending on the Elbe, which is a very long way. They covered three thousand miles and fought two dozen actions while they were about it; and this from the battalion-eye viewpoint is how they did it.

The trouble about writing this kind of book is that when a war is over the last thing anyone wants to think about is the past: while you wait to be demobilised you dream about the future. Then everybody goes home with his tales untold and all the evidence – the how and the why and what it felt like – is scattered. This book was possible because John Sym, who commanded the 5th Seaforths towards the end of the war, realised that it would happen as usual unless he did something about it. He knew I had written before the war. He knew the Battalion would remain intact for the six months it would take for demobilisation to get under way. If he let me off all parades after the shooting stopped, would I write him a history? I found a cottage in Altenbruch near Cuxhaven and began writing, with the Battalion billeted around me and eye-witnesses on call by the hundred. I finished in November on the day before I was demobbed. Soon after that everyone had gone.

The readers I had in mind were the men of the Battalion and their relatives and friends – people who would want to remember who had done what; and there was the Regiment, which would want a true account for its bookshelves. So it had to be a proper history, with the names and the times and the places. But it seemed a pity to leave out the way to brew tea in the Desert, and the Pipie's beard, and what a barrage felt like, so I put these in as well. The book was published under the title *Sans Peur*, the Battalion motto. It was soon out of print, and has remained so ever since.

Looking at it now, half a century on, I am struck by the length of the tale. I set out simply to record the facts; but the facts piled up, battle after skirmish after battle, and there we were still slogging along, still with battles ahead, still regarding it all as normal. It is this, the endlessness of what we were called upon to do, that I hope comes through to the modern reader.

There was talk at one time of rewriting *Sans Peur*, but I was against it. The old story was true and it was told as we saw it at the time. There are passages that jar today (for example those on our attitude to sniping: we actually kept a Game Book, labelled as such), but that was how we thought then, these were the people we were. So I have added a glossary, subtracted nothing, and since only a handful of old men like myself cares what the Battalion motto was I have given the book a new title to fit its modern purpose, which is to tell what it was like to live in a tightly-knit family and fight a war

ALASTAIR BORTHWICK
Barr, Ayrshire. 1994

GLOSSARY

ADJUTANT Had many functions, but mainly responsible for the battalion's paper-work, for example translating the Commanding Officer's orders into written form and then circulating them to those concerned. He might be called (perhaps not very accurately) the Commanding Officer's private secretary.

A.P. / A.T. Armour Piercing / Anti-tank.

BATTALION Infantry unit of 972 officers and men. It was divided into four rifle companies and a headquarters company which administered various specialist sections and platoons such as Signals, Carriers, Intelligence and Mortars. Each rifle company was divided into four platoons, and each platoon into four sections.

BEATING RETREAT Ceremony performed by pipes and drums

BESA Heavy machine gun.

'B' ECHELON The Battalion's supply and maintainance organisation.

BUFFALO Amphibious armoured troop or general purpose carrier.

BRIGADE Three battalions and supporting arms.

BAZOOKA German hand-held anti-tank weapon.

CROCODILE Flame-throwing tank.

COMPO Individual rations for fourteen men.

DIVISION Three brigades and supporting arms

DOOVER Australian term for a covered slit trench or foxhole(U.S.).

F.O.O. Forward Observation Officer. Artillery officer working well forward to observe the fall of shot and then radio corrections back to the guns.

H.D. Highland Division

H.E. High-explosive

I.O. Intelligence Officer. Responsible for information, interviewing prisoners and route-finding, but in practice the C.O.'s dogsbody.

KANGEROO A tank, with its turret removed, used for troop-carrying.

KAPOK BRIDGE Floating bridge stuffed with kapok.

L.C.I. Landing Craft Infantry

L.O.B. Left-Out-Of-Battle Personel. Composition varied – usually included the Second-in-Command.

O.P. Observation Post

PIAT Projectile Infantry Anti-Tank. British hand-held anti-tank weapon.

PIPIE Pipe-Major

R.A.P. Regimental Aid Post. The Battalion's own casualty station.

R.S.M. Regimental Sergeant-Major

REGIMENT The parent organisation to which the battalion belongs. Each regiment (The Seaforth Highlanders, The Black Watch, The Sherwood Foresters etc.) has a home-based headquarters which is responsible for the provision and training of recruits which it supplies to its battalions at home or abroad.

S.P.GUN Self-Propelled Gun

SCHUMINE German anti-personel mine, made of wood to defeat mine-detectors.

SPANDAU German light machine-gun.

STONK Concentration of artillery or mortar-fire.

TATTIE-MASHER German stick-grenade.

TELLERMINE German anti-tank mine.

T.C.V. Troop-Carrying Vehicle.

TIGER TANK German heavy tank equipped with an 88mm. gun.

WEASEL Light run-about with very broad tracks to support it safely over boggy ground and anti-tank mines.

BATTALION

BEFORE ALAMEIN

(previous page)   *Mr Churchill inspects the Highland Division in Egypt in 1942.*

CHAPTER ONE

Before Alamein

I

IT HAD been warm in the old Bergensfjord as we sailed up the Red Sea; but now, crammed into the tenders, we knew what real heat was. There were no awnings. The sun beat down on the mass of kit, and weapons, and men, and the thought of marching when we reached shore appalled us. Even the breeze caused by our progress over the water did not help: it was a hot breeze, and already it was bearing unbelievable smells. The Bergensfjord dwindled astern, for all its discomfort a last symbol of home; and Suez grew ahead. It was August 14, 1942.

This history could begin at an earlier date – we had been mobilised since the beginning of the war – but no Territorial battalion really wants to be reminded of those first dreadful days when all was chaos, when a pay parade occupied the concerted efforts of every officer for days on end, when we trained with wooden mortars and imaginary brens, and sergeant-instructors learned Lesson Two on the Rifle while they taught Lesson One. Nor do we much want to remember the nights when we defended the coasts of Scotland against Germans who, thank God, never came; nor ponder too deeply over those ''schemes'' where the sole military objective appeared to be to diddle the umpires. Let us say simply that the Battalion was mobilised at Golspie in the county of Sutherland on September 1, 1939, that by dint of bitter training, extended over nearly three years, had been transformed from a collection of well-meaning civilians into a fighting unit, and that we were now going into action for the first time.

We stepped ashore on a quay where the heat bounced off the stonework and hung quivering in layers; and after a delay of only three hours (practically on time, by Egyptian standards) we found ourselves in a train of sorts, ambling through strange and exciting countryside where there were camels, canals, water-buffaloes, and similar novelties. The afternoon passed quickly and we were soon at Quasassin Station. There we were met by guides, superior persons full of their three weeks' service in Africa, who led us in trucks to our camp at El Tahag.

No one liked Tahag. Tahag was a hell-hole. It was a bare, bleak, flat, gritty stretch of desert inhabited in times of peace only by flies and ants. When it became a base camp, water-towers had been built every half-mile or so along the single tarmac road which ran from horizon to horizon, and round them colonies of tents had grown up, each tent dug a yard into the ground as protection against bombing. Parallel to the road and about half-a-mile from it ran a line of latrines. We were on the bare bones of the earth. We lived there for the next ten days in great misery.

As in our childhood we had had to pass through the successive stages of measles, whooping cough, and scarlet fever, so at Tahag we had our childish ailments. In the first place, we looked ridiculous: we had to wear topees, which branded us immediately as new boys because after their first week all incoming troops were allowed to discard them. Our faces peeled, our lips cracked, and our bare knees itched. The flies were intolerable, settling in millions on any food which was left exposed for a second. Our eyes ached with the glare. Sand seeped down into our sunken tents, covering our clothes, our kit, and our food; and dust-devils came sweeping like waterspouts across the camp, smothering everything in their way and carrying stray garments far out into the desert. But these were lesser evils. Of all the plagues of Egypt, gyppy tummy was the worst.

In the politer histories, gyppy is written off in a sentence. This is wrong. It filled our minds, in some cases to the exclusion of anything else, throughout our early weeks ashore, and to anyone who fought with the Eighth Army it is a memory which will remain when much else has faded. Gyppy tummy was dysentery in any of its forms, but was most commonly used to describe the mild type which was a mortification of the flesh and spirit but was not positively crippling. It was spread by the multitudinous flies, and could develop within a few hours. One might eat a good tea, feel a little off colour at dinner, and be anything from uncomfortable to raving two hours later. The normal attack lasted three or four days, during which the victim had acute diarrhoea, no appetite, and a constant feeling of nausea; and, though the throat and mouth remained apparently normal, cigarettes had such a disgusting flavour that it was impossible to smoke them. Few of us escaped. Hundreds went to hospital, and life for the gallant few who remained was one long trek across the desert to the latrines. We never became immune to gyppy; but after the first fortnight only a few of us had it at any one time, and then seldom badly enough to remain off duty. Still, it was always there in the background, a nagging accompaniment to the day's work, and the second-worst torture of the campaign was to have gyppy tummy and be compelled to drive in a truck over the bumps of the Western Desert. The worst torture was to drive a motor-bike.

These difficulties notwithstanding, we trained at Tahag. There were route marches, tactical exercises, night compass marches. We paraded and drilled. We were visited by the Prime Minister, who had added a topee to his already remarkable collection of hats. And while these things went on we gradually began to learn about the desert. Meanwhile, let us have a look at the Battalion. There were nine hundred and seventy-two of us, and we were one of the nine infantry battalions in the 51st Highland Division. We were nearly all from the far north of Scotland, from Wick, Lybster, Dornoch and the Caithness hinterland, with a sprinkling from Morayshire and a strong contingent from the West Coast. We still had a high percentage of the old Territorials, and many of us had known each other before the war. The commonest name in the Battalion was probably Macleod or Macdonald, and among the Gaelic names the Norse stock showed in the Isbisters and the Gunns. Our commanding officer was Lt.Col. J.E.Stirling, a man who knew what he wanted. The men called him Jumbo. Thanks to his ability, drive, and explosiveness, the Battalion was fit to fight. The second-in-command, Major J.H.Walford ("Juicy" to the men), was a less forceful character, with a quiet manner and a habit of taking time to come to the point.

He tended to be overshadowed by the Colonel. The third member of what might be called the staff was Captain W.L.Mackintosh, the adjutant, who held that all successful adjutants made life hell for subalterns, and did his best to conform. These three were the fixed stars in our firmament. None of us could have foreseen that soon the Colonel would be a brigadier, that Billy Mackintosh would have lost his life, and that the quiet Major Walford would have led the Battalion with such success in battle after battle that by the end of the war he would be a legend.

Commanding Officers of the 5th Battalion The Seaforth Highlanders: (above left) Lt.Col. J.E.Stirling D.S.O. who commanded up to the Battle of El Alamein; (below) Lt.Col. J.H.Walford D.S.O. who led us through the campaigns of the Desert, Sicily, Northern France and Holland; (above right) Lt.Col. J.M.Sym D.S.O. who led us in the Reichswald, the Rhine Crossing and our final battles of the war in northern Germany.

II

Our transport arrived, and on August 24 we drove through Cairo to Mena Camp, which was on the Fayyoum road just beyond the Pyramids. It was clean desert there, not previously occupied, and so the flies were not quite so bad as they had been at Tahag; but there were no water-towers on the Fayyoum road and for the first time we knew what a water ration meant. We each had two gallons a day, far more than we were to have again that side of Algeria, yet we grumbled. It was impossible, we said, to do anything with two gallons. The time was not far distant when we were to be happy on two pints.

As a battalion we were never able to taste the much-advertised delights of Cairo, though the city was only five miles away. A few leave passes were granted, and then there was an alarm. The moon was approaching the full, and it was thought that the Germans might take advantage of it to slip through and attack Cairo. At this time the Boche were within fifty miles of Alexandria, stretched from El Alamein on the coast to the Quattara Depression, an impassable salt-pan forty miles inland. Our main defensive line was holding this bottle-neck, but there was always the chance that Rommel might send some of his Afrika Korps on a wide sweep inland round the south side of the Depression and make for Cairo. So we dug in, and prepared to sell our lives for the Sphinx. Alongside us were the other two battalions of our brigade, the 2nd Battalion The Seaforth Highlanders and the 5th Battalion The Queen's Own Cameron Highlanders, henceforth to be known in this narrative as 2nd Seaforth and 5th Camerons. However, nothing came of the scare. The full moon came and went, and nothing happened. We hoped for Cairo leave again, but before any could be granted we were off to the Western Desert.

They called it "going up the Blue" in those days, a tribute equally to the vastness of the desert and to the sky which composed nine-tenths of its landscape; but the vividness of the phrase was lost on us during our journey. We spent the first night by the Cairo/Alexandria road, and on the second struck off into the desert along "C" Track. There was nothing blue about "C" Track.

It must be explained here that the desert in no way resembled those postcards in which camels trudge, with a fine eye for composition, along the crests of gigantic dunes. By far the greater part of the desert was flat or gently rolling country composed of rock, with only a thin layer of sand or dust on top of it. One result of this was that all desert tracks were bumpy, the sand hiding the rock ledges underneath: and another was that as truck after truck followed the same line of least resistance, the sand became ground to dust which, as Major Jack Davidson so excellently described it, was 'so fine you could pour it like water'. This dust was diabolical stuff. It was orange in colour. A truck driving in it threw up a bow-wave as if it were ploughing across an orange water-splash, and behind each vehicle it rose in a billowing cloud which was slow to disperse. It settled on the skin, smooth as face-powder; and before long skin, hair, and clothes were in colour and texture a uniform matt orange. Eyeshields of some kind were essential. If some hundreds of vehicles were driving along at once, and if the wind happened to be blowing from the head of the column towards the rear, the effect was cumulative and half way down the column there was certain to be a dust-cloud which would have put a London fog to shame.

These were the conditions we struck when we turned off the Alex road on to "C" Track. The whole Division was on the move and thousands of vehicles were ahead of us, throwing up a cloud that darkened the sky. Visibility most of the way was not more than five yards, and almost immediately we were covered from head to foot in the thick orange pall. Trucks lurched and bumped, the drivers able to see even less of the lie of the rocks than the sand usually permitted, and many drifted from the column and set out in little convoys of their own in the wrong direction, leading the others after them. Occasional breaks would come in the cloud and the clear sky would show through. The stragglers would find themselves in a little patch of unmarked, trackless desert, and would turn and hurry back into the cloud again. The men, especially those in the backs of the trucks where there were only bare boards to sit on, were bounced about incessantly; and as we bounced we sweated. The sweat mixed with the dust to form mud, caking our faces like masks and streaking our shirts with patches of darker orange.

After nearly forty miles of this we reached International Corner, a piece of desert no different from any other piece of desert except that it was decorated with signposts and the dust was churned even more finely than usual. There we swung right to El Hammam Station, where we picked up guides as darkness fell. They led us through minefield gaps, and in almost total darkness we found ourselves manning our first desert positions.

When daylight came we saw that we could have been very much worse off. Our area was clean, and the people who had been there before us had dug deeply and well. Also, the Boche were miles away. We were simply giving depth to the main defences ten miles ahead, and nothing short of a major breakthrough could touch us. It was a good place for us to find our feet and become accustomed to a life and a landscape unlike anything we had known before. The country round Hammam was a fair sample of our surroundings for many months to come – bare, wind-swept desert supporting only a little dwarf scrub, a few scorpions, and many flies. It undulated gently for a thousand miles and more, each hummock so like its neighbours that even the most accomplished map-readers were baffled and trucks had to be navigated by compass, like ships. The nights were clear and chilly, and a heavy dew fell. We slept in holes with bivouacs rigged over them, occasionally finding a scorpion sharing the warmth of our blankets. Half an hour before dawn we stood-to, huddled in greatcoats and feeling damp and chilly. The light grew. We could see a few vehicles dispersed around us, each with its crew standing dismally beside it. Shadows began to form in the lee of the rocks and the sun came up, striking so directly through the clear air that one could hold out one's hands to it and warm them. The dew sparkled on the bivouacs and the scrub. Suddenly we were hot. The dew was disappearing as we watched, and the flies were out in clouds. We shed our coats and pullovers, and settled down to breakfast. We learned many things there, not the least of them being how to cook. The days of 'Come and get it' in the dining-hall were over, and we knew that soon even company cooking would be impossible. Much better, we thought, to learn now rather than later. Rations were issued down to sections (usually about ten men), and shortly after dawn each morning the desert was dotted with earnest little groups mastering the technique of the Benghazi cooker. The Benghazi was a simple device, and owed its popularity to the fact that petrol at that time was easier to come by than water. Each section carried a tin in which holes had been stabbed with a bayonet. This was half filled with sand, and a pint or so of petrol was stirred into it so that it formed a thick paste. A match thrown from a safe distance was all that was necessary after that. It would burn for half-an-hour with no more attention than an occasional stir with the point of a bayonet. On these fires we were soon cooking excellent meals.

Another of our lessons was in the uses of the four-gallon non-returnable petrol can, a most important subject at that time. The War Office in its wisdom had decided that the ideal container for petrol was one which could be thrown away after it had been emptied and to this end had caused to be manufactured out of the thinnest of tin many millions of square cans. These littered the desert wherever the British Army had fought, and many were their uses. They made excellent Benghazis, and half of one well cleaned made a pot which would hold ten men's rations with ease. They could be used as seats, or cut into fly-traps, lamp-shades or wash-basins. Filled with sand they were indispensable: trench walls could be revetted with them and from them almost anything could be constructed. Commanding officers reared themselves mighty latrines dedicated to their sole use (there is a famous story of one colonel in the Division whose palace collapsed about his ears at the ungodly hour of three o'clock in the morning); cookhouses were built; and there was even a case where a mess capable of seating fourteen was made from eight hundred cans and a tarpaulin. The four-gallon non-returnable petrol can was the desert brick, the basis of all architecture. It was ideal for almost anything except holding petrol.

Unfortunately the Germans had a much better design, the Jerrican, which could be refilled again and again and lasted a lifetime. Our own were so clearly useless (as much as half the petrol was apt to leak out before it could be used) that after Alamein we used nothing but captured German ones and had to exercise our ingenuity in new directions to find our building materials.

We learned to tolerate the heat, to save our shaving water for the washing of socks, and to drink in the morning and in the evening – the only times, we discovered, when the drink was not sweated out in minutes, leaving us thirstier than before, and with a fresh crust of salt on our already gruesome shirts. We learned one of the chief military lessons of the desert, which was that a man in the dark without a compass inevitably lost himself inside three hundred yards and had generally got well on his way round a circle inside one hundred. We learned that American tinned bacon was tastier than British, that empty beer bottles left lying about by our predecessors could be sold to the NAAFI at Hammam for a piastre a time, that the North African coast had the finest bathing beach in the world, that fresh green gherkins were good for neither man nor beast, and that if our weapons were to fire at all they must be kept absolutely free from oil. We learned how to lay and lift mines, and drive trucks in desert formation. We mastered the sun-compass. In short, we shook ourselves down, adapted ourselves, and began to acquire the desert soldier's flair for travelling light and being at home wherever he might stop. We were not quite such new boys when we went up and relieved a Royal Sussex battalion in "E" Box on September 8.

We were in the forward defences now, though not quite in the front line. This was Rommel's highwater mark before he fell back and consolidated on the Alamein Line, and all round us were burned-out tanks, crashed aircraft, fragments of equipment, and the general litter of battle. The Box itself was invisible, but it existed none the less. In country where tanks were free to roam anywhere, both sides were forced to adopt the box system whenever the line congealed for any length of time. Thousands of mines were dug in, forming a series of huge rectangles each big enough to hold a brigade; and these boxes could be entered only through a few carefully marked gaps. If an attack threatened, the gaps too were mined, and each brigade found itself in an invisible fort. There were many accidents in these places. In the dark, or even in the dusk, it was fatally easy to miss the gaps and drive into the minefields; and few battalions who lived there escaped without casualties.

Our area in Box "E" was called Stuka Valley, probably in memory of some outstanding dive-bombing attack rather than the shooting down of a dive-bomber, because there was no sign of a Stuka in it. It was hardly a valley at all, but even a slight depression in the flatness of the desert counted as a valley there. On one side rose a bare rocky promontory called Abu Shamla's Tomb, and down in the dip were a few lonely wooden crosses. A small wind blew most of the time we were there, carrying a shifting carpet of grit over our trenches. Occasionally a 'plane came out of the blue sky and machine-gunned us, and on one unlucky occasion near "M" training area a bomb near our carriers caused our first casualties. The training and hardening process continued. We began to feel confident.

III

On the last day of September Colonel Stirling held a conference and told us that on October 2 we were going up to relieve the Australians in the front line – the next stage in our pilgrimage towards real action. There had already been a series of attachments of officers and N.C.O.'s to the Aussies and experience had been gained thereby, but this was the first time that the Battalion as a whole was due to go up. Advance parties went off next day, and late on the afternoon of October 2 we followed in a fleet of R.A.S.C. lorries.

It was a simple enough job we had to do and nothing untoward happened while we were doing it; but it was our first time and so has left a deeper impression on our minds than probably it should have done. We had been waiting for something like this for three years, and took it all very seriously. Now, looking back, it is strange to remember how excited we were. Major J.H.Davidson, O.C. "D" Company, wrote an account of it afterwards, and as it is both vivid and typical it will tell the story for all the companies.

'I remember embussing, and the Company Sergeant Major giving a last reminder about silence and no smoking,' he wrote. 'Off we went along a bumpy, pot-holey route which called itself "O" Track and led to a distinguished and dusty highway known as the Bombay Road, which in turn led to the overworked and decaying tarmac of the Coast Road, which runs uninterrupted from Alexandria to Algiers.... The night was dark and, of course, there were no lights. We were due to meet our Australian guides near Alamein Station, and sure enough they were there awaiting us. I shall always remember "D" Company's guide – a figure in the dark with a huge slouch hat and a very pronounced Australian accent. I never saw him, but his confident attitude and cheerfulness were infectious; and as he stood on the step of my truck navigating us through gaps in minefields, along dusty and almost non-existent tracks and past slit-trenches, I felt a sort of inexplicable feeling of confidence and almost jealous admiration for that little Australian figure in the dark. If I remember correctly, he was the company commander's batman.

' "Much farther to go?" I asked presently.

' "Nearly there now, sir," came the answer, and with that reply came the most frightful explosion and blinding flash – from underneath the truck, it seemed to me. I nearly jumped out of my skin, and wondered if I had been seen. There was another explosion, and then another.

' "Reckon that's our mediums. Just pulled in to shoot up the Quattara Track tonight," said the calm nasal voice at my side....

'At last we halted, and another Australian voice came out of the darkness asking: "Is that the Scotties?" This time it was the commander of the Australian company we were to relieve.

'By some freak of good fortune I found that our company was present, and the unmistakable figure of the C.S.M. was strutting about asking for the Aussie C.S.M. My platoon commanders were taken over by the Australian opposite numbers, and they creaked off one by one in the darkness to their new platoon areas. I was taken to the company H.Q., a unique one: an upturned three-tonner provided the roof, and the ground underneath had been dug out to form quite a roomy little office-cum-bedroom. There was a light there which enabled us to study jointly the layout of the company - the positions of ammunition dumps and so on. I found a most complete picture laid out before me clearly....

'Presently noises outside announced the arrival of the Australian platoon commanders: the relief was almost complete. After a cup of tea had been produced it was deemed quite complete; and standing outside my Company H.Q. I regretfully watched our Dominion friends clamber on board our three-tonners and disappear into the night, again guided by my figure-in-the-dark. I can still hear the exact words of the Aussie company commander as he shook me by the hand

' "Well, good luck. It's all yours now."

' "It was quite still as I stood there, eerily still. There was the noise of the troop carriers growing fainter in the distance. The outline of my headquarters loomed behind me. I could distinguish the dim shapes of some men of Company H.Q. moving about uncertainly. I knew that the platoons were there, there, and there; and that the Boche was there, four thousand yards away. It was all mine. I don't think I was filled with the pride of ownership, but I longed for the dawn so that I could see my new possessions. I looked at my watch. About 0230. Then my platoon commanders appeared. Lieutenant Robertson assured me that the guard on the minefield gap was in position. No, he doubted if he could find the place again in the dark: better not go in case we got lost. Ian Houldsworth said he would show me 16 Platoon area, and boldly we set out. He was certain that it was "just down here" – but it wasn't. After a bit we gave up, and not without trouble found Company H.Q. again. It was quite clear that nothing could be gained from these fruitless expeditions. The C.S.M. and myself talked until the sun came up, and then all the mysteries became simple. There was 16 Platoon only a few hundred yards away, 17 over on its left, and 18 just visible at the far end of the barbed wire fence. And there, plain as a pikestaff, was the track to the minefield gap.

'We were not under observation and could move about freely. The C.S.M. was just remarking that it was a quiet bit of the line when half-a-dozen shells landed about a hundred and fifty yards behind us, obviously aimed at the mediums, but then they had pulled out before first light. A sliver of hot metal churned up the dust quite near. Then I remembered I had to send shelling reports to Battalion H.Q., so I seized the hot sliver of shell and despatched it to Pat Nairne, the Intelligence Officer. After all, these were our first "malice aforethought" shells, and this was our first time in....

'We improved our slits, relieved our guard, and I had got back to Company H.Q. A quiet West Coast voice at my elbow, Corporal Aird's, asked me what I wanted for lunch. I realised that the day was passing: in fact it was mid-afternoon. I said: "Corporal Aird, can you make some really good porridge?" My lunch-cum-afternoon tea this day consisted of a plate of porridge made only as Corporal Aird can make it, supplemented by ration biscuits, and honey which I had bought in Alex, and tea.

'We had found our feet.... Confidence grew, and we just blinked the next time some shells came over.... A few days later found us due to be relieved by another fresh unit. We modelled ourselves on the Aussies, and one would have thought we had been in the line for years if the way in which the men of the company handed over was any guide. The figure in the dark was there, this time a Seaforth; and as I drove away I said to the incoming Company Commander:

' "Well, good luck. It's all yours now." '

IV

During this tour of duty in the line, patrols were going out nightly to discover all they could about the German positions and minefields; and once again we learned our lessons. It was nervy work. The usual dress was pullover, shorts, and desert boots or sandshoes. Faces were blackened, and no equipment was worn: a few rounds in a shirt pocket were sufficient. A woollen cap-comforter was preferred to a steel helmet, partly because it was less conspicuous but mainly because the slightest wind playing on the overhanging steel brim made hearing difficult; and hearing, on a dark night, was the sense upon which a patrol most relied. When the men were close to the enemy they crept forward twenty or thirty yards at a time, then lay still in a circle, facing outwards and listening for as long as half-an-hour before moving on again. Sound travelled far in the desert, and this method always gave them warning of the enemy: a cough, a clink of equipment, a few words spoken quietly in German could be picked up a long way off. Sometimes it was the enemy we were looking for, sometimes their mines. The patrols would lie out in the minefields, tracing the boundaries and scraping away the sand to discover which types had been laid. The big tellers, the anti-tank mines, were not dangerous; but there was always the chance of meeting S-mines, anti-personnel mines which jumped into the air before exploding. We were lucky, and had no casualties. We lost only one man, and then in a manner which may seem odd to anyone who has not been on patrol. It is a fact that prolonged nervous strain induces sleep: the brain, being stretched to breaking-point, seeks some means of escape. Sleep is the most convenient one. This subconscious desire for escape grows until the victim, unless he has been forewarned and is putting up a conscious resistance to it, reaches a state in which his natural sense of fear is completely overcome. He will then fall asleep anywhere, no matter how great the danger. This happened to the "escape-man" at the tail of one patrol. He just disappeared and was never seen again. We could only assume that he had dozed over during one of the listening halts, failed to wake until after the others had gone, and then wandered into the German lines.

On the night of 7/8 October we moved back to Stuka Valley, where we stayed until the 18th. Then we moved back into the line again, and prepared for the battle of El Alamein.

EL ALAMEIN

(previous page) A mortar team under artillery bombardment at El Alamein (probably a staged publicity picture which skilfully captures the atmosphere of the battle).

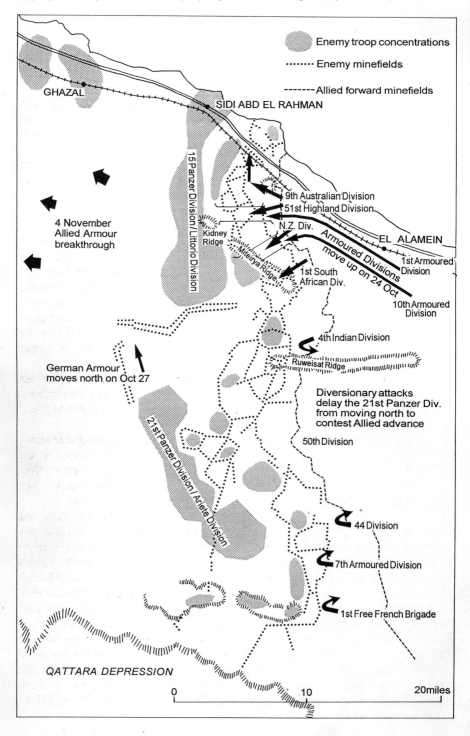

Enemy troop concentrations

Enemy minefields

Allied forward minefields

GHAZAL

SIDI ABD EL RAHMAN

15 Panzer Division / Littorio Division

4 November
Allied Armour
breakthrough

Kidney
Ridge

9th Australian Division
51st Highland Division

N.Z. Div.

Miteirya Ridge

EL ALAMEIN

Armoured Divisions
move up on 24 Oct

1st Armoured
Division

1st South
African Div.

10th Armoured
Division

4th Indian Division

German Armour
moves north on Oct 27

Ruweisat Ridge

Diversionary attacks
delay the 21st Panzer Div.
from moving north to
contest Allied advance

21st Panzer Division / Ariete Division

50th Division

44 Division

7th Armoured Division

1st Free French Brigade

QATTARA DEPRESSION

0   10   20 miles

CHAPTER TWO

El Alamein

I

THERE WAS a time when a man could stand on a hilltop from dawn until dusk, and in that narrow scope of space and time see a battle. He could watch every move and counter move; the pattern of the attack would be clear; and he could be certain that before he slept the fighting would be over.

Modern war has its pattern too; but it is so vast that it is only within the range of the senses after it has been plotted on a map. No man can see it all, and no single day can hold it. Each separate move in the master-plan is a battle in itself, and the flank attack which was once launched by a handful of men in a matter of minutes is now an affair of divisions or even corps. It follows from this that any unit so low in the Order of Battle as a battalion seldom has any but the most slender idea of what is going on over the whole front. The "big picture", the plan for the Army front as a whole, is a few lines on the Commanding Officer's map-board; and once the battle has been joined even these will probably be inaccurate, for few battles are fought as they are planned. The battalion fight, the thing the infantryman sees, frequently bears no resemblance to the big picture he reads in the newspapers afterwards, and is often difficult to reconcile even with the story told by the battalion on his left or right. The battle of El Alamein was not one battle but many; and, like every other unit taking part, we have our own particular version of it.

The battle began on October 23, 1942, with the German Afrika Korps under Field-Marshal Rommel almost at the gates of Alexandria. It ended on November 3 with the Afrika Korps in headlong retreat, started on its long trek which was to end in annihilation two thousand miles to the west.

The big picture showed two small armies of roughly ten divisions apiece facing each other on a line running north and south from the Quattara Depression to the sea. On one side were Germans and Italians; on the other British, Australians, New Zealanders, South Africans, Indians, and a few Frenchmen and Greeks. The details of the big plan need not concern us here.

The essence of it was that, by means of troop movements, dummy tanks, and diversionary attacks, Rommel was to be led to believe that our main blow was coming against his south flank whereas it was in fact going to come frontally on the northern half of the line. While his attention was engaged in the south by a junk-yard collection of old trucks mocked-up to look like tanks, we were going to breach the minefields near Alamein, form a bridgehead on the far side, and hang on until our armour (lying behind us and disguised for the time being as trucks) could pass through. If that could be done, we had won: no army in the desert could survive with tanks running amok in its rear. It would be a hard fight, because the line was nowhere lightly held; but if, once the battle had begun, the German armour could be kept facing the ancient wrecks in the south convinced that our northern attack was only a diversion, we would be able to establish our bridgehead before a decisive counter-blow could be launched against us. This plan was successful. Rommel held his armour until it was too late.

The little picture, our own, is easily described. The Highland Division was part of the force which had to break through and form the bridgehead. There was desert for four thousand yards, and after that there were minefields and Germans. No subtleties of ground or cover existed. The desert was absolutely flat, and on the map the drawing of our lines of advance was a draughtsman's job. A straight line was not only the shortest distance between two points: it was the best route as well. We had two tasks to perform in the battle, and the first of them was a direct result of this flatness.

Obviously, the initial attack would have to take place at night: we should be slaughtered to no purpose if we tried to advance in daylight. Equally obviously, many thousands of men trying to form up without landmarks and in darkness on our start-line (which was a thousand yards out in No Man's Land) would become hopelessly lost before the battle began unless steps were taken to prevent it. Our Battalion's first task was to lay white tape along the whole of the Highland Division start-line, a distance of two thousand five hundred yards, and from there tape back nine separate routes by which the other battalions could advance on to the line. After that their fate would be in their own hands, but at least they would start in order.

It was not an easy task. If we laid all the tape – and there were nine miles of it – on the night before the attack, any German patrol stumbling on it would know what we were up to. If we waited until the night of the attack before laying it and then spent too much time over the job, the assaulting troops would be caught by daylight before they had dug in on their objectives. However, by planning and much practice, a solution had been found. We and the rest of the Division had already fought the battle three times in "M" Training Area behind our lines, and after a good deal of trial and error a drill had been evolved.

We began work on the night of 19/20 October. The first difficulty was to pinpoint the ends of the start-line. If they were wrongly placed the whole layout would be wrong; and the only way to fix them in surroundings as featureless as the ocean was to have several officers start with compasses in their hands from known points behind our trenches and pace carefully along on bearings until they converged. Once these key points had been fixed, a drum of signal cable, invisible in the dark, was unrolled along the start-line and tied to short metal pickets which we hammered in every fifty yards. It was unlikely that the Boche would find the cable, and if they did it would not tell them much.

Sixty men finished this part of the job in one night. On the night of October 21/ 22 we were out again; and by dawn the nine routes had been plotted, the nine cables laid, and the pickets driven in. We still had a night in hand before the attack; and Colonel Stirling, who had practically lived in No Man's Land since the taping began, spent it in guiding representatives of the other battalions along the cable to show them the layout and allow them to mark their own boundaries and centre-points. It was found by pacing that the routes delivered units on to the start-line very accurately throughout its length.

The spade-work was now complete. On the night of the battle, parties went out at dusk with drums of white tape, unrolled them, fixed the tape to the cable at intervals so that it could not be blown or dragged away; and ninety minutes later the nine miles of start-line and routes were clearly marked.

II

Our job was done. Our own brigade was not taking part, but was acting as a firm base from which the other brigades could be launched. The long lines of infantry began to move through us. We added the finishing touches to our doovers (Australian, derivation obscure, for slit trenches with roofs on them) and settled down to watch. The night was cool now, but we all had raging thirsts and were tempted to drink more than we could spare from our waterbottles. There was little shelling from either side. The silence was oppressive, and for some reason we had taken to talking in whispers. We thought of the thousands shuffling into position on the start-line. As 2140 hours approached we sat with our watches in our hands, then swung round and looked to the east where our gun-lines lay.

Captain A.Grant Murray was out with a patrol, covering the start-line while the attack formed up.

'The hands of my watch seemed to creep round as we lay listening and watching,' he wrote afterwards. 'To our front all was quiet apart from a verey light or two and some machine-gun fire.... As zero drew near I twisted round and looked back towards our own lines. Suddenly the whole horizon went pink and for a second or two there was still perfect silence, and then the noise of the Eighth Army's guns hit us in a solid wall of sound that made the whole earth shake. Through the din we made out other sounds – the whine of shells overhead, the clatter of the machine-guns ... and, eventually, the pipes. Then we saw a sight that will live for ever in our memories – line upon line of steel helmeted figures with rifles at the high port, bayonets catching in the moonlight, and over all the wailing of the pipes.... As they passed they gave us the thumbs-up sign, and we watched them plod on towards the enemy lines, which by this time were shrouded in smoke. Our final sight of them was just as they entered the smoke, with the enemy's defensive fire falling among them....'

We were shelled that night but took no hurt, and on the following night moved forward to the first enemy minefields and dug in again. We stayed there until the 27th, taking no part in the fighting which was still going on to the north of us, but simply remaining in reserve and keeping our heads down. We had a few casualties from shelling, but although the battle had been raging for four days we still could not say we had been in it. At this stage the front was being consolidated. Our infantry had punched the hole in the line and formed their bridgehead; but an unmarked minefield on Miteraya Ridge had held up our armour when it tried to fan out beyond, and the front had stiffened again. A second assault was being prepared, and while this was going on our neighbours were holding German counter-attacks and cleaning up the odd pockets of resistance which still existed in the bulge which was now British territory.

The battle of Alamein for us was to be this second attack, the breakout from the bulge; but before it took place we had to play another passive role, this time not so pleasant. On the night of the 27th we moved up to Sniper Valley, near Tel el Eisa, and relieved the 2/27 Battalion of the 20 Australian Brigade. We remained there until the 30th in a purely defensive position. Sniper Valley was a demoralising place, as are all places where one is hit without being allowed to hit back. We were accustomed by this time to moving about as little as possible during daylight, but here we could not move at all.

'It was about midnight when we arrived to take over,' wrote Corporal G.S. Parkinson, "D" Company's clerk, 'and, being only a few hundred yards away, Jerry became suspicious. In a few minutes the sky was lit by his flares and spandaus began to clatter, the bullets passing dangerously close. One man was hit in the chest, and thenceforward all movement was restricted to a minimum.

'The Australians seemed quite cheery, but it had been a costly position for them, and the night we took over one of their officers had been killed by a sniper. Company H.Q. had quite good trenches but there were hardly enough of them; and, as the snipers were beginning to get accurate and we could not dig fresh ones, three men had to share a trench. I was with a runner and a stretcher-bearer. Immediately in front of our trench was a big oil-drum, and any movement was clearly outlined to the enemy and brought bullets whistling about our ears.

'During our period in this sector we developed a really healthy respect for the German snipers. They were expert marksmen and we were forced to keep our heads well down all day long, the only time we dared to venture out being at night. The forward platoons were even worse off....

'Our platoon commanders tried to pinpoint the snipers positions and sent fire orders by telephone to Company H.Q., where we had a mortar detachment. Scores of mortar bombs were hurled into their lines, but all to no avail: a careless movement still was answered by the snip of an automatic rifle fitted with telescopic sights. Nerves became frayed, and even at night one became fearful to move. One chap was so bad that he lay for two days at the bottom of his trench afraid to move and too fearful to come out for food. He was taken to hospital on the third night and we never saw him again.

'Private Holmes of 18 Platoon was hit in the eye by a bullet and required immediate attention. Private "Happy" Third, always willing to be in the thick of things, volunteered to run across to Company H.Q. for a stretcher-bearer. He arrived flushed with excitement, and then set off back to his platoon area with the stretcher-bearer. We saw him hesitate a little as he tried to get his bearings, and then he made a final dash, closely followed by Piper Duff, the stretcher-bearer. There was the inevitable staccato report of the rifle, and we saw Happy fling his hands into the air and drop to the ground, shot through the temple. He died within a few minutes....

'Later the same day a sergeant on a nearby gun peeped over his trench to talk to one of his gun crew; and, though he only showed his head, he was hit squarely between the eyes.... We had to eat, sleep, and live in our trench for three days.... We could neither wash nor shave, and we had about a week's growth on our faces.... It was with a sigh of relief that we learned we were to be relieved by the New Zealanders on the 30th.

'As we prepared for the take-over, Jerry got the wind up and sent up his flares. Bullets once more whistled past our heads, and for part of the way we had to crawl on our stomachs. As we passed Battalion H.Q. I well remember the C.O. and the Adjutant standing there giving us encouragement. The latter said: "Cheer up, lads. You'll get a smack at them tomorrow night." '

III

They say a man's first battle is always his best, that he does not have the experience to assess risks accurately, and so does far more than is expected of him. This is probably true. Most of us have felt immortal the first time: the people who fell were not real people; the shells which exploded were not real shells; the din, the whining, the crashes, the dust were at once confusing and exciting, and we did things we were never to do again so lightheartedly. The night of 1/2 November was the first time, not for a few, but for all of us. We were to fight more skilful actions and achieve more for less cost. We were to learn guile. But never again were we to go in as we did that night, with so much verve.

Of course it was a wasteful action. It had to be. We were raw troops with more spirit than sense, and we chose a bad night to grow up. There was nothing wrong with the plan: men just threw their lives away. Yet it is a night we may look back upon with pride and not a little wonder. It had a quality. Out of the death and mutilation came a corporate courage, something solid, and heartening, and unselfish, which was felt from one end of the Battalion to the other: we had trained for years, and this was it, at last. It was very difficult to be a coward.

It was to be a two-brigade attack, 151 on the right and ourselves (152) on the left. We were to advance two thousand yards, pause for half-an-hour, then advance another two thousand yards and dig in. Then the armour would come through. The attack was successful. The armour did get through, and the Afrika Korps broke and ran.

On the morning before the attack Colonel Stirling had his arm in a sling: he had cut it on a signal cable, and it had gone septic. After breakfast he gave out his orders sitting in his jeep with the company commanders gathered round. He looked worn and tired and in pain, but his voice was as incisive as ever: 'The Battalion will attack.... "C" Company right forward; "B" left forward; "A" and "D" right and left rear.... Transport will move under command of Captain J.L.Butler.... Battalion H.Q. will move between the two reserve companies.... The ground is flat and very little is known about it: our objective is just a pencil line the General has drawn on the map. We may meet anything or nothing....'

Afterwards there was a Brigade conference, and a hurried lunch. It was hot, dusty, hectic, everyone trying to hide his excitement and appear businesslike and normal. At 1630 hours, Captain Farquhar Macrae, the M.O., had another look at Colonel Stirling's arm, and shook his head. It would not do. He had hung on too long already, and these things moved fast in a hot climate. With only two-and-a-half hours to go before we moved up to the assembly area, the Colonel was packed off to hospital; and Major Walford, at that time miles to the rear with the L.O.B. (Left Out of Battle) personnel and clean out of the picture, was sent for.*

The battle had almost started before he reached us, Billy Mackintosh and Jack Davidson were the only ones with a firm hold on the plan, and thanks to them we were shepherded on to the start-line in time and in order. The moon was ten days on the wane, and there was not much light. The men knelt ten yards apart along the white tape, black silhouettes against the sand; and among them officers and N.C.O.'s moved, whispering last instructions... don't bunch... keep close in to the

---

* The Second in Command was usually "Left Out of Battle" ready to take over should the need arise.

barrage... don't lose sight of your neighbours. We gripped our rifles and waited. It was 0055 hours on November 2. Suddenly the sky was bright with flashes, our barrage was moaning overhead, and we were walking forward.

A barrage, even if it is not one's first, is a difficult thing to write about. It cannot be taken apart and described in detail, and in the mass it is so overwhelming that no broad picture of it can possibly be convincing. The noise is unbelievable. If one shell be fired from one twenty-five-pounder gun at night, the infantryman first sees a flash far behind him and a few seconds later hears the sound of the gun. Again there is a slight pause; and far overhead a shrill sound, somewhere between a whine and a sigh and a small wind blowing across the strings of a harp, grows in volume and deepens in tone until the shell roars into the ground ahead of him. There is a red flash, and an explosion which has a distinct metallic clang in it. If the shell falls at some distance, the clang has an almost bell-like quality. Most of the fragments travel forward, and raise long scuffs of dust which are distinct from the dust of the explosion itself. The noise of the explosion is very great.

When some hundreds of guns are firing at once, the high shrill sound grows until the whole sky is screaming; and when the first shells land the earth shakes, clouds of dust and smoke arise, and the immense crash drowns the approach of the shells which follow. The infantry man is a fly inside a drum; and only occasionally, when for a few seconds the guns seem to draw breath, can he hear the twanging of harps which heralds the next salvo. The uproar swells and fades and swells again, deafeningly, numbing the brain; and through it comes the enemy's reply. That night, for the first time, we heard the crump of mortars around us; and, ripping through everything, the crack of bredas and the vicious *pup-turrrr, pup-turrrr* of the spandau, the German light machine-gun.

Clouds of dust and smoke arose, blotting out the desert which so short a time ago had seemed so vast. Each man found himself in a diminished world inhabited by himself and at most three or four others. Somewhere near him was an officer or sergeant with a compass, trying to walk a straight course through the inferno for more than two miles to an objective which was only a pencil line on the map. Inevitably groups divided and subdivided. Some companies remained intact, moving on their appointed courses. Others lost a section or two. Some lost a platoon. But there was a compass in nearly every group, and most of those who survived the barrage did reach the objective. It was, unfortunately, a question of surviving the barrage. Through inexperience, the forward companies took too literally the injunction which had been drilled into them, and kept so close that until they reached the half-way line they were under our barrage instead of behind it. German shells and mortar bombs were landing too, and casualties were heavy. Therefore of the Battalion as a whole it can be said only that we reached our objectives without meeting a great deal of opposition, and dug in. The real story of the battle can only be told through the small groups which fought it, each in its own small dusty world, and each with its own adventures.

Here, for example, is an instance which could be duplicated a dozen times, the story of Sergeant Carnduff. Carnduff, a big, slow-speaking, able fellow who ended the war as a company quartermaster sergeant, was at that time sergeant of 14 Platoon under Lieutenant A.B.McLeod.

'We had only gone four or five hundred yards,' he said, 'and the stuff was coming down all round us, when Lieutenant McLeod was killed. A shell burst

Scenes during the Battle of El Alamein: (above) The artillery barrage; (below) The desert offered little cover – daylight advances like this were rare.

fairly close to him; and from the way he fell we thought he was getting down deliberately, to let the barrage move away from us. So we got down too. After a while I thought there was something queer about it, so I went over to him. He was dead, lying on his face with his hands under him. It was dark, but I knew he was dead. He had the only compass in the platoon, and it was in his hand. I had a hell of a job getting it out from under him. By that time, of course, the rest of the Company had disappeared, so we set off on our own, extended to ten paces in a long line.

'We'd done about two thousand yards when the section on the left shouted: "Tank in front". I couldn't see the damned thing, so I told the others to lie down while I went to see what was happening. It was a tank all right. It was dug in, with its gun sticking out just above ground level; so we crawled round the back, where we could get at it easier. It was very dark, and we couldn't see much; but all at once someone started screaming. Three Ities were crawling out from under the tank. God knows what they were doing there; but anyway they seemed to think they were going to be murdered, and one of them was screaming like a woman. We took them prisoner and were feeling pretty pleased with ourselves, when all at once the tank machine-gun opened up. The gunner inside can't have seen us, because he was firing straight ahead and we were behind him. He must have heard the screaming and shouting, I suppose, and just loosed off. He wasn't so lucky. He'd left the hatch open, and we'd plenty of grenades, so that finished that off.

'We were close up to the barrage by this time, but we still couldn't see any of our chaps. We pushed on for a long time, and I began to wonder where the hell we were. We hadn't seen a soul except Italians for over two hours. Lieutenant McLeod's batman was with me, a wee lad from Kilbarchan... Smith, I think his name was... and he said to me: "Sergeant, I think you're passing trenches with folk in them." I asked him how he made that out, and he said: "Well, I'm positive something moved in that last slit we went by".

'So we went back, and found a slit, and there was a man in the bottom of it with his head under a blanket. You could just see him and no more, but you could make out that the blanket was shaking a wee bit. We hunted about on that line and found eight more, all the same. Well, the boys had been moaning about having to carry the big anti-tank grenades. So we got rid of them.

'After that we carried on again, and pretty soon we saw people, and there was Colonel Meirs of the Camerons. He didn't know where half his own companies were, never mind ours. He said to dig in with him until we knew the form. It was the following night before we got back to "C" Company. When we arrived, all that were left were Lieutenant Robertson and seventeen men....'

The companies all had similar stories to tell – of dust, and moonlight, and shells, of Italians coming out of the darkness with their hands up, and tracer bullets streaming through the night. Captain Gaston of "B" Company was wounded almost on the start-line, carried on, and was wounded again: on the half-way line Lieutenant Laurie McGillivray (his front teeth knocked out by a bullet) gathered the remnants and found the Company was down to half strength. "C" Company, which had started a hundred strong, was in even worse shape: five of the seventeen men who reached the objective were strays from Battalion H.Q. However, the two rear companies had not suffered so badly and reached their objectives almost intact.

One of the best accounts of the advance comes from George Green, commander of H.Q. Company, who by the end of the battle was the only captain left on the field apart from the Medical Officer. George makes no bones about it: he was lost. This being so, his story has a wider range than most of the others, because he wandered so industriously that by dawn he had visited half the companies in the Battalion and, although he started in the rear, it seems highly probable that at one stage he led us all.

'I remember a rum bottle,' he said. 'I'd been dishing out the ration on the start-line, and then the barrage opened up, and there I was with this bottle in my hand. It was still half full. I couldn't possibly drink it all. I took one good swig out of it, and then laid it down very carefully all by itself in the middle of the desert. I've often wondered what happened to it.

'Donnie Munro was on my right when we started. The dust was so thick you couldn't see ten yards either side, but up above it wasn't so bad and you could still see the moon. The noise was simply hellish. I kept on going, and after a while Donnie had disappeared and so had everybody else. I must have gone too quickly, because all at once the barrage was coming down on top of me: it seems impossible, but I could actually see big silver slivers of metal flying about. The bursts were all round. I lay down and began to crawl backwards. Then I saw Jack Davidson of "D" Company lying about three yards away. He heaved his flask over to me, and I was glad of it. It seemed we were on the half-way line. The barrage was to halt in front of us for half an hour, forming a screen while we re-organised; so if I'd gone on I would have had it.

'I tried to make my way back to Battalion H.Q. and landed in the middle of "C" Company, who were roaming around blazing away with tommy-guns into every hole and corner they could find. I decided this was no place for me, and set off again. It was a cold night, but I was sweating like a bull. The sand made walking very tiring.

'The next one I ran into was Farquhar Macrae, who was in a little scoop of sand working on the casualties. There were a lot of wounded Ities in the background, howling dismally; and I found about twenty of my own chaps near them, unwounded but lost. How Farquhar worked out in the open, with the racket and the dust and the darkness, I don't know. He just had to, I suppose. He was even doing amputations. I gathered my chaps and we set off, leaving him to it, and had another shot at finding Battalion H.Q. The barrage was moving again, so we moved with it and went to where we calculated our objective should be. We hadn't worked it out too badly, either because the verey success-signals went up not far away. This business sounds chaotic; but it wasn't, really. We were nearly all split up into smaller groups than we had planned to move in – it was inevitable with visibility the way it was – but the Battalion was still holding direction and we weren't far apart. We just couldn't see each other. Later on, when daylight came, we found that the plan had been carried through to the letter – much to our surprise, I admit, but carried through it was.

'However, that came later. At that time we imagined we were alone. We began to dig in, but before we had got down any distance a German armoured car appeared and went around and round us, blazing away with a machine-gun. I don't think he could have seen us clearly, because most of his shots went wide. Then he belted off at a tangent, still firing, and disappeared into the smoke. It was that kind of battle: things kept popping on and off in a casual sort of way. I heard later that the same car bumped into Farquhar and his medical orderlies next. They were unarmed, of course. They tried to get away, but Private Gallacher was killed and the rest were taken prisoner. They escaped before dawn – trust Farquhar!

'Anyway, it was 0430 hours by the time we reached the objective, and the whole Battalion was digging in. The dust had subsided, the sun would soon be up, and the German guns were feeling for our range. This was when the real trouble began. The ground was like iron, and it was almost impossible to dig down more than two feet without striking solid limestone.

'We couldn't get down at all. For the next five hours my group just lay as the shells came over, heavily and accurately. They were dead on the range. All this time we were trying to dig. It was the worst ever. Stuff was landing continually within twelve yards of us, and some shells were as close as four feet. I never got my head right down: it was just level with the surface. We began to have casualties. One or two went bomb-happy about the second hour and started to scream. There was a chap hit in the mouth, and we couldn't move him. In the afternoon we found some Italian trenches fifty yards behind us – we'd never had our heads up far enough to see them before – and after that it wasn't too bad....'

Lieutenant H. S. Robertson, the only surviving officer of "C" Company, tells the end of the story. 'I dug in a shellhole where the limestone crust was broken,' he said. 'My batman and runner were sharing it with me, and I left them to get on with the digging while I tied up our front with Laurie McGillivray who was still in great form with all his teeth knocked out. A bonny sight he was, too. When I got back my batman was dead and the runner was knocked stupid. A shell had burst on the lip of the trench. I shook some sense into the lad – a sandbag had hit him a crack on the head – and we dug the deepest doover on the battlefield. We were glad of it. At dawn our tanks came up and began fighting their battle right in amongst us, manoeuvring for position and firing while what seemed like every tank and anti-tank gun in the Afrika Korps fired back. Solid shot was ricochetting all over the place, and there was H.E. too. The whole show was fantastic. Some of our lads had to skin out of their trenches several times to avoid being run over. One Sherman backed towards me. The Tankie saw me, worked round my trench, and stopped a yard or two away. I looked up, and there was a ruddy great gun-barrel hanging over my head. There was one hell of a bang, and showers of sand came down on top of us. The Boche fired back, but missed: we heard the shell go by a few feet away. I thought my runner was going to crack – he'd had a fairly eventful morning – but he was a good lad and hung on. Then the tank went away.... I saw thirty of our own tanks brewed up in that small area, and as many Boche ones were blazing and smoking a thousand yards away on the Tel el Aqqaquir Ridge. In the middle of it all, Major Walford came tearing round our positions in a jeep, of all things. Yes, in a jeep. In the middle of the tank battle....'

The tanks retired, and left us to a second night of shelling. We adjusted our positions and sorted out the men who had linked up with the wrong companies on the previous night. Protective listening patrols were sent out. By dawn we were organised and solid, and the tanks were coming through again to fight the final and decisive half of their battle. To our relief they passed right through us. Again the German eighty-eights opened up, again the air filled with the crack of solid shot;

but as the day advanced the columns of black smoke which marked the kills drew farther and farther away, and by night our armour had broken through. The battle was over.

The cost had been bitter. Twelve officers and one hundred and sixty-five men of the Battalion had been killed or wounded. Captain Murdo Swanson had laid out in the desert with his leg off, cracking jokes with a man who lay near him. He died. Johnnie Butler, O.C. 4 Platoon, could not bear the screaming of a wounded man and went out to get him. He was killed. Billy Mackintosh was killed on the third night as he sat outside his trench. There were many others. We looked around us, saw the gaps in a team which had existed almost unchanged for three years, and were appalled. It was a new idea, then.

Up on the Coast Road the traffic was streaming, nose to tail, towards the west.

DESERT JOURNEY

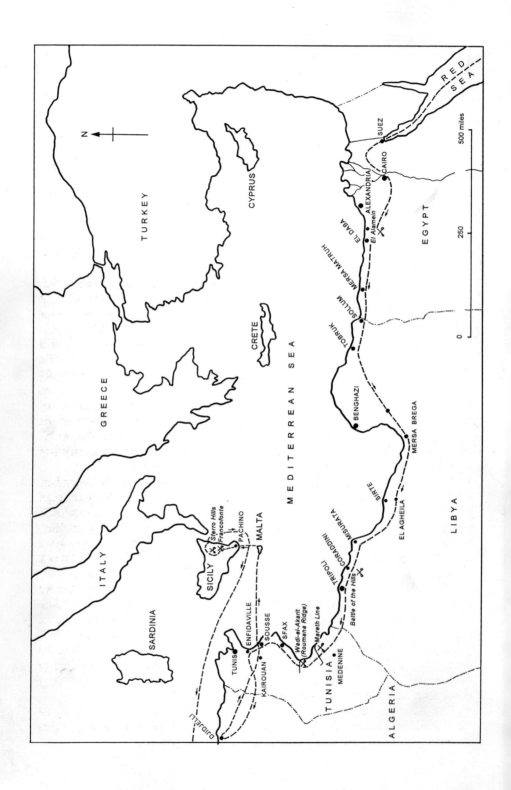

CHAPTER THREE

Desert Journey

I

SINCE 1941 the war had been swinging back and forth like a pendulum across Libya, Cyrenaica and Egypt, first one side and then the other attacking until it had outrun its supplies and was forced to stop. It was in the nature of things that this should be so. Distances were great and the advantage lay with the side which was retreating towards its supply bases rather than with the one which was stretching ever farther and farther out into the desert. Sooner or later the stiffening defence was too much for the attackers, the advance petered out, and the race to build up for the next attack began – with the odds heavily in favour of the side which had lost the previous battle.

The aim of both sides, naturally, was to build up so great a superiority that momentum could be maintained until a decisive victory was won; but with the whole north coast of Africa to play with this meant mobile war of a scope never before attempted. There was almost no limit to the distance to which either side could retreat. True, the Axis had a definite aim: if they could reach the Suez Canal it was difficult to see how we could continue to maintain ourselves in the Middle East. But where was the point at which we could pin the Axis against the wall? Tripoli was no good: they could retreat far beyond that. Tunis? Algiers? Was there any real reason why they should not retreat all the way to the Atlantic. Either we had to surround them where they stood (and annihilation on these terms could not be depended upon) or we must set some limit to their retreat, a limit within which our own momentum could be kept going. If we stopped before final victory was won, Rommel would have us back to Alexandria at the next throw.

The answer to this problem was the North African campaign. In December, 1942, American and British troops landed on the western shores of the Mediterranean and began to attack towards us from Algeria and northern Tunisia. They met stiff resistance in difficult country; but that was relatively unimportant. The great thing was that the wall was there and the limit had been set. If we could keep going we should pin the Afrika Korps against our friends, and the pendulum would never swing again. The distance we should have to travel was two thousand miles.

We set out on the first big stage of this journey on November 21. Before then we had been recuperating from the battle, moving up the coast by easy stages to Sidi Haneish while the chase was taken over by 10 Corps. We had licked our sores, received reinforcements, and even suffered a period of spit-and-polish which culminated in a Brigade Motor Show. Senussi tribesmen, looking down from the escarpment in the middle of a five-day dust-storm, were edified by the sight of hundreds of painfully clean vehicles sitting for judgment in the wilderness. They shook their heads in wonder and returned to their camels.

Troop-carrying transport arrived, and for three days we followed the Coast Road until we reached Acroma, not quite three hundred miles on our way. There we waited four days, preparing for our first long desert journey.

The Coast Road, that ill-used stretch of tarmac which ran all the way from Alexandria to Algiers, was by any peacetime standard a very bad road indeed. It was crumbling and bumpy and full of pot-holes, and the Germans had sown it generously with mines. But it was a road. It was clearly defined, and it led somewhere. It was not two feet deep in dust. Limestone ledges did not lurk on it to jolt the unwary. It was one of the few signs of man's handiwork in all the desert, and its slender black ribbon unwinding across the miles of sand and rock was a sight which cheered both the Germans and ourselves. It was the one living stream in a dead ocean. Along it our journey to Acroma had been in the nature of a sight-seeing tour, interesting and not strenuous, with the blue Mediterranean on our right hand, the haze of the desert on our left, and all around us the litter left in the wake of the retreating Axis army.

West of Acroma, Cyrenaica bulged out into the sea carrying the road with it, and there we took to the desert, heading straight across country for Agadabia.

When old age comes upon us and our grandchildren have taken to drifting quietly away whenever the desert is mentioned, we shall no doubt have convinced ourselves that the African campaign was a romantic episode instead of the dirty business it was. We shall chuckle over the jolly patrols we did and the brilliant way in which we dodged the shells, and sigh for a sniff of desert dust or one sip of that wonderful water we had at Marsa Brega. All of which will be nonsense. Here and now we should be well advised to give our problematic grandchildren permission to call us fools and liars if we start off on that tack forty years hence. On one subject, however, we should claim exemption, and that is desert navigation. Desert navigation was fun. The father of the art was Ralph Bagnold, an Army officer who pottered about the Western Desert in a truck in the early 1930's, evolving a new technique as he went along and afterwards writing an excellent book about it called "Libyan Sands". The principal tools bequeathed to us were the sand-channel and the sun-compass, and in their uses we had been slowly acquiring skill since we landed in Africa. Now we were to put our experience to the test.

As has already been pointed out, the Western Desert was as devoid of landmarks as the North Atlantic and trucks crossing it had to be guided like ships as soon as they left the road or tracks. There were three distinct problems in navigation; first, the formation in which the battalion would move; second, the method by which the individual vehicle would move; and third, the method by which direction would be maintained.

The battalion moved in desert formation. That is to say the vehicles scattered themselves over the desert, widely dispersed as protection from air attack, travelled in parallel lanes, and took their direction from the navigator's truck. When they stopped for the night they lagered, came together in a tight ring like the ox-waggons on the veld so that the crews could dig in and protect them. Lagering was always done after sundown so that the stopping place could not be seen by the enemy, and it was broken before dawn brought the dive-hombers over.

This was all very well in theory; but in practice the neat parallel lanes seldom happened. The going varied. Vehicles stuck. Desert formation became elastic, the columns constantly expanding or contracting as the leading vehicles met firm ground or soft. This brings us to the individual vehicle. Each truck carried two sand-channels and many shovels; and each driver, if he knew his job, kept his eyes skinned for the best going. Smooth yellow sand, attractive to the uninitiated, was deadly: unless it was of short duration and taken at speed the truck would bog to the axles. Pebbly going was usually good, but sometimes it was a deceptive crust with soft sand underneath which only the experienced eye could detect at a distance. In some places the desert was smooth and firm as a race-track for miles on end and in every direction: in others it was treacherous as treacle. Even the good driver could not always get through.

Back in the early days, if a truck bogged we tried to drive it out. This was fatal. It only dug deeper. The only sure way – and often it was a slow and exhausting way – was to dig the sand out from around the rear wheels and insert the sand-channels, which were two sheets of steel a foot wide and as long as the wheel-base of the truck. If these were placed in front of the rear wheels they formed, in effect, a little five- or six-foot road along which the truck could be driven. If, after being driven the six feet, the truck had gained sufficient momentum it could continue slowly on its way while the crew ran after it, flung the channels in at the back, and bundled on board while the truck was still moving. If, on the other hand, the truck had not gained sufficient momentum, it simply ran off the end of the channels and bogged again. The whole heart-breaking business would then start over again and continue in six-foot bites until the obstacle had been crossed. It was chilly enough in the mornings in November, but by noon the sun was as hot as ever and the flies were iniquitous. Trucks always seemed to bog at noon. There is no thirst in all the world greater than that of the man who, pestered by flies and with his shirt sticking to his back, has just inserted the sand-channels for the fifth time at twelve o'clock mid-day in the Western Desert. Many similies were invented to describe this state, but none can be repeated here.

These problems were, of course, shared by the navigator too, and to an increased degree because he had to assess the going across the whole battalion front and not just ahead of his own vehicle. He also had special problems, the chief of which was to handle his sun-compass correctly. The sun-compass was a brilliantly simple invention. There were several models – the Cole and the Bagnold were the ones most commonly used – and the principle on which they all worked was that of the sun-dial in reverse. If a sun-dial is set up so that it points to the north, the shadow will tell the time. Let us, said Bagnold, Cole, and the others, set up a sort of sun-dial so that it points to the time, and then the shadow will tell us where north is. It was as simple as that. The Cole sun-compass, which was the type we had, was a six-inch metal plate with a needle rising vertically from the centre of it and the hours of the day marked round the edge. It was set for the bearing the convoy wanted to follow and, after a few adjustments had been made, all the navigator had to do was drive his truck in such a manner that the shadow of the needle fell across the correct time.

Difficulties naturally arose when bad going was encountered and the truck could not hold to the bearing. These detours were carefully plotted by the navigator, who had constantly to watch new bearings, the hour of the day, and the mileage clock in the truck. When opportunity offered, he cut back on to the old bearing again. It was an anxious job, but a fascinating one.

See then George Green leading the Battalion to Agadabia. His truck had a little seat built high behind the driver's cab, so that the roof of the cab was in front of him like a desk and he squatted above everyone else like a rather worried Buddha. By his left hand, screwed to the roof of the cab, was the sun-compass. In his right hand was his ordinary compass, for there was as yet no sun. In his pocket were an enormous notebook, many pencils, protractor, and a wad of squared paper; and draped round his person was the mass of equipment, binoculars, map-boards, waterbottles and so on which he perpetually carried about: George was bulky, but he never seemed to have enough space for all his gear. Behind him were one hundred and fifty Battalion vehicles. Ahead were two hundred miles of desert.

The Germans were making a stand at Marsa Brega, and the whole of the Highland Division was moving forward to bolster up the handful of British troops and tanks which had so far reached that point. The first leg of our journey was to take us beyond Bir Hachim, the fort where the French had held out so gallantly during the big attack in July, 1942. We started at seven o'clock in the morning on November 28 feeling cold, miserable and wet, for it was actually raining. For days we had studied diagrams and sand-table models representing our layout on the move; but visibility was poor and it was some time before we had sorted ourselves out. One half of the Battalion, under Major Walford, was far behind, acting as rearguard to the Brigade. The rest of us formed the advance-guard. Hence the worried look on the face of Major Green, who had visions of leading over a thousand vehicles astray.

The first day passed without incident, except that our rearguard fetched up several miles ahead of everyone else and was gravely disturbed next morning by the sound of an ''enemy'' army starting up behind it. The bad weather cleared. At four o'clock in the morning we were off on the second leg, heading along the so-called Msus Track, which was no track at all. Starting up was hectic. The Brigade in lager covered two square miles of desert. The night was still black; and there had been a theory, entirely without foundation, that if all vehicle engines were warmed up for a few minutes the whole Brigade would be able to move off together. In actual practice there were many vehicles, especially the Diesel ones, which had to be towed before they would start. The drivers of these vehicles and those which were towing them knew perfectly well that if they were left behind for as little as five minutes, dawn would find them lost in an empty desert. Excited figures ran about in the darkness wailing for tow-chains. Engines revved and died. Exasperated sergeants stormed at delay. At last we were ready and began feeling our way through the maze of slit trenches to the open desert, straining our eyes for the vehicle ahead or for the tiny green light which Major Green carried at his mast-head. The morning was fresh, and cool, and as we gathered speed and rumbled along together there was excitement in the air. Gradually we opened out as the daylight grew; and when the sun came up we were scattered as far as the eye could see, each vehicle with its little plume of dust, each with its nose pointed towards the west.

It was exhilarating, that journey. The desert rolled on and on, unchanging, a world of white glare and blue sky with a wind which in a journey of a thousand miles had not found one smell it could carry to our nostrils. In battle there were smells, but where this wind had come from there was none. It was sparkling, arid, dead as a diamond. We stopped for breakfast. All over the desert little figures jumped from their vehicles. Smoke arose. In half an hour the meal had been cooked and eaten and we were on the move again, ploughing along past mile after mile of sandy shingle, flat and trackless and broken only by an occasional salt-pan or patch of scrub. As the day grew the mirage flickered on the skyline, squashing the leading trucks into little black puddles, elongating them absurdly until they advanced like pencils standing on end, or swallowing them in lakes of blue water or forests upside down. In the late afternoon we had our last meal, and as night fell began to close in again. Engines seemed to roar more loudly now, and the dust-clouds merged. We began to peer again, anxious for slit trenches but determined not to lose our leaders. Then it was dark, and we were digging in, and George Green was climbing stiffly from his throne, worried about the route for tomorrow.

Late on the evening of December 1 we arrived at our new location west of Agadabia, with the enemy a few miles up the Coast Road on the Marsa Brega line.

II

The rest of this chapter should tell of a battle, but there was no battle. The enemy withdrew before we could get to grips with them, the chase was taken over by the New Zealanders and the 7th Armoured Division, and we were left to celebrate Christmas in peace though not in comfort. This period, however, was not all turkey and NAAFI beer. We went straight into the line when we arrived on December 2 and remained there until the 8th, a period which most of us, and in particular those who went out on patrol, are never likely to forget. The Germans had arrived with some time in hand, and they had employed it in laying mines.

We did not have many casualties from mines, but the threat of them was enough to put everyone on edge. They were beastly things, and in the sandy desert there was almost no place where they could not be buried easily. There were many varieties, but only two main types – the anti-tank, which we already knew; and the anti-personnel, which we were now to meet in bulk for the first time. We were foot-sloggers, and anti-tank mines seldom bothered us much: we could walk over them in safety, and by the time our vehicles advanced the Sappers had generally been able to sweep a path for them. We had our accidents, but not many. Anti-personnel mines were another story altogether. The least touch set them off. In those days the *schumine*, a small wooden mine which could not be picked up by detectors, had mercifully not been invented; but even so, detecting was so slow a process and the distances to be covered by our patrols were so great, that it simply was not practicable to sweep ahead for traces of the metal S-mines then in vogue. The patrol just had to go out and take its chance.

The S-mine, or Jumping Jimmie, was a nasty piece of work. It was about the size of a two-pound pot of jam, and was filled with ball bearings. Three tiny antennae projecting from the top were all that showed once it had been laid. When trodden upon it jumped into the air and exploded at chest-height, scattering the bearings far and wide. One of the most hideous features of these contrivances was the cumulative effect, because, as they were nearly always laid in clusters, one casualty only too frequently led to others. Despite the necessarily inhuman orders laid down, few men, when it came to the pinch, could bear to leave their comrades wounded and untended. They went in after them, and they too were blown up.

Often as many as three or four men were killed or wounded in this way on successive mines. S-mines were sown in thousands in front of Marsa Brega, and our orders were to patrol.

The Battalion was on the right of the Brigade line, with the sea only a few hundred yards away. It was a delightful spot, Boche permitting. Our positions were among silver sand-ridges, and ''A'' Company even boasted a few palm trees and a spring of brackish water. From our observation post among the dunes we could see a sweep of blue bay with a grounded schooner and a wreck piled up on the dazzling sands; and from the end of the bay, forming our horizon, a ridge ran inland. On it was Marsa Brega, the usual mud-brick coastal village, with a mosque surrounded by a high crenellated wall on the right, a square white building we called the Inn on the left beside the Coast Road, and the odd mud-hut and palm tree between. The place was three thousand yards away. On the slope below it the line of the enemy wire could easily be seen through glasses.

On the night of the 3rd we had two patrols out investigating the wire, one under Lieutenant F.C.H. Paxton and the other under Lieutenent A.J.Dimach. Both came back undamaged and with information. Next day the Divisional Commander, Major-General D.N.Wimberley, D.S.O., M.C. (better known as Big Tam, King of Scotland) came up to see our observation post, the fame of which was beginning to spread. As his badges of rank were covered by his jersey, he was told to keep his bloody 'ead dahn by Private Harrison who was then in residence and had no desire to have shells drawn about him by anyone showing on the skyline. The General very properly obeyed, joined him, and chatted for half an hour.

'Oo's Tam?' asked Harrison afterwards of a petrified sergeant. 'Cripes! Thought e was a ruddy subaltern. Still, 'e didn't oughter 'ave stood up on them long legs of 'is. Not outside *my* O.P.'.

That night Lieutenants I.G.H.Houldsworth, A.J.G.Offin, and Dimach were out with patrols; and on the 5th, Lieutenants H. S. Robertson and Houldsworth. On the 6th, Captain G.A.Willock, Second-Lieutenant D.J.M.Robertson and twenty men from ''D'' Company crossed No Man's Land to investigate enemy positions, and repeated the performance on the following night, when Graham Offin was also out again. By that time we had a good idea of the enemy dispositions, and we had laid a minefield of our own. Three men had been killed and one wounded; but this was a light loss compared with some of those suffered by other units on the front. Every day brought fresh stories of explosions in the dark, scattered patrols, and heavy casualties. Mines were everywhere, and we could count ourselves lucky to have escaped at so little cost.

On the night of December 8 we were relieved by the 1st Black Watch and went back to an area near Agedabia to prepare for the attack on Marsa Brega.

III

This attack, as has already been said, never took place. On the 13th we moved back to our old positions in the line with all plans complete; but that same night the Germans retreated, mining the Coast Road as they went. For some days there was talk of us following immediately, but in the end the mine situation proved to be so bad that we were told we should be left in peace until the Engineers had cleared the road. Apart from one minor journey of fifteen miles along the coast, we had nothing more to do until Christmas had come and gone; and even then our job was nothing more exciting than another short journey and unloading supplies on Ras el Ali jetty – vitally important, and work at which we broke a few records, but hardly what we been led to expect in the grim days among the Marsa Brega minefields.

'Imagine a straight tarmac road,' wrote Paddy Nairne of the first halt, 'whose monotony is relieved only by kilo stones leaning drunkenly and by telegraph wires needing repair. Picture a brown rocky ridge stretching for four hundred yards north of the tarmac road to a marshy flat coloured like milk chocolate. Then let your mind's eye cross the flat and pass over the undulating grassy dunes, reminiscent of a first-class bunker, until it rests on the grey sea that is the Gulf of Sirte. The Battalion lived, stretched out from east to west, in the edge of the sand dunes. We slept to the roar of the waves. Hector Macrae (the Quartermaster) and "B" Echelon camped under the ridge on the road side of the flat and cynically watched the marshy two hundred yards between them and Battalion H.Q. become impassable for vehicles as a result of the December rains. Here we stayed for nearly four days, and here we passed Christmas, 1942....

'It has always been a regimental custom for the companies to enjoy a special dinner on New Year's Day.... This year the occasion was Christmas Day – for operational reasons, some said, but chiefly, we thought, because the pork would have been bad by January 1. NAAFI had supplied pork, a few turkeys, plum duff, and half a bottle of beer for each man. George Willock had collected it all from Marble Arch on Christmas Eve: the supplies had been flown up from the Delta, he said. Some companies had made elaborate dining "halls" by digging a broad rectangular slit trench and using the sand left inside as a table. Petrol tins were cut and used as platters. The Commanding Officer (Colonel Stirling had returned from hospital by this time), accompanied by the Adjutant and R.S.M., was piped into each company area, where with a glass of whisky he proposed the company's health. His speech inevitably became longer with each company he visited.... He arrived at H.Q. Company to the tune of the Company March and on the shoulders of two strong men. He spoke cheerfully, with a tendency to repetition....

'At four o'clock the pipes and drums beat retreat on the edge of the marshy flat. The sky was the colour of lead: it was to pour with rain within two hours. The pipes and drums were the only sound in that waste land. It was a dreary and yet distinguished spectacle. We were fascinated as we stood there, charmed like snakes by the pipes and by the desert landscape. No cloud moved in the sky; not a blade of grass rustled in the dunes; no bird flew. Only the band playing and marching on the unechoing sands....

'Later... I climbed the hillock on my way to bed. Rain had stopped and the moon was up. The sand was glistening white, like icing on a cake. I tried to pretend it was snow. I thought of Britain. Was there snow on the ground at home? Had the village church bells been rung in the morning? Was it a good year for holly berries? Home thoughts from abroad are usually sentimental nonsense. No doubt it had been a mildly rainy day in Scotland.... I went to bed. There was a wind flapping the sides of the bivvy. I reckoned it would be raining on the morrow.'

THE ROAD TO TRIPOLI

(previous page) The combined pipes and drums of the 2nd and 5th Seaforths parade at Tripoli.

(above) C.S.M. Durrand who was in the thick of the Battle of the Hills ... 'Yon was the worst business I was ever in.'

(left and below) General Montgomery and Winston Churchill take the march past of the Highland Division.

CHAPTER FOUR

The Road To Tripoli

I

LEAVING THE Battalion for the moment to unload petrol on Ras el Ali jetty, let us consider the situation from the Axis point of view. A few divisions of first-class German troops, somewhat knocked about, were retreating westwards with an equal number of Italians who, whatever their personal charm, were militarily speaking a dead loss. If this army turned and made a determined stand it would be surrounded: open desert stretched inland for a thousand miles, and no matter how far it extended its flank we would always, given time, work round it. The Germans could, of course, run away faster than we could follow, especially if they mined the road; but that policy had a limited future. These things being so, the best they could do was compromise. They would run, but run slowly. Wherever the ground was in their favour they would make a stand, force us to deploy and prepare a set-piece attack, and retire again before the attack materialised.

Fortunately for us, the places where this could be done were few. Marsa Brega had been one of them, a bottle-neck where the Coast Road squeezed between salt marshes. Now they were digging in on the Wadi Zemzem, a dried-up watercourse two hundred miles to the west.

We did not think they would stay there. Their best defensive chances lay far to the west in Tunisia, and it was unlikely that they would risk any major part of their force on a position so relatively untenable as the Wadi. The usual formula of a week's patrolling in the line, followed by artillery preparation, followed by attack would only give them warning; and when the attack did come we should find empty trenches in return for our wasted week. How much better, it must have seemed to General Montgomery, the Eighth Army commander, it would be if we were to wade right in, break what there was of the Zemzem positions, and make a dash straight for Tripoli.

And so, in early January, the rumour began to filter round that something big was in the wind. On the 11th we left Ras el Ali without regret, and by night were in the Marble Arch staging area. That day we heard Colonel Stirling had left us to take over command of 154 Brigade, and that Major Walford was our new colonel. Next night we were at Nofilia, on the 13th at Sirte, and on the 24th reached our new positions on the Wadi Chebir. The whole Division was there, with 154 Brigade actually in the line and 153 and ourselves lying a little in rear.

The plan had all the elements of a Wild West thriller, with more than a hint of the Charge of the Light Brigade thrown in as well. To appreciate how we felt about it, it must be understood that to us Tripolitania, the scene of Mussolini's most ambitious colonial experiment, was the Promised Land flowing with eggs and dates and tunny-fish, where houses were built of materials more enduring than mud-brick and there was at least one town with more than a single street in it. Tripolitania, which would have broken the heart of any British farmer, was civilisation; and we were going into it. We were going a long way into it.

On the night of January 15/16, 154 Brigade was going to provide a firm base from which one battalion of 153 Brigade, the 1st Gordons, would attack. When the

Gordons had made a hole, our brigade was going to line up in its vehicles, move through the gap, and make a dash for Misurata without more ado. Misurata was exactly a hundred miles away. At the same time, 7th Armoured Division and the 2nd New Zealand Division, which were operating in the south and already beginning to curl round the German flank, would make a bee-line for Tripoli. And the other divisions? There were no other divisions. These three – 7th Armoured, the Kiwis, and ourselves plus 22 Armoured Brigade – were the only effective fighting force available in the Eight Army at this time, so great were the distances we had covered and the difficulties of keeping us supplied. We three, with nothing behind us, were to be launched into the blue.

The night came, the guns opened up in support of the Gordons, and we moved off in our trucks to the Wadi Ues-ca, our marshalling area for the advance. It was a moonlit night, bitterly cold, and the trucks raised a cloud of dust which made driving very difficult. We reached the Wadi after being bombed on the way, and settled down to wait.

The night was an anxious one. The whole plan hinged on the Germans imagining that an attack by one battalion was an attack by half the Eighth Army; and if they stayed to fight the Gordons instead of running away we should find ourselves being thrown in to help. Meantime we could only dig, hope, and, if possible, sleep.

With dawn came the news that the Gordons had succeeded. We were put at one hour's notice to move, keyed ourselves up for the big advance, and, as so often happened when there seemed to be no doubt about the immediate future, something went wrong and we did not move after all. During the morning we sat dozing beside our vehicles in the Wadi while white clouds sailed in a blue sky and the Light Brigade remained obstinately inert. It was early afternoon before our orders came through and we were on our way with the 5th Camerons leading. We crossed four or five miles of stony undulating desert, through a minefield gap churned with dust and strewn with the signs of battle, and past the Gordons, dug in and resting beside the positions they had taken. A few shells landed among the Camerons. Our route lay almost due north. The Zemzem was a wide and straggling wadi, filled with tall grasses and scrubby undergrowth which made it difficult to keep either formation or direction and caused many halts. It was no place to meet an enemy dug in and waiting, and we took no chances until we had reached more open country. Soon it was evening, and we began closing in to lager. It was an eerie landscape in the moonlight, and as the German rearguards still hanging on behind us were sending up their usual firework display of verey lights, we were conscious of our isolation. Misurata seemed a long way off, as indeed it was. We stopped, and dug in, and tried to sleep.

We moved off again next morning before dawn, a time of day when even the most exciting plan is apt to be viewed with no enthusiasm at all. 'There is a mild literary tradition,' wrote Paddy Nairne of that morning, 'that a few hours' sleep under the Wide and Starry Sky (preferably, I understand, in a casual ditch) brings refreshment to the body and inspiration to the soul. I always think there must be some misunderstanding about this. We struggled from our slit trench beds, as on many mornings before and since, with dew-sodden hair, blear eyes, and stiff limbs. Everywhere engines were being warmed with a roar, and men were stamping cold feet as they adjusted their equipment and munched a quick biscuit. A little more than fifteen minutes after reveille our column had started.'

Our spirits rose with the sun, and once it was fairly up and we had breakfast inside us the doubts of the night vanished and we were prepared to bash on indefinitely. War can scarcely be classed among the more exhilarating pastimes but it does have its rewards, such things as the feel of a good stiff drink in the calm after a battle, or the comfort of a good bed found by chance, or the luxury of emerging from a dust-storm into an Alexandria leave redolent of baths and cream-cakes. Such pleasures, however, are pleasures of contrast, on a par with the man who hit himself on the head with a hammer because it was so pleasant when he left off. The true pleasures of war are very few, but undoubtedly the unopposed breakthrough is one of them. The dust is less dusty because it is enemy dust, the scenery more beautiful because it has been stolen. Speed is intoxication. To watch the miles slip by in enemy territory is one of the major excitements of life. The sun shone in a pale blue sky over a landscape of brown sand and dark green scrub; and spread across the land, as far as the eye could see, were trucks two hundred yards apart rolling along to Misurata. Everything was right that day. There were even wild flowers in the wadi near Churgia landing ground where we stopped to brew lunch.

We halted once during the afternoon while the advance-guard made a show of force which produced a hundred prisoners from an Italian ammunition dump – good news, for it meant our sudden advance had taken their lines of communication by surprise. Before last light we stopped again to brew the evening meal; and once more the order was 'Bash on.'

It is impossible to describe accurately or in order the events of that most muddled night. I think we may take it that at no time did we encounter the German main body (which had fled, leaving only rearguards in the Wadi Zemzem). Once again I must fall back on Paddy Nairne.

'There was no real fighting,' he writes, 'not even by the advance-guard. But there were many alarms and excursions, and often a fog of dust and sand. There was also a certain amount of that inconsequential dash which one finds in the battle scenes of a Shakespeare play. A film director who wished to convey the right impression could only give his audience a succession of confused shots – of George Green standing on the seat of his truck, greatcoat buttoned to the neck, placidly playing the part of that Man of Iron, the Unshakeable Navigator; of the first white farms of Tripolitania appearing like ghosts in the moonlight; of Colonel Walford standing on the track as he discovered that the back half of the column had mistakenly passed the front half at a halt; of the undefended anti-tank ditch which the vehicles had to cross in single file; of the Intelligence Officer, despatched to recover the back half of the column, driving hopefully and hopelessly into the night; of flares and demolitions lighting the sky like fireworks from the direction of Misurata; of the Commanding Officer and Intelligence Officer, separated by three or four miles of featureless sand, trying in vain to explain to each other over the wireless where they were; of a party of military government officers shaken and excited after a party of Germans had sniped them in the village of Crispi, which the Brigade had bypassed; of the Pole Star, which was our guide, gazing impassively on the troubled desert land below; and finally, when the Battalion had halted, of silent sentries posted and men sleeping peacefully on the chilled dewy ground till daybreak.

'Then next morning, as the gladdening sun of Monday, January 18 arose and shed its glow on the Promised Land, the bogeys and anxieties of the darkness disappeared like bad dreams. Before our eyes lay fields of tall green asphodel, trim white villas, high water-towers, small green trees; and scarcely two miles away stood Misurata, gleaming white, romantic and seductive through the black olive trees.'

As Paddy points out, this would have made a good final curtain; but real life, and especially real war, is a messy business and is unhelpful in this respect to the writers of histories. We had barely shaved and begun to think of lunch before we were ordered to carry on for another fourteen miles to Garibaldi. This we did, and the rest of the day and the better part of the night were spent in searching the area for Germans. Next day, January 19, we were left in peace, surrounded by seemingly inexhaustible supplies of water. We washed our clothes: and ourselves, and felt much the better for it. In the evening we thought of sleep, a little wistfully as befits those who know from experience when a thing is too good to be true. We did not sleep. Instead we moved ten miles and rejoined the Brigade at a place called Zliten.

II

If there is one thing the pious infantryman prays to be spared, it is a hurried attack. Modern war is a complicated business, with many pieces which must interlock if the picture is to be complete; and unless each piece knows its place there is a mess. The artillery may shell its own side, the tanks become divorced from the infantry, battalions take the wrong positions and find themselves shot up from the flanks. Knowing this, the wise commander likes time to plan accurately, seeing the ground for himself, discussing it with the commanders of his supporting arms, tying up everything, having the lie of the ground and the moves which are to take place upon it clear in his own mind and in the minds of his subordinates. The process is lengthy, but it pays. A set-piece attack is seldom costly.

In a pursuit, however, such attacks are frequently impossible. Both sides are moving fast, and the pursuers constantly run against small rearguards left to delay, if possible, the entire force. In these cases there is often only one thing to do if the enemy is not to escape – fling in one or two battalions immediately, root out the opposition, and allow the main body to pass through unimpeded. There is no time for reconnaissance or elaborate conferences. After the bare minimum of planning, the attack goes in.

The Battle of the Hills, which was fought on January 21, 1943, was one such attack. The Highland Division was advancing along the general line of the Coast Road, with Tripoli, our goal for so long, almost within its grasp, when the enemy elected to leave a strong rearguard astride the road west of Homs. The Division's advance-guard bumped this resistance after dark. It was all very awkward. The country was broken up by deep wadis and rocky hills which did not appear on the small-scale maps which were all we had at that time. The moon was admittedly bright, but it was no substitute for a good map and broad daylight. Still, the position had to be taken quickly; and General Wimberley ordered an immediate attack by two brigades. 154 Brigade plus 2nd Seaforth were to make a wide outflanking movement to the right, and the rest of our own Brigade was to attack frontally. Zero hour was to be 0630 hours on the 21st.

While all this was going on, we were driving slowly up the road from Zliten in the dark, comforted by the knowledge that 154 Brigade was ahead of us and with not the smallest hint that we were about to be pitched-forked into a battle. Presently the column stopped. Rumours spread of a hold-up. We heard that 154 were doing a right hook, but still did not feel that we need be embroiled. The column started again and we passed through Homs, a ghostly place in the darkness. Still the miles clicked up on our dashboard clocks. Nine, ten, eleven. This was getting serious. Suddenly the sky split, and we were passing through our gun-lines. We crept along for another two miles, resigned by this time to the worst. The guns behind us were still firing (had we only known it, they were trying to register their targets by moonlight) and the shells were passing directly overhead. No, things did not look too good. Suddenly Major Davidson was shouting from the roadside:

General Wimberley briefing officers of the 2nd Seaforth before the Battle of the Hills.

'In there on the left... disperse... debus... get ready for battle... "O" Group here immediately... O.K.?'

'O.K.' we said, without enthusiasm.

In five minutes we had gathered and were being told that we were to march forward to an assembly area a mile along the road. The Colonel, it seemed, was off on a recce with the Brigadier. A recce at this time of night? Yes.

From this point on, the story of the battle had best be told by Captain J.A.F. Watt, O.C. "B" Company, who was in the thick of it throughout and, having ample leisure in a hospital bed, wrote an account of it afterwards.

'At the assembly area we met the C.O.,' he wrote. 'We were to attack two sharp conical hills we could see faintly outlined against the sky two or three thousand yards away. One of them was farther away than the other and to the left as we looked at them. The attack would therefore be in two phases. The two leading companies – "A" right and "B" left – would take the first hill; and on their success signal the two rear companies – "C" right and "D" left – would pass by their left and take the second hill. An artillery concentration would be laid down on the two features to help us forward – if the guns could be brought up in time. Tanks would support the leading wave – if they arrived in time. Two three-inch mortars would be in support of each company. Battalion H.Q. would move between the two rear companies.

'From what we could make of the maps and what little we could see of the country, it seemed as though the road ran past the right of our objectives. This assumption proved to be wrong. The road in fact curved sharply to the left across the line of our advance, then right again between the hills. On our way back from orders we met John Thornton, the Brigade Intelligence Officer, who was taking bearings, and he warned us that there was something fishy about the map and that we might have to cross the road....

'About 0515 hours we began to get the men awake and ready to go. They were in good spirits and ready for anything. A message came round postponing the start, and we began to worry about what time would be left us to dig in on the objectives before first light. All this time the mediums kept pounding away at the enemy, wakening him up thoroughly; and soon his fixed-line spandaus firing tracer were carving lanes of light down the line on which we should have to advance.

'Through the din we began to hear tank noises, and our hearts lifted as the tanks crawled into their appointed places behind the two leading companies. There was no time to liaise with them – just a brief shout as we started to move up to the start.

' "We're off now. Follow on."

'Their engines roared into life, but they did not move. The ground was too broken, but at the start of the attack we thought they were with us. We reached the start-line just at zero and crossed it in perfect line, a little bunching here and there perhaps, but otherwise in good formation. The two rear companies were held up by the failure of the tanks to get forward, and the distance between the two waves was more than it should have been. Battalion H.Q. moved at the correct time, and was about half-way between the two waves.

'The enemy, thoroughly aroused by our shelling, was firing everything he had. From our first objective mortar bombs began to drop uncomfortably close, but he was only guessing at our position and we had no casualties. After the first few hundred yards we settled down to a steady and pretty rapid advance. The line was unmistakable. Three spandaus firing tracer very conveniently marked the flanks and centre-line of our advance.

'Half-way, and still no casualties. A deep wadi blocked "A" Company's advance. A halt until Captain David Murray could find a crossing-place and reform on the other side, then on again. A steep ridge in front.

' "Up we go. That centre spandau must be trimming the grass on top."

'It was, but there were still no casualties as we went down the other side. The vicious chattering of the spandaus became louder, and others not firing tracer began to pour in their contribution from somewhere on our left front.

' "There's the road, and over we go." – and with the words the gun on the left sent a long burst down the road.

' "O.K. Cross now, and go like hell.'

'Between the bursts we got across the road.

' "Don't bunch on the left.... Don't bunch!... For God's sake don't BUNCH."

'On the lower slopes of the first objective, a momentary halt to take stock. Then up the last three hundred yards. The centre gun which had been such a great help all through the advance now became a definite embarrassment, as we should have to go straight for it. The bullets were crackling over our heads, and we could picture the gunner lying behind his gun just over the crest in front of us, very soon now to have the shoot of his life.

'We went on steadily, up the steep slope to within fifty yards of the gun. A deep breath.

' "All right, chaps. In we go."

'Down came the bayonets, and as we broke into a run the gun stopped firing and the Jocks let loose their horrid battle cry. Two dark figures rose out of the ground ahead of us and scuttled away into the darkness followed by a hail of bullets. That must have been the gun crew. Yes, there was the gun in the pit. A quick examination showed spent belts and empty cartridge cases, but no live ammo. Providence had been working overtime....

'But it was only the first false crest we had reached. On down the other side into a steep-sided wadi and a hellish concentration of mortar fire. Now we were getting casualties, particularly on the left.

'At this stage Colonel Walford appeared from nowhere, right up with the forward platoons. It was a habit he had. Daylight was coming in fast, and the thought of how we were going to get dug in was an ever-present nightmare. On the top of the next ridge were more Boche positions, and with grenade and bayonet we cleared and occupied them.

'In the meantime, Battalion H.Q. had been moving along in the correct position relative to the forward companies, but as day began to dawn they moved more and more to the left, following the line of the road. The forward companies had disappeared over the ridges, and exactly where they were there was no means of telling, as light automatics were blazing all along the front, the stammer of brens mingled with the high-speed rattle of the spandaus. On they went....'

But this is C.S.M. Durrand's story. At that time he was advancing down the wadi with the rest of the curious force which made up Battalion H.Q. that morning. The whole Battalion had been on the move before the battle began, and so the customary sorting-out of essential and unessential men had not taken place. H.Q. was nearly double its normal battle size; but, being the administrative department, its bulk added little to its fire-power. The clerks, signallers, intelligence men, and pipers who composed it, carried only rifles.

'We never crossed the road,' said Sergeant-Major Durrand. 'We didn't know it bore off to the left. As near as we could make out from the map it went to the right, and that was where we wanted to go. So we followed down the near side of it. There was a lot of tracer flying about and we were well spread out, but after a while we came to a narrow wadi that gave good cover. We closed in, and the whole lot of us got into it and followed it until it gave out on to open ground. The moon must have been obscured, because I remember it was very dark. I was with Captain Budge, the Adjutant. All we could see was a hill – just a wee hill – about a hundred yards ahead, showing up fine against the sky.

' "We'll take that hill, and then sit tight," says the Adjutant.

'We spread out again and started to go forward, and when we were fifty yards from the top every bloody thing in creation opened up on us. Point blank, it was. There were three machine-guns dug in on top of the hill, and the Boche were heaving tattie-mashers at us too. There was a sniper out on the right, but at that time it was dark and he was just shooting at the noise. We got down. The first burst had killed six or seven, and wounded two or three. The ground was too hard to dig, and anyway we were far too close for that. It was getting to be daylight, and the sniper on the right got busy....'

Meanwhile, let us return for a moment to Jimmy Watt and "B" Company, perched on their hilltop in the left forward position. They were in a bad spot, with the enemy in strength both on their flank and in front of them; and it soon became apparent that the Boche meant business. A counter-attack began to boil up, the first move being made by a small column of about a dozen who doubled into the open with their hands up. Lieutenant A.J.Dimack climbed out of his slit trench and went forward to accept their surrender. He was promptly shot, but managed to crawl to a trench and sham dead until we retook the position and the battle was over. The rest of the company fired everything they had, and the Boche went to ground. But this was only a preliminary. Soon a half-tracked armoured troop-carrier hove in sight, an ugly clanking thing impervious to bullets, which came on and on until it was within throwing range, whereupon a shower of tattie-mashers was launched from inside and behind it, and all was smoke, and noise, and confusion. The Germans who had been advancing under cover behind the half-track got in amongst our slit-trenches, and the company suffered more casualties. C.S.M. Elder, who was in a slit trench with Colonel Walford, was killed at this stage. A period of very close fighting followed, and then the Germans began to melt away. For the reason we must return to Sergeant-Major Durrand.

'When it was daylight, we saw we were pinned. We were on a rough slope covered with stones and bits of scrub but nothing you would call real cover. If we lifted our heads the machine-guns in front got us, and if we lay still where we were the sniper got us. We could hear a terrific racket coming from "B" Company over the hill, but we'd enough to think about without worrying about them. The sniper was only two hundred yards away, and he was deadly. First he got Sergeant McKirdy of the Intelligence Section right through the head. Then he wounded Mr. Nairne, and Mr. Ross the Signal Officer. One or two others got it too. He was just picking us off.

'The Adjutant says: "We'd better get out of here."

' "Ay, sir," I says, "but how are you going to do it?"

'It was open ground behind us, d'you see, a machine-gun had the entrance to the wadi taped. Still, he was right. We had to get back to the wadi some way.

' "We'll never make it if we all rush," he says "We'll have to get out in threes. Pass the word back. The ones farthest back go first."

'We were all spread out, but the word got back. The first three were Joe Younger the R.S.M., Gunn the piper, and a fellow from the 2nd Battalion who'd been lost and tagged along with us. I don't know his name. They got up and ran, and I saw the sand pumping up all round them. The three of them were dead before they got ten yards.

'We could hear somebody away in the distance behind us shouting: "Come back. Come back." There was a good number of us left at that time. We told the next three to spread out and try a different route. They were Sergeant Clark the Signal Sergeant, Ross the runner, and I forget the third. I think maybe it was Dougal of the Intelligence Section. Ross had a message to take back, asking for help. They ran for a ditch beside the road. Clark was killed, but the others made it. The next three tried to follow them. They were Lance-Corporal Wares, Dunbar the H.Q. Company clerk, and another lad. Wares and Dunbar were killed. Round about that time one of the sanitation men, Private Mathieson, was killed at my side by the sniper. It went on like that. We kept on putting them out three at a time, and about one in three was killed. A lot were wounded too – Bowie, Bannerman, Bruce – the M.O. was a busy man that day.

'When there were only the Adjutant and myself and about a dozen left, Jerry began putting down smoke. We couldn't make it out at all. We thought he must be going to attack, so the Adjutant says: "Let's get out."

'There were some wounded, so while the others tried to get them back the two of us kept blazing away into the smoke with all the rifles we could lay our hands on. The smoke was all round us by this time and we couldn't see a thing, but we thought the shooting might slow them down if they were attacking. We heard the others reach safety, and then we turned and ran for our lives. We missed the wadi in the smoke, but I saw a low irrigation bank ahead, and I knew that if I could only reach that I'd be safe. We went like hell. We could hear the others shouting: "It's a grand place. Come on in here."

'I just threw myself over the bank when I got to it, and went right down. It was only about two feet high, but it was enough. Captain Budge's foot tripped on the top of it. If he'd only let himself drop, he'd have been all right; but he tried to correct himself, and straightened up. A burst got him in the back. He was dead before he knew what hit him. The dyke was in the form of a square, and I collected all I could and began to lead them to the far side of it. In the end the lot of us got down behind it absolutely exhausted. I was gasping away there when I heard someone say: "What's wrong?"

'I looked up, and Captain Hunter of "C" Company was standing there. He knew the Boche were on the run, but I didn't.

' "For the love of God, get down," I said.

' "It's all right, laddie," says he.

'I lost my rag. "Don't call me laddie," I says.

' "Where's the Adjutant?" says he.

' "He's dead."

' "Good God! Well, the Signal Officer'll do." '

' "He won't," I said, "He's wounded." I was getting real wild.

' "Get me the I.O., then."

' "Wounded."

' "Well, the R.S.M."

' "Killed. And if you don't get down yourself, sir, you'll be the next."

'Then he told me. That was the end of it because, you see, the smoke hadn't been put down for an attack at all. The Boche were pulling out. Our rear companies had made straight for the second objective and had been pinned down before they reached it; but the counter-attacks hadn't shifted the forward companies, and "A" Company had begun to work round the Boche rear. What with that and 154 Brigade coming round the right as well, the Boche had had enough. So they went. After a while I went forward to look at the three gun positions that had given us all the trouble; and, without a word of a lie, all three of them were ankle-deep in spent cartridge cases... Yon was the worst business ever I was in.'

By nightfall, Sergeant-Major Durrand was our new Regimental Sergeant Major, Captain Douglas Findlay-Shirras had come from the 2nd Battalion to be Adjutant, and we were filling all the other gaps in our ranks. We had lost six officers and seventy-five men killed and wounded.

Next day our forward troops, racing neck and neck with the 7th Armoured Division, entered Tripoli.

THE ANTI-TANK DITCH

(previous page) In the Anti-Tank Ditch, Mareth Line, 22 March 1943.

(above) Short back and sides – Private Dow and Captain Grant Murray in the Wadi Zessar.

CHAPTER FIVE

The Anti-Tank Ditch

I

IT HAD BEEN a long way. We had come fifteen hundred miles from Alamein over ground which for centuries had been considered impassable to armies; and for the past week we had been averaging thirty-five miles a day against enemy rearguards and demolitions with our lines of communication stretched as they were never to be stretched again. Some trucks arrived in Tripoli towing half a dozen others, from each of which the last few precious drops of petrol had been syphoned to keep the leading truck going. And now, after months of supplying ourselves from the tin-pot harbours of the coastal villages, we had a port in our hands.

As a symbol Tripoli had its value: it was, after all, the capital of Mussolini's African Empire. For months it had been a milestone, something solid at which we could aim beyond the sand and the mirage and the desert sores and chlorinated water, a half-way mark that would put limits to the desert and prove to us that it was not utterly without end. But to those in charge of supply, Tripoli was not a half-way mark: it was a fresh start. The harbour had been wrecked and block ships sunk, but the damage was not irreparable. At first lighters, and later ocean-going ships, entered it; and a new supply base came into being. We could go ahead again with confidence, with all the things we needed.

We remained in or near Tripoli from January 25, 1943, until February 17, during which period Ian Robertson left us to become Brigade Major and we were, as usual, a good deal busier than we were when in action. There were guards, ceremonial church parades, fatigue parties, Divisional Highland Games much playing of the pipes, and a great pressing of trousers and polishing of cap-badges. Secret stocks of boot-polish were unearthed in the town, and it was rumoured that the first ship to enter the harbour carried a cargo of blanco. Our billets were of all kinds, one part of the Battalion even living in the Law Courts. The big event of this period was the Divisional march past before Mr. Churchill and the Commander in Chief General Sir Harold Alexander, which took place on February 4 and was enhanced by the fact that the Italians appeared to have built Tripoli expressly to form a background for this sort of thing. Down by the seafront, flanked by palms, rose the twin pillars topped by the Tripoli Ship and Romulus and Remus. From them a wide avenue led past the old fort and up through the shopping centre, with its arcades of Roman arches. Our tanks were drawn up in line along the sides of the avenue, yellow in their desert camouflage. The massed pipes marched. The sun shone. It was all a great success.

Two hours later we were grubbing in the holds of lighters, unloading stores.

On the 17th we set off westwards once more still marching along the one lonely road which wound along the north coast of Africa. Ahead of us were still many miles of desert or semi-desert; but the flatness to which we had become accustomed was soon to change. Beyond the Tunisian frontier lay hills, admirably suited to defence and containing positions which had been prepared for many years. The French had owned Tunisia before the Germans walked in; and, after hearing some of Mussolini's more eloquent speeches, had not unnaturally taken steps to safeguard their southern frontier where it marched with Tripolitania. They had built the Mareth Line, a strong system of fortifications which stretched across the narrows where the hills most closely approached the sea. This was some way within their own borders; but between the frontier and the Line were many minor hills and wadis, all of them good rearguard positions. In this area, and for an equal distance on the Italian side of the frontier, the road was lamentable. Both countries had left it so in case the other should attack.

The Germans were falling back on the Mareth Line, spinning out the process as long as they could and leaving rearguards wherever a rearguard could be left. While we had been lying at Tripoli the 7th Armoured Division had been harrying them; and now we were moving up to a concentration area near the frontier town of Ben Gardane, which was to serve us as a base for future operations.

For three days we marched, and on the fourth drove in trucks to Ben Gardane. Slowly the ground had become less and less cultivated, dropping back from green fields to palm and olive groves and eventually to flat, wind-swept marsh where the sand glittered with salt. An outpost detachment of carriers under Gordon Begg had preceded us by a week, and since then had lain on bare, mine-strewn dunes feeling sorry for themselves and becoming accustomed to the old gritty feeling again.

'Ben Gardane,' said Gordon when we arrived, 'is a loathsome thing, God wot.'

We carried on to Medenine next day and rested there on the 23rd while the C.O. and the Intelligence Officer recced the country round the Wadi Zessar, only one of the many wadis which seamed the surface of the desert like cracks in a dried-up pond. Four or five weeks later it contained the bulk of the Eighth Army's transport and was crossed and recrossed by well-marked tracks; but at that time it was new ground and it was our job to recce and patrol it. The Germans were now behind the Mareth Line, too tough a nut to crack without careful preparation, and it looked as if we were in for a period of line-holding and patrolling while behind us the supplies built up and the rest of the Army deployed for battle. The Highland Division was to hold the Zessar with 22nd Armoured Brigade on its left flank and 7th Armoured holding the sector south of the Medenine/Mareth road. Our Brigade was to occupy the southern sector of the Divisional front, and we were to be the centre battalion of the Brigade. This defensive area was known as Fort George.

In retrospect, the month which followed is one of perpetual movement from one wadi to another, of alarms and threatened counter-attacks, and patrols without end. It cannot be recorded in detail here: it is sufficient to say that our function throughout the period was to protect the preparations going on behind us. The Germans were enjoying the luxury of a secure base for the first time since Alamein, and counter attacks were therefore always a probability. One was, indeed, launched on a considerable scale along the whole front on March 6; but in our sector artillery broke it up before it reached us.

For us it was a time of digging complicated doovers into the sides of wadis which, no sooner had they been made fit to live in, were abandoned. We became connoisseurs of wadis. There was the Wadi Zeuss, for example, a pleasant enough spot with running water and shrub-covered banks which gave a little shade in the heat of the day; and, at the other end of the scale, the Wadi Melah, which was midge-infested, boggy, and stank of very ancient sea-water. This Melah water, strangely enough, was the home of a species of small turtle; and before we left, numbers of the unfortunate creatures were wandering about with "H.D." carved on their backs: the Division always did have a reputation for self-advertisement (by the end of the war huge and splendid H.D.'s were painted on most vacant walls for three thousand miles) and we had already acquired the title of Highway Decorators.

Sometimes we were shelled, and sometimes we were not. Sometimes we wired, and sometimes we mined, and always we patrolled. A book could be written on the patrols alone, and I suggest that some day Gideon Rutherford writes it. He was the champion then. He was out most nights, and he always got what he wanted. These things apart, the only event of interest during this period was the departure of Padre Levack who, after surviving much stickier parts of the campaign, was badly concussed when the C.O.'s jeep nose-dived into a shellhole and bounced him out on his head. He did not come back to us. His place was taken a fortnight later by Padre Ironside Simpson, who remained with us until the end of the war.

This was our life until March 21, when we were ordered to move forward and take over from the 7th Green Howards in an anti-tank ditch beside the Wadi Zigzau. It seemed to be just one more move of many, another place to dig a hole and settle in. We had no suspicion when we moved off that we were going to remember the anti-tank ditch for a long, long time.

II

We did not attack from the anti-tank ditch, or even patrol from it. We were not counter-attacked. All we did was sit there for forty-eight hours, keeping our heads down. Yet to this day, despite the number of other holes in the ground the Battalion has lain in or scrambled over or fought for, 'the anti-tank ditch' in conversation can mean only one thing – March 21, 22 and 23, 1943. It remains in the minds of those who were there as an experience worse than the battle of Alamein.

There were several reasons for this, most of which will be dealt with as they occur in the story; but the principal one was the fact, not perhaps obvious from the events, that the hardest thing to do on a battlefield is to take punishment without giving any in return. Give a Jock a rifle or a bren gun and allow him to use it; and however frightened he may be, he will face up to most things. Put him, inactive, in a trench, and danger becomes progressively more difficult to bear. Fear is insidious, and it grows in inactivity. Let us be honest about it: we were frightened in the anti-tank ditch.

We went there on March 21. On the 20th we had heard that the long-awaited assault on the Mareth Line was to begin that night, and that we were to have a hand in the second phase of the operation. It was not a difficult job on the face of it. The main attack was being made by the 50th Division, in action again after a long rest, and we had only to follow up behind them and hold what they had gained, a task which seemed all the easier when reports came through early on the 21st that the Boche defences had been penetrated as far as the famous Wadi Zigzau and that the attack was still going well. At mid-day Colonel Walford (who had just been awarded the D.S.O. for his conduct with the forward platoons in the battle of the Hills) left on reconnaissance, followed later by the "O" Group. The rest of the Battalion moved off in TCV's at dusk along the causeway road a mile or two inland from the sea.

(above) Battalion H.Q. in the Anti-Tank Ditch.

As the ground rose beyond the salt-flats the mine-infested area began, and instead of the occasional wrecked truck by the roadside there was a row of carriers and jeeps, overturned or reduced to tattered strips of metal by the mines. 50 Division had evidently had a bad passage before they could sweep and tape their gaps. The farther we went, the greater the congestion became (50 Division were rushing their carriers and anti-tank guns up to support the bridgehead they had seized over the Zigzau, and we had to use the same track) and when at last we reached the debussing point there was neither the space nor the light for proper dispersal. We were glad to be quit of the trucks. The Germans were shelling them, and there were several hits.

The situation we found as we prepared to march forward was as follows. The 7th Green Howards, from whom we were to take over, had found themselves in a bare and stony place and had taken cover in the German anti-tank ditch which strengthened the Zigzau obstacle at this point. They had been out of touch with their Brigade H.Q. all day. The only way to the place lay through an exceptionally deep minefield by a narrow gap made on the previous night and now well registered by the German guns, so that anyone occupying the ditch was out in the blue, pinned against the mines, and with only the most tenuous communications to the rear. It did not sound too good. Still, we felt, it was a ditch. There would be cover. Maybe it would not be too bad after all.

Our last illusions faded as soon as we saw it. After a nightmare trip through the minefield, stumbling along a grubby length of tape in the darkness while the Boche, well knowing what we were up to, plastered the gap with shells and mortar bombs and raked it with spandau fire, we arrived in the ditch and knew the worst. Except for an occasional gentle dog-leg it ran straight throughout its length; and it offered practically no protection at all except from shells dropping short. The wall nearest the Germans was vertical and about six feet deep, capped by a parapet of varying height and thickness. The rear wall had no parados, and sloped down at forty-five degrees until it met the foot of the front wall. There was thus no level floor, and the depth made it impossible for anyone to fire out of it. The ditch could be defended only by men lying on top of the wall, under the parapet and with nothing but empty air to protect them from shells and bombs bursting behind them.

Our natural reaction, once we had reached the place and sorted ourselves out, was to dig: not only were shells falling close, but an enemy bomber was patrolling up and down, firing streams of white tracer into the gap behind us. But no sooner had we unhitched our picks and shovels than a fresh complication arose. The ground was like iron. Naturally hard, it had in addition been soaked by the winter rains and then baked to a brick-like consistency which made digging almost completely impossible. No matter how much effort we expended in the two days that followed, we never achieved anything which gave protection from a shell dropping on the parapet or into the ditch itself. Individual slits did not exist. The ditch was one big slit, and the whole Battalion was in it.

At that time, however, we were not unduly worried. Indian troops were guarding our left flank, and to the right and forward of us was the 50 Division bridgehead which, we had every reason to hope, would be so expanded by morning that we should be left behind and be free to dig where we willed. Even when we discovered that the Indians had not arrived and that our left flank was flapping helplessly in the air we were not disturbed. The nearest troops on that side were the 2nd Seaforth, two miles to the rear; but, we said, it would be all right in the morning. And anyway, there was nothing we could do about it.

We spent the night in fruitless attempts to scrape slits in the rear wall. When dawn came we could see the last stages of 50 Division's attack on the Ouerzi and Ksiba defences. Valentine tanks were working forward across the slopes on our right, mopping up in a leisurely way, and grey strings of Italian prisoners were winding their way to the rear. The heat of the battle was over. Only a few shells were dropping. No one seemed to be much worried about anything, except the prisoners, who broke into a trot every time a shell fell within a mile of them. It was a scene we had watched many times before. 50 Division had obviously done well. We stood down.

The enemy guns continued to search our ditch and the minefield throughout the morning, but it was mid-day before we realised that something was seriously wrong. The shelling, instead of tapering off, began to build up again; and as it increased, small and then bigger and bigger parties of khaki-clad figures came filtering back over the slopes on our right. At first we thought they were stretcher-bearers, but before long there were too many of them. Clearly all was not well with 50 Division. Those of us who had not already realised the hopelessness of digging in our present surroundings made a last despairing assault on the sloping floor of the ditch.

With the possibility of counter-attack looming up, our communications became increasingly important; but, although relatively speaking our bad time was only beginning, communications were already in a delicate state. They were to be our greatest worry throughout our stay in the ditch. Our telephone cable to Brigade had been cut by shelling almost as soon as it had been laid, and as fast as it was repaired in one place it was cut in another. In the end it simply was not possible for linesmen to work at it under the fire coming down on the gap. This meant we had to rely entirely on radio, which, under battle conditions, was not quite such a simple matter as might be assumed. Our No.2 set had to be manhandled through the minefield, and the signallers had been able to carry only one bank of batteries. If these batteries were to become exhausted before replacements could be brought up after dark and if during that time we were to be counter-attacked, we should be unable to warn Brigade or call on our artillery for help.

We watched the khaki driblets coming back over the slopes, and knew with certainty that we were for it. Instead of being in the rear we were the front line, and we had no left flank.

During the afternoon, accurate shelling all along the line of the ditch by guns of varying sizes became almost continuous, and sniping began from points which, try as we might, we could not pick out. To dodge round the ditch's only landmark, an up-ended Green Howards truck which stood on its nose at Battalion H.Q., became a certain signal for a "ping" overhead; but although the truck itself was often hit, no one was unlucky.

Twice "A" Company at the left end of the ditch reported German infantry and tanks forming up for an attack on their front; but both times the fire of our supporting guns, called down through our single wireless link with Brigade, was enough to disperse them before they came within small-arms range. If they had been close enough to shoot at, I think it might have helped. As it was, we could only lie and wait for the next shell – an event which, considering that the Boche knew exactly where we were, was seldom long in coming. Here, for example, is a snippet from one man's day, part of an account written by Corporal Parkinson of "D" Company. He was lying on the parapet, with Company H.Q. immediately behind and below him.

'I remember hearing the whine of a shell, followed by an awful crump, as one burst no more than two yards away and directly in front of me. I ducked, and in that split second another shell landed immediately behind me and right in the centre of the sloping wall of the ditch. I felt myself being lifted and carried through the air by the blast, and then I landed on top of C.S.M. Aitken and Mr. Gammie. I was dazed and startled by the suddenness of it all... blood stank in my nostrils... I grabbed the C.S.M. by the tunic and shook him, but his head dropped to one side... he must have died instantaneously.

'Confusion reigned everywhere. I sat where I was, and wept.... Lieutenant Gammie seemed to be trying to speak, but in less than two minutes he too was dead. Two of the stretcher-bearers were killed outright also.... The third was badly hit.... Four of us nearest the explosion and on the ledge were blown off by the blast, and two of us – Lance Sergeant Bert Brooks and Pat Davidson – were hit in the lung by small pieces of shrapnel. Captain Robertson was wounded in the legs... and of the sixteen men in Company H.Q. only three of us escaped injury.

'I could scarcely credit my good fortune, and gingerly felt myself over. My pack on my back was riddled in four or five places; and, taking out my mess tins, I found two jagged holes in them. One piece of shrapnel had ended up in the middle of a bar of chocolate, and another in my cheese sandwich. My water-bottle was like a watering-can. My blanket was used to cover the dead....'

This went on all day. By dusk, German tanks were prowling over the ground where we had seen the Valentines in the morning, and before long they had the gap under fire and were beginning to shoot along the ditch in enfilade. Darkness made it possible to adjust our lay-out, though there was not a great deal we could do. The left flank was thickened up a little by setting "B" Company to dig in on some high ground outside the ditch, but apart from that we were still just a thin line along the edge of the minefield. Carrying parties brought up food, and the signallers collected a spare set of batteries which had been dumped in the gap on the previous night. One of the batteries had a bullet hole in it, but it worked: for a few more hours our communications were assured. Moving, digging, and carrying seemed to fill the hours until stand-to found us cold and weary. We had had no sleep. With daylight, shelling began again as heavily as ever, and now there was mortar fire as well.

During the night the Camerons had put in an attack on our right in an attempt to regain some of the ground lost by 50 Div., but when we saw our guns change from high explosive to smoke we knew they were in trouble. When daylight came we could see their wounded and dead lying out on the bare, bullet-swept plain; and there was nothing we could do for them. Some crawled back to us, badly hit as they were. One was led in blind. Farquhar Macrae worked on them all day in the bed of the ditch.

This second day was probably worse than the first, but by now our brains were becoming numbed and much of it failed to register. Stray horrors remain – the direct hit on "A" Company's Observation Post; the man, struck by a shell which did not explode, who had what was left of his arm cut off by Farquhar and tossed over the top into No Man's Land; the Cameron who crawled in with his heels shot away – but noise and lack of sleep had blunted our senses and now all that is left is a memory of incessant din, of shells bursting on the lip, of heat, and smell, and thirst, and stretcher-bearers stumbling interminably along the sloping floor of the ditch. There was no shade. The sun beat down on wounded and unwounded alike. We could not bury the dead. The sentries lay in their precarious posts on the parapet, and the day dragged on.

At dark a Liaison Officer from Brigade arrived with orders for our withdrawal that night. It appeared that hope of making a bridgehead in that part of the line had been abandoned, and the policy now was to draw back into less exposed positions and await the results of a left hook which had been launched farther inland.

We left eleven dead in the ditch and carried out the wounded. We carried every scrap of equipment and ammunition we had: not a round was left. The gunners put down smoke to cover us – it was a night of bright moonlight – and we slipped away through the mines. By 0300 hours on March 24 we were out – not clear of shelling, but at any rate in open country where a position in depth was possible and we could dig in properly.

It may seem wrong, in retrospect, to make the ditch one of our great occasions in Africa. We had three others – Alamein, the Hills, and the last fight at Roumana. Lying in a ditch for two days hardly seems to qualify – until one adjusts one's standards to the battalion level. The Field Marshal may think of battles in terms of their significance to the campaign as a whole, and grade them accordingly; but the private soldier cares nothing for causes or effects or relative importance. He remembers what it felt like. That is why the anti-tank ditch will never be forgotten so long as there is a man left alive who lay in it.

THE FIGHT FOR ROUMANA RIDGE

(previous page) The slopes of the Roumana Ridge.

(below) Roumana Ridge – the German positions overlooked the intervening desert.

CHAPTER SIX

The Fight for Roumana Ridge

IT WAS WARM April weather. The winter rains had performed their miracle, and the desert was covered by a multitude of wild flowers stretching away to the low ridge of hills which jutted out of the plain on the horizon. The hills lay in a blue haze, quivering in the heat. They were not very big. According to the map the highest point, Djebel Roumana, was barely six hundred feet high, but rising as they did from a perfectly flat landscape they were doing their best to look like mountains. The Afrika Korps was there, digging in for yet another rearguard action.

They had abandoned the Mareth Line on March 28, outflanked on the left by our armoured columns. This place was twenty miles north of Gabes, and we had followed them there by easy stages while another formation had done the harrying. Finally, we had gone out on the usual patrols, studied maps, made recces; and now we were ready to attack again.

The plan was simple and straightforward; and like most successful plans, war being what it is, it came unstuck and succeeded in a way which had not been foreseen. Beyond the Roumana ridge was another long, open stretch of plain, and it seemed obvious that once the ridge was firmly in our hands nothing could hold out beyond it. We should command everything. That was the first consideration. The second was that, with the Axis for the moment commanding everything on our side, the approach march would be a long one and would have to be done at night. The third consideration was that when our new line had been consolidated, it would have to be given depth. Depth on our side of the ridge was useless because if a counter-attack succeeded our own plain would once more be commanded. Therefore our forward troops would have to dig in on the plain beyond Roumana, while the troops in depth manned the heights.

It was a tidy plan. The Battalion was to cross the start-line at 0330 hours on April 6, with "A" Company right forward, "B" Company right rear, "C" Company left forward, and "D" Company left rear, and advance on a bearing of 318 degrees. They were to advance very slowly for approximately two thousand yards; and then, at 0415, our barrage would come down on the objective. The companies would then scramble up the ridge, capture it, and consolidate along the crest. After daylight, when we could see to take advantage of our commanding position, we should advance down the other side and dig in a thousand yards farther on.

This second advance was never completed. The Germans counter-attacked just as it began, and the battle of Roumana (the better-known "Wadi-Akarit" was the title given to the Corps battle over the whole front, of which ours was only a small sector) was in the end fought and won among the rocks round the highest point of the ridge. But that is getting ahead of the story.

We crossed the tape at 0330 hours and began to advance through the long grass at the rate laid down in the plan - one hundred yards in four minutes, or rather less than a mile an hour. The grass was wet with dew. No one spoke, and probably few of us were even thinking much: before a battle there might be heart-searching and worry, but apathy was apt to take over once the start-line was crossed, leaving only a tightness in the pit of the stomach, and a blank mind. One just plodded on. Far away on our left the guns were rumbling where the Indians were already attacking the Fatnassa feature, but the only immediate sound was the swishing of feet through the grass. We tramped slowly, so slowly. Roumana lay ahead, silent as the Sphinx. We hunched and made ourselves small as enemy planes came over, dropping flares; but though we felt naked they did not see us, and passed on their way. There was silence again. Suddenly the ground shook and the smell of cordite was in our noses. The artillery barrage had begun.

5th Seaforth Officers (l to r) Jimmy Watt, Jack Walford(seated), unidentified, George Green, Jack Davidson (seated), Douglas Findlay-Shirras and D.J.M.(Big Robbie)Robertson.

Dawn was breaking when we reached the foot of Point 198, the highest point on the ridge. The barrage was climbing the rocks ahead of us, the flashes not so vivid now in the growing light, and smoke hung in the gullies which seamed the hillside. There was the usual uproar. Behind us were the 2nd Seaforths, who were to swing right-handed and go for the east end of the ridge as soon as we were on our way to the crest; and ahead, all over the broken face of the hill, men were scrambling upwards, following the trailing curtain of the barrage. At 0545 hours we disappeared over the crest of Roumana.

The story of the fight for Point 198, the vital height upon which the success of the whole battle depended, centres round one man, Major J.H.Davidson, who commanded "D" Company. Jack Davidson was a farmer from Caithness, and those who knew him before the war say he was a very good farmer. He was a big man, beautifully built, a born fighter and leader of men, but a hater of war. He was intelligent. Most of the things which are usually said about people in obituary notices could be said about Jack Davidson with complete sincerity: and if he had lived I do not doubt that he would have commanded a battalion, only to wash his hands of it with relief when the war ended and he could go back to his farming. He was a good and brave man.

He and perhaps twenty others fought the Roumana battle almost alone. This is their story from the beginning.

When the Company, under strength through previous battles and only about forty strong, first reached the lower slopes at dawn they surprised a number of Italians variously assessed at seventy and two hundred. Certainly there were not less than seventy of them. They had all been in bed, were too terrified to do anything about getting dressed, and were last seen heading for the Prisoner of War cage in shirt tails or pyjamas, delighted to be out of the war. The Company carried on, seeking the best route through the rocks and crags which rose sharply above them. Point 198 was reached about 0545 hours, just as the 2nd Seaforth swung into their phase of the attack and the moving thunder of the barrage, echoing and re-echoing among the crags, halted in a protective wall on the reverse slope of the hill. They were on their objective and, thanks to the Italians, had not had to fight for it.

There followed a quick reorganisation to resist counter-attack; carrying parties were sent for extra ammunition to the foot of Roumana; and Jack Davidson began to scout about the summit, sizing up the ground over which he would have to attack again at 0900 hours. So far everything was normal. The Jocks found themselves holes among the rocks – the ground was too hard for digging – and began to think of breakfast. Out on the right, covering an uncomfortably wide frontage, were "A" and "B" Companies in positions which were without cover and completely overlooked both by Point 198 and by the hill much farther to the right which was now in the hands of 2nd Seaforth. Somewhere to the left rear was "C" Company; and left again, across a wide gap, were the Camerons. So far, so good. Provided Point 198 and the 2nd Seaforth held, the front was sound.

This provision, however, was apparent to the Germans as well as to ourselves, and they set about pushing us off the two heights. At 0700 hours they opened up with their mortars.

We did not like mortars. Statistics proved that nearly all front-line casualties were caused by them (bullet wounds, for all the millions of rounds expended, were rare); but it did not require a statistician to appreciate their effect, then or at any other time. As the bombs dropped vertically, a trench offered incomplete protection; the rate of fire was terrific (one mortar could have twenty bombs up at once, sailing through the air like beads on a string); and, worst of all, we could not hear them coming. Out of a clear and peaceful sky they would come slamming down like, as Paddy Nairne once described it, a charwoman beating a carpet. The concentration on Roumana was dead on the mark, and Jack's recce became a nightmare of tip-and-run from rock to rock. When he returned to the Company he found a few men wounded, but was relieved to see that Captain Ian Mackenzie, his second-in-command, had everyone tucked away as safely as the ground would allow. Spandaus had now chimed in and the din was deafening, but he continued to plan his advance.

At 0900 hours they were off again, Ian Mackenzie and Lieutenant Dixon on the left, and Jack and Sergeant Mackenzie on the right, with our barrage coming down on the very broken and rocky ground which lay ahead. Then came the first hint of trouble. Under cover of his mortar barrage the Boche had succeeded in moving up machine-gun teams which were now lying hidden among the rocks close to our positions, and they opened up on the Company within the first hundred yards of the advance. Outflanking moves were tried, but despite excellent work by Sergeant Mackenzie, Sergeant Chisholm, and Private McGrath, the guns could not be dislodged. There were too many of them, and they were firing from too many directions.

Colonel Walford, as usual, had left his headquarters and was sniffing the morning air with the leading platoons. He saw that the position was precarious. The whole of the ridge would become untenable if the enemy reached Point 198, and so long as a counter-attack threatened it would be folly to go on with the small numbers at our disposal. He went off to raise reinforcements, and "D" Company returned to the rocks on the summit, organised to hold on until help came.

Paddy Nairne, also a great believer in seeing things for himself, had returned from hospital and was up with "D" Company at this stage. He writes:

'We saw a fascinating sight, the sight one reads of others experiencing. Away in the sunlight on the western slopes of the 2nd Seaforth objective on our right a group of men appeared.

' "2nd Seaforth prisoners," I said.

' "Can't see their hands up," said Major Davidson, looking through his glasses, "I expect this'll mean heavier mortar fire."

'Our ideas soon changed. Behind the group appeared a party of men in close formation, a party of men in grey uniform who deployed and began moving along the ridge towards us. It was the start of the German counter-attack.'

It was clear that 2nd Seaforth had been pushed off their objective, and that "A" and "B" Companies must, in consequence, be in trouble. Point 198 was the only position of any importance holding out on the ridge, and as Jack Davidson had only a handful of men left there the outlook was not too bright. Wireless communications were bad, and the positions of "A", "B" and "C" Companies were obscure. Battalion H.Q., established in the foothills immediately below and in full view of the summit, did the little that it could do: Gordon Begg took a party up the high ridge on "D.'s" right, and Paddy took nine men on to the foothills two hundred yards to the east so that he could control the eastern slopes. All over the hillside shooting broke out as the Germans closed in on their objective. Our twenty-five-pounders joined in, and Colonel Walford glued on to an independent New Zealand Honey tank he had found roaming about looking for trouble. The fighting became confused, neither side knowing exactly where its own troops lay. The only certainty was "D" Company, by now clearly visible just below the crest, holding on while Germans bobbed on the skyline. Brigade, shaken by the news which was coming in over the field telephone, appealed to Division. The 5th Black Watch were sent out of reserve to reinforce us.

Here is Major Davidson's own account of what was happening on the ridge:

'I ordered a defensive position on Point 198, which was occupied about 0930 by the remnants of the Company – about a dozen men in all, just enough to man the flanks and watch the front. Ian Mackenzie had disappeared. He was afterwards found well forward. He must have been cut off, but had fought to the last. There were three dead Germans lying near him.

'Shortly after occupying this position, I became aware that the enemy had penetrated right forward and had at least two positions within forty yards of us, immediately above our heads. We tried to climb the last few yards of the crest to get at them, but were at once machine-gunned from the right. From then on it was a case of hanging on and being as offensive as possible. Magazine after magazine was fired from our brens. Private Bridges was magnificent. Corporal Mitchell was wounded, but another gunner took his place. Corporal Thompson and Bain shot incessantly. Private Smith from Caithness and myself watched the crest above our heads. Sergeant Mackenzie moved about from place to place and was a tower of strength. About 1230 hours a determined German attempt was made to get round our left flank, and a party of nine was seen getting into position behind us. We gave them all we had and they withdrew in disorder, leaving three dead and assisting two wounded. We got one or two reinforcements from Battalion H.Q., who were immediately below and could see every move that both we and the Germans were making. The New Zealand Honey on the plain, directed from Battalion H.Q., did invaluable work pumping solid shot into the German positions above us. I reckon it made all the difference.

'About 1500 hours the situation was getting desperate. I could hear German voices above me, and I knew my right was vulnerable. Just then George Willock from Battalion H.Q. appeared with a bren and helped a lot; but the Germans above had crawled forward silently and started to let us have a shower of stick grenades. I gradually moved the Company back about a hundred and fifty yards to another position and succeeded in re-establishing ourselves there, and managed to prevent the enemy getting Point 198. The 5th Black Watch arrived about 1800 hours and took over. We relaxed and heaved a sigh of relief....'

This exercise in understatement gives, of course, no real idea of what the fight

German machine guns and light artillery pieces captured at Roumana.

involved. Apart altogether from his own feelings (he told me afterwards that from first to last he was certain that he was not going to come out of it alive), there are two notable gaps in the narrative. One is a point not emphasised, and the other is not mentioned at all. The first is the timings, and the second is the fact that the attack was made by approximately one hundred and fifty Germans. With his dozen men, helped out towards the end by George Willock and another half-dozen, he fought those Germans at close range for *eight hours*. Also, the ground was so broken and visibility so close that the Germans could infiltrate from almost any direction. Throughout most of that time, his were the only men on the crest of the ridge, and if they had not remained there the whole Brigade attack would have failed and possibly the Divisional one as well.

'We were firing nearly the whole time,' said Private S. Hailwood, one of the survivors, 'I can't remember a time when it was quiet. The ground was all covered with rocks, and we couldn't dig in. Neither could the Germans. We just lay behind what we could find, and moved about a bit if they got our positions taped. It was very confusing to fight like that. You would see a Boche bob up from behind a rock maybe thirty or forty yards away, and then you'd be shot at from three hundred yards away, or from the next hill. I'll never forget the sound the bullets made, smacking off the rocks. The Boche were in little groups all over the place, and there was bags of cover. You never knew what was going to happen next. Look at that bunch that got round behind us – we chased them all right, but they'd shot one of our lads in the back before we nailed them.

'We'd plenty of food, but I don't think any of us ate at all. I know I didn't. I had nothing to eat for twenty-four hours, and I didn't feel hungry. I was thirsty, though.

'There was a bit of a panic when the tattie-mashers came over. We weren't expecting them. The lad beside me had the back of his head blown in, and I was

The Seaforth Cemetery below Roumana.

half stupid with the blast. Then I heard Major Davidson shouting: "Over here, over here!", and we went back a hundred yards or so, and then he stopped us, and we managed to hold them again. Not many officers could have stopped that move back once it had started. We thought a lot of the Major.

'I don't know how word got up to us that the Black Watch were on their way, but I remember someone telling me. I didn't believe it. I said: "Ay, they'll be up here next week, maybe." It didn't seem possible that they could arrive in time to do any good, because we were just hanging on by the skin of our teeth, and there only seemed to be about half-a-dozen of us left. There were more, of course, but you couldn't see who was there and who wasn't, among the rocks. About five minutes later the lad next to me said: "Look at that!", and I looked round, and it was the most wonderful sight I ever saw. The Black Watch were coming across the plain behind us, stretched out in two lines, all neat and tidy, like an exercise. You could even see how they were split up into platoons and sections. I knew then that we'd made it. I can't tell you what a wonderful sight it was.'

While this had been going on, the Camerons on our left had been gapping a minefield; and in the late afternoon our tanks broke through to the far plain. Although mortaring and shelling continued until midnight, the battle was over. We reorganised on a defensive line. By morning the Germans had gone.

Our losses had been five officers and twenty-seven men killed, and five officers and ninety-one men wounded, a heavy blow to a battalion already badly depleted. Major Davidson was awarded the D.S.O. for his stand on the ridge, Captain Willock and Lieutenant I.J.C.Grant the M.C., Sergeant D.Polson the M.M., and Private Bridges a bar to his M.M.

In the narrow sector in front of "D" Company's positions on the crest of Roumana we buried forty Germans.

FRESH START

(previous page)   The 5th Seaforths wading ashore in Sicily, July 1943.

(below)   Briefing at Sousse for the Sicily invasion.

CHAPTER SEVEN

Fresh Start

THAT WAS THE last battle. We had a fortnight in the line near Enfidaville (four days were considered an ample tour of duty for fresh troops, and we were far from fresh); but on May 5 we came out for the last time and left the final rounding up of the Afrika Korps to units less exhausted than ourselves. I do not think we could have attacked again. We had had few reinforcements, and some of the companies had dropped in strength from a hundred men to twenty-five. Behind us lay two thousand miles of desert and the toll of death, wounds, jaundice, and dysentery. We were very tired.

We lay on the fresh spring grass and looked across the plain to the hills about Tacrouna, where we had last held the line and where shells were still dropping on the Free French who had relieved us. We washed, and laundered, and slept, trying to believe that it was all over. We had been told we should not go in again, but one never knew. The Axis front was crumbling in the north, where the First Army had been hammering away for so long. Bizerta and Tunis had fallen, and the enemy were hemmed north and south into a tiny pocket; but opposite us they still hung on. We decided we should believe nothing until it happened.

We were kept in suspense until the last minute. On May 10 we were told we should move on the following day to Algeria, far from the fighting. We should move at 0730 hours. We packed, slept, and awoke to a clear sunny morning, lined up, and got into our trucks. The trucks began to move, then stopped. A barrage began to fall in the distance, away to the right of Tacrouna.

We sat in our trucks and watched it while horrid rumours spread up and down the column. It was said that the Free French were attacking, and that we were being held until the results of the attack were known. If the French failed, so rumour said, we might be called upon to help. Half-an-hour passed, an hour, an hour-and-a-half. The barrage died. We kept our eyes fixed on the smudge of smoke which still stained the distant frieze of hills, and kept our fingers crossed. At last a message arrived. The column began to move, and at the end of our track it turned south. We heaved a huge sigh of relief.

We were four days on the road, through scenery which seemed all the more magnificent for the news, received late on May 12, that enemy resistance in Africa had ceased. More news trickled in as we went. A hundred and fifty thousand prisoners had been taken from the final pocket, and the booty was tremendous. Von Arnim, who had taken over from Rommel, was in the bag. It sounded to us like a good clean sweep. We felt pleased with ourselves. The corn of the plains gave way to the cork forests of the mountains as our road switchbacked up and down through Kairouan, Tebessa, Ain Beida, Setif, over country where there was no war and Roman ruins lay honey-coloured in the sun. The scenery on the last day of the journey was probably more varied and spectacular than any most of us had ever seen, alternating between hot plains of corn and mountain passes where the air was cool and clear and the next ridge hung like a curtain before us. Even the Kerrata Gorge did not exhaust the possibilities of that wonderful day: after winding down a road which was half tunnel and half a ledge cut in the side of the cliffs (*IT IS FORBIDDEN TO SHOOT THE MONKEYS* said a notice), we swung down on to the Mediterranean coast and by late afternoon were looping back and forth along an even crazier cliff road with the blue sea a hundred feet below. By evening we were erecting our bivvies near a town which bore the improbable name of Djidjelli. We had ended one campaign and were about to begin another.

Djidjelli was a good spot and it would be pleasant to linger over it; but there is no space for that. We rested there for a little, bathing in the sea and occasionally driving into the town, where there was nothing to see, nothing to do, and precious little to drink. Soon we were training again, and this time we trained with ships.

With Africa cleared, the time had now come for the Allies to tackle Europe; and even at that early stage, when we knew nothing of the big plan, it was obvious that the shaky end of the Axis was going to be dealt with first and that our destination was Italy. Down at Djidjelli the harbour swarmed with craft we had never seen before, bearing (for the Navy had the same habits as the Army in these matters) strange initials on their bows. There were LCI's, LST's, DUWK's, LCA's, shallow draught vessels capable of discharging their cargoes of men or vehicles on to open beaches. For some weeks we practised loading and unloading ourselves into and out of these craft (the Landing Craft Infantry was our particular type); and at the same time certain unfortunates were taken up to a school in the mountains and dangled on ropes over cliffs, the idea being that if we ever landed on a rocky coast we should have some trained climbers available to help us off it.

It was a green and pleasant land, and we enjoyed it. Our chief memories of it are probably of the red rocks dropping sheer from the lighthouse down at Phare Io and the cork forests behind us covering the mountains like green foam. Lesser memories are the nights when the Luftwaffe came over from Sicily and the sky above Djidjelli was criss-crossed by streams of tracer. There was also the wine. It was coarse, tangy red stuff, very good with cheese; and even after a disastrous series of object-lessons the Jocks never seemed to understand that although it drank like beer it acted like whisky. The P.R.I. bought it in bulk and sold it at fivepence a pint. The men used to line up with their mess-tins for their ration, and they had to drink it in the immediate neighbourhood, where Sergeant Sinclair could see them if they tried to slip into the queue for a second helping. One pint, and Africa was wonderful; two pints, and Africa ceased to exist. My batman once drank three, but that is another story.

Several drafts of reinforcements arrived there, and we were soon up to strength. On June 18 the Battalion moved to a concentration area on the outskirts of Djidjelli, and on the 24th we embarked in LCI's and sailed round the coast back to Sousse, in Tunisia, taking our bren carriers with us. The rest of our transport travelled by road. Here we stayed until we were ready to sail for Sicily.

Sousse had changed for the worse since we had seen it last. The spring flowers had gone, leaving behind country which combined all the disadvantages of the desert with those of cultivation, and had the advantages of neither. The desert had been clean and spacious. We now found ourselves in country much confined by cactus hedges, country even more dusty than the desert, and entirely covered with prickles of one kind or another. The sun had withered all vegetation except the indomitable cactus, and the earth was a dusty brown blanket filled with burrs, spines, needles, spikes, barbs, thorns, and a peculiar yellow grass which discharged broadsides of tiny spears into the legs of anyone brushing against it. Even the ordinary flies stung there. We lay in a field which had not so much as an olive grove to redeem it, under a drifting cloud of dust thrown up by traffic on a nearby track, and sweated prodigiously. When the chocolate ration arrived, we tore a hole in the paper wrapping and sucked out the chocolate. One day the khamseen wind blew and all Farquhar's thermometers burst. They were in their cases in the shade, and they registered up to a hundred and ten degrees. Against this background we planned our part in the Sicilian campaign.

No one knew for certain that it was to be Sicily, but it was difficult to imagine where else we could be going. Extraordinary efforts were made to keep our destination secret. We were issued with maps and aerial photographs, works of art complete in every detail except that of proper names. Our routes were marked, defences shown, types of 'going' indicated (*SAND DUNES: TRACKED VEHICLES ONLY; ROAD 10FT., DIRT SURFACE; CORN: GOOD GOING FOR ALL TYPES.* There was even a field marked *VINE STAKES: UNSUITABLE FOR PARACHUTISTS.*); but one village in the middle of a plain would be labelled *BIRMINGHAM*, another *NEW YORK,* and dried-up streams would be called *GANGES* or *MISSISSIPPI.* As each commander received only the maps of his own immediate area it was impossible to be sure of our destination, though one could guess. Still, these maps made it possible for us to plan the opening stages of the operation in the minutest detail, right down to the objectives to be tackled by individual platoons, without large numbers of people being let into the secret until the last minute. No one except Colonel Walford knew exactly where we were going until after we had sailed; but long before then every man knew what his first task was to be.

For days the officers crowded in relays into the mess-tent and pored over photographs while the Colonel explained the landing plan. The tent was suffocatingly hot, and we crouched there (the sloping walls made it impossible for most of us to stand upright) while our shirts stuck to our backs and the sweat dripped off the tips of our noses. After three or four days of this we felt we had lived on the wretched beaches all our lives and could find our way off them blindfold if need be; but still Paddy Nairne was called upon to explain the ground once more. Here was the tunny factory, and here the jetty where the gun-post was. This was Green Beach and this was Amber Beach. If we landed on Green Beach, we should go this way, and if we landed on Amber then *this* was the route. This patch here was the Assembly Area... 5th Seaforth here, 2nd Seaforth here, and the Camerons here. And of course, this was the Vehicle Park. If, on the other hand, there were mines.... In the end we could see the ground with our eyes shut, and dreamed about it at night.

While all this was going on, ships were being loaded. The details are much too complicated to be more than hinted at here; but something of the planning involved can be appreciated when it is realised that not only had the cargoes to be so arranged that the most urgent stores were on top for rapid unloading, but that cargoes of a similar type had to be distributed over many ships so that the sinking of one would not paralyse any particular branch of the operation. Thus no battalion had all its vehicles on a single ship, or even all its vehicles of one type on a single ship. Furthermore, we were not all travelling in the same convoy or on the same date. The fighting troops led with supplies to last them two days. Supply ships came next. Other ships brought the battalion vehicles which would carry the supplies. Battalion transport which had hitherto worked as a single unit had to be drastically reorganised in consequence. And so scattered were the dates of sailing that our Left Out of Battle personnel were not due to join us for three weeks. It was all immensely complicated, and the commonest sight at the docks in those days was that of a harassed officer dashing about with an inch-thick wad of loading instructions in his hand.

The final briefing was done in an olive grove a short distance from our camp, the only place in the neighbourhood which offered any shade. Brigadier G. MacMillan, who had succeeded Brigadier George Murray as commander of 152 Brigade, came and talked to officers and sergeants, dealing with the plan as it affected the Brigade. Then Colonel Walford outlined the Battalion plan. Finally we went away and briefed our companies and platoons. On July 5, 1943, we marched down to Sousse docks and embarked. There were few regrets about leaving Africa.

The Highland Division was going to land on the south-east tip of Sicily in the neighbourhood of a town called Pachino. Other British landings were to be made to the north, and west of us were to be first the Canadians and then the Americans. The general idea for the campaign as a whole was to drive straight up the east coast to the Straits of Messina, and so cut off the garrison, which was mostly concentrated in the western half of the island.

Our detailed planning had been designed to take us as far as our assembly area beyond the beaches, and after that various tentative plans had been prepared to cope with varying types of opposition. The other brigades were landing ahead of us, and if they met stiff opposition our likeliest job would be the taking of Pachino itself. These plans need not be discussed, because opposition was negligible at first and Pachino had been taken by the time we landed.

The LCI's we sailed in were flat-bottomed, box-like contrivances which we were horrified to hear were capable of crossing the Atlantic. As they rolled in the slightest sea and in rough weather pitched off the crests of the bigger waves like tin trunks falling downstairs, the mere possibility of such a voyage appalled landsmen like ourselves. They held two hundred men each, in four separate troop-spaces, and in even a moderate sea the Jocks were apt to lie being sick in bundles of fifty. The first leg of our journey, which took us to Malta, was mercifully calm. We disembarked at Valetta on the 6th and marched off to three different camps. There we lay, alternately bathing and planning, until we re-embarked on the evening of the 9th. We sailed for Sicily at 1230 hours on July 10.

That night it blew, and by 0930 hours we were far gone in seasickness and only slightly comforted by the news that the ridge south of Pachino had been captured by 153 and 154 Brigades and that our tanks were advancing on the town. Over the surface of the choppy sea our convoy was spread, the escorting destroyers seeming enormous beside the tiny LCI's. Ships were everywhere, hundreds of them, ploughing quietly and steadily on. The sea abated a little and our spirits began to rise. We crowded to the rails. We became excited. We might have been on a pleasure cruise, so little sign was there of war. Twice an air-raid alarm was given, but nothing happened. Slowly a thicker patch of haze on the horizon became solid, and by noon we knew for certain that it was land. Soon we were laughing to each other and pointing out the ridge, and the tunny factory, and the lighthouse, and all the other places we had studied for so long in the tent at Sousse. Ships were thick round the beaches, and we could see little specks of men toiling to unload them. A few shells were dropping on the ridge, but that was all. There was no battle on the beaches, no guns overlooking us as we came gently in and prepared to disembark. We heard later that the Italians had been so staggered by the arrival of our first wave that they had surrendered without offering anything more than token resistance. Our troops were already miles inland and had nowhere met the enemy in force.

The landing went through without a hitch. We waded ashore thigh-deep at 1345 hours, and by 1700 hours were on our way to the concentration area. An hour later our fighting vehicles were ashore and had joined us. Our first landing on enemy-occupied Europe had cost us no more than a slight wetting as we waded from the ships on to the sands of Amber Beach.

AMBUSH AT FRANCOFONTE

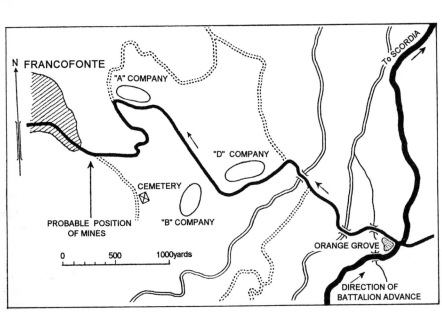

DIAGRAM A

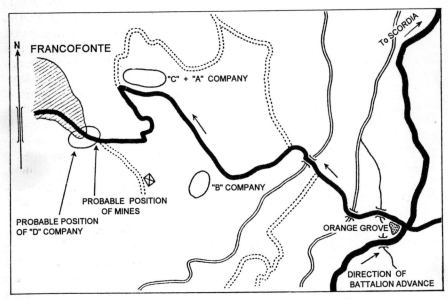

DIAGRAM B

CHAPTER EIGHT

Ambush at Francofonte

I

THE BATTLE OF Francofonte was a second Battle of the Hills, a text-book example of what can happen to a battalion when it is launched into the blue over ground which has not been adequately reconnoitred. It was not one of our brighter efforts; but, given the conditions under which it was fought, it is difficult to see how it could have turned out otherwise. Three hundred paratroopers, the pick of the German Army, selected the best defensive ground they could find and then lay in wait for us; and we, ordered to push on quickly and knowing nothing beyond what the map could tell, walked into the trap which had been laid.

It was a complicated fight, so complicated that the battle had been over for some time before we could piece together the various events and discover what had happened; and so, if this account is to be understood, I must explain now what we did not know at the time – the precise nature of the trap. The lie of the ground is shown in *Diagram A*. The road to Scordia ran along the right, or south side of a shallow valley and was overlooked from the left by the village of Francofonte. The village itself was barely visible. It lay on the crest of a hill, but was so surrounded by olive and orange groves that only a few roofs could be seen from the road. These groves covered most of the hillside, which was encircled in the typical Sicilian fashion by terraces rising like enormously wide staircases from bottom to top. Up the hillside ran a branch road, a tortuous affair cut into the slope, winding among the terraces with a high wall on its left, or uphill side, and an equally high drop on its right. Where it left the Scordia road there was a particularly dense orange grove, and where it neared the crest there was a hairpin bend. In the grove there was a 37mm anti-tank gun, and along the top side of the hairpin was a strong German position. Other positions were sited near a cemetery on the south side of the village.

As the hill on which Francofonte was built was no different from a score of other hills in the neighbourhood, the Germans could rely on the attacking force continuing along the Scordia road until it was halted by the 37mm in the orange grove. By this time it would have passed below the cemetery, and the machine-gunners lying doggo there would be able to open up and take the column on the flank. If this were not sufficient, the troops in the grove could retire to the village, which was a strong natural fort, and the entire garrison could hold out there and at the same time continue to dominate the Scordia road, thus holding up our advance. It was very pretty, and it worked.

Now consider it from our point of view. We had landed on the 10th. That night our brigade, with the Camerons leading, was directed on the Rosolini/Noto road and was held up after a short distance by light opposition. This was easily dealt with by the Camerons next morning, and the advance continued. The roads were narrow, dusty, and lined by the same old cactus hedges, the country dry and wrinkled as a worn-out carpet dumped down on a rockery, covered with thin, parched soil and untidy little hills from which limestone ledges projected. If it had not been for the terraced fields we might still have been in Africa; and so, for all the good the country appeared to be doing them, might the Sicilians. They were a poor, drab lot and seemed uninterested in our arrival. They just carried on in their wretched fields, and looked up apathetically as we passed. Every now and then three-foot letters painted on a gable told us that Mussolini was *Always Right*, or that one must *Believe, Obey*, and *Fight*. They were almost the only traces of the new order we saw in Sicily: the place did not seem to have changed much in a thousand years.

That day our Carrier Platoon set off to make contact with the 1st Canadian Division on our left, and took forty prisoners in Rosolini on the way. Siracusa had fallen by this time, and in the evening we had orders to advance north of Avola so that the general British advance up the coast towards Lentini and Augusta might be helped on its way. On the morning of the 12th, half the Battalion was ferried in trucks to positions near Cassibili, where we relieved a battalion of the 69th Brigade. The rest followed in the afternoon.

So there we were in the early hours of July 13, with three days in Sicily behind us and not a shot fired. The Brigade was on the move again by 0500 hours, heading for Scordia by way of Palazzolo, Buscemi, Buccheri, and Francofonte; and we were the advance guard. At 1230 hours a Brigade Provost party which had gone on ahead to sign-post the route reported that they had been fired on near Francofonte. The fire, they said, had come from a few snipers.

II

We were in trucks, with the Carrier Platoon and "C" Squadron of the Royal Tank Regiment nosing cautiously on ahead. There was still no sign of the enemy, at that time bundling north as fast as they could: but we knew that sooner or later we should bump into a strong rear-guard. We were at that awkward stage of an advance when the enemy may be ten miles away or round the next corner, and the rate of advance must be based on the assumption that they are ten miles away. There is no time to search every wood or house: the enemy may be digging in a day's march ahead, and every minute wasted is to their advantage. In these circumstances the advance-guard must simply push on until it makes contact.

At 1400 hours the leading carrier rounded the bend below Francofonte and was knocked out by the gun in the orange grove.

The column stopped, piled up in a long line which started short of the bend and extended in a cloud of dust for a mile back down the road. We began to clamber out of our vehicles, and the Boche in the cemetery opened up. It was a thoroughly unpleasant situation. The cemetery was in the trees high above us, and it was quite impossible to see where the guns were firing from. We crouched in ditches, or behind trucks, or wherever we could find cover, firing back into the general area of the crest but unable to find a real target. I believe that if the average infantryman at any period of the war had been given the choice of being shelled or machine-gunned, he would have chosen the shells without hesitation. There was something much too personal about a spandau. It did not aim at an area: it aimed at *you*, and its rate of fire was prodigious. It had a vindictive sound. Each burst began with an odd hiccup before getting into its stride, so that the crack of the first round was distinct and all the others ran together like the sound of tearing calico. Their *pup-turrrr, pup-turrrr* was the most distinctive noise on any battlefield; and on this day at least a dozen of them were sniping down at us from the olive groves.

Colonel Walford decided to mop up the 37mm post in the orange grove before dealing with Francofonte itself, and sent off ''C''Company (Captain J.L.Paterson) to outflank it on the right, a task which happened to be easy, as the Germans withdrew as soon as they saw their flank being turned. Off went the carrier screen again with a troop of the tanks, this time up the branch road to Francofonte. Behind them came the Battalion, with ''A'' Company (Captain J.R.Roberts) on the right of the road, ''B'' (Lieutenant G.A.D.Inches: Captain Pat Agnew was already dead) on the left, and ''D'' (Captain D.J.M.Robertson) in reserve. The carriers and the leading companies came under a hail of automatic fire as they neared the crest, and were held up. This stage of the attack ended with ''A'' along the down-hill leg of the hairpin, ''B'' beside the cemetery, ''D'' in reserve farther down the road, and ''C'' on its way back from the far side of the valley, where it had gone on its original outflanking move. These are the positions shown on *Diagram A*.

It was obvious by this time that we were up against very good troops indeed, though we still had an idea that there were not very many of them. Paddy Nairne, eyes gleaming with professional glee, had identified them as the 2nd German Parachute Regiment, which should by rights have been in the south of France. This was the first anyone had heard of their being flown over to meet us. We were impressed by their quality. They fought fanatically (of the three hundred in the village, more than half were found dead when it was eventually taken), but did not permit their devotion to the Führer to cloud either their judgment or their skill. They were particularly good at using alternative positions, an unpleasant change from the average run of German who dug a hole and then clung to it: a heavy burst of fire from several weapons would come from a point which, when engaged, was found to be empty. Meanwhile they were blazing happily away from another position a couple of hundred yards off. It was a game of hide-and-seek among the olive trees, and we could make no headway against it. The attack bogged down.

The second phase began when ''C'' Company arrived. Hamish Paterson was ordered to take his company up the road, pick up one platoon of ''B'' Company, drop two of his own platoons, and with the two platoons left to him make an outflanking attack on the right. We were still labouring under the delusion that a few determined men on the outskirts were making a great deal of noise, and that the village was either empty or very lightly held; and on that basis the plan was reasonable. When Hamish reached the lower leg of the hairpin he found what was left of ''A'' Company, but no one knew where ''B'' was. He therefore dropped only one of his platoons there, and ordered the other two to stand by ready for action while he went off to make a recce. It was probably the least healthy recce he ever made.

'I took Sergeant Findlay of the Mortars with me, and a runner, and Gordon Angus, and Sandy McLeish,' he said. 'It was about half-past five or a quarter to six by this time, and getting late. The five of us left the road and cut across the hairpin until we landed on the top leg of the loop. It was the same as the leg below – a big wall along the uphill side, and nothing but these damned olive trees all round. Well, we looked over the wall, and there was the village, and Gordon Angus says: "Hell! It'll take a brigade to take this." I thought he was about right. It was a gloomy dump, like a Durham mining village by the looks of it, and there were far too many houses. I don't like houses.

'We were just beginning to take this in when we heard something swishing about in the grass. I thought it was cows. We saw something moving in the ground mist, and so help me it was a dozen Boche, colossal big so-and-sos, coming straight for us. We ducked down, and they came over the wall and walked past us only ten yards away. They were so close I could see the magazine on the leading man's schmeiser.

'So far as we could make out they were heading for the ground between the two legs of the hairpin. Behind us, mind you. Between us and the Company. So there was nothing else for us to do but go forward into the Boche lines. There was a field we crossed, and then a gully. We were bearing to the left, trying to get down on to the road where the column had been sniped in the afternoon. We saw a gun fifty yards away, and had to work round it. Then we reached the terraces above the road, and after that we just ran like hell....

'When we got back to the company, after coming all the way round by road, we found them scattered, shooting back at the characters who'd passed us, up above them in the olive trees. We pulled them together again.... Then I got a bullet in the leg....'

The time was now 2000 hours, and the third attempt had begun. "D" Company, under Captain Robertson ("Big Robbie" to distinguish him from Hugh Robertson, who was "Wee Robbie") had been sent round on the right. No one had as yet seen many Germans and comparative quietness followed the company's departure, so Colonel Walford was optimistic when he left soon afterwards, summoned to attend a Brigade "O" Group. When he returned he was greeted with the news that Big Robbie was wounded, and that nothing had been heard of his company. It had simply vanished. As this state of affairs persisted for nearly twenty-four hours, our condition when darkness fell was as follows (see *Diagram B* on page 86): At the hairpin, "C" Company and the remnants of "A"; at the cemetery, the remnants of "B"; vanished, "D". Tanks in hand, three: the others had broken down. Officer situation, bad. "A" had lost Lieutenant Borwick killed and Lieutenant Taylor badly wounded; "B" had lost Captain Agnew and Lieutenant Baillie killed. Hamish Paterson and Big Robbie, the other two company commanders, were both wounded; and three company sergeant-majors were dead. The snipers had not been picking their targets at random.

Now let us investigate the mystery of "D" Company, last seen 2000 hours making a right hook on the village. The story is told by Private J.F.Moir of 18 Platoon.

'When we left the bottom arm of the horseshoe,' he said, 'we made a wide loop to the right, and then swung in until we joined the road again just short of the village. It was nearly dark, and there was some mist. We didn't see anything. We followed the road until we were about three or four hundred yards from the place we had started from, and then we found six rows of tellermines. They weren't buried, just laid on the surface of the road. We tiptoed through them and carried on.

It was so difficult to see anything that I'm not certain where we were, but it seemed to me that our road skirted the village. There were houses over on the left, but we were never actually beside them. The road kept bearing round to the left, and so far as I could make out we got round behind the village, so that when we stopped it was between us and the rest of the Battalion. But we may have been only half-way round it. I don't know. It was too dark.

'All this time we hadn't seen a soul. Everything was dead quiet. There was a lane and a fence down the back of the village, and we started to dig in there, fairly scattered. Ours was the last platoon: both the others and Company H.Q. were about a hundred yards farther on than we were.

'I don't know what Captain Robertson's plan was. It seemed to us that there was nothing in the village, but the wireless wasn't working so we couldn't let Battalion H.Q. know that. I expect he meant to send a runner back while we dug in, and then just wait. I mean, we'd been told to do a right hook and attack, but there just wasn't anything to attack. Anyway, the runner never went because things began to happen. My platoon was beside the road, with a guard out: there was Corporal Twine and two others in the guard, maybe fifty yards away up the road. All of a sudden I heard them challenge, and then all hell was let loose. Corporal Twine was wounded in the first burst, and I don't know what happened to the other two. The Jerries rushed forward, firing as they came. You could just see the red flashes, and hear the shouting. We opened up. I remember emptying a magazine into them. Then they disappeared. We lay wondering what was going to happen next, and which side they were going to come from. They must have worked round the back of us, because a minute or two later a dozen of them tried to rush the lane, between us and the village. Williamson was up there with a bren gun. He got a lovely shoot right down the lane, and the Jerries disappeared again.

'Our Platoon Commander was Lieutenant Hutton Bremner, and he had been up at Company H.Q. when the fun started, so I went to report. He was with Captain Robertson. I told the two of them what had happened.

' "Are you sure they were Germans?" said Captain Robertson.

' "Positive," I said.

' "I'm going to see for myself," he said. "Come on, Hutton."

'He grabbed a bren gun and went off with Mr. Bremner and Company Sergeant Major Bates. And that was the last we saw of them. There was a lot of shooting a minute or two later. We didn't know at the time – all we knew was they'd disappeared – but we found out later that the Sergeant-Major was killed, and the other two were put in the bag. Captain Robertson escaped later by hitting a Boche over the head and running towards the Battalion. That was how word got back that we were in a jam. He was wounded a wee while after that. Mr. Bremner escaped too, but that wasn't until next day.

'There was shooting all over the place by this time, and nobody knew what was happening. There was only one officer left, and that was Mr. Cochrane; so when the others didn't come back I went to look for him. He was with the farthest-out platoon and hadn't a clue about what was going on. I told him. He didn't believe they were Germans either. He said he couldn't make a plan until he knew what was what, and he asked for volunteers to go with him and find out. Like a damn fool I volunteered, and another lad called Taylor came too. 18 Platoon was pulled in closer to the others, and then the three of us set off, leaving the others digging.

'We went about two hundred yards over the fields more or less the way we had come, and after a bit Taylor got a stray shot in the neck. We left him lying. Then we reached the road. There was a hedge beside it, and when we peered through we could make out a hell of a lot of people on the other side. It was impossible to count, but there were a lot. We thought maybe it was ''C'' Company, so Mr. Cochrane shouts out: ''Who's that?''

'A voice shouts back: ''You are our prisoner. Surrender.''

'So Mr. Cochrane shouts: ''Surrender be so-and-soed,'' and empties his revolver into them. ''Come on,'' he says, and we legged it back in the dark across the fields. We picked up Taylor on the way and lugged him in somehow.'

'Moir hasn't got the story quite right,' said Dougie Cochrane. 'I wasn't the only officer left: I was the only one he could find in the dark. There was still Lieutenant Duff Dunbar, and we bumped into him on our way back from this escapade. He'd been trying to find us for some time. I told him what I'd seen, and he decided we were too scattered to defend ourselves properly. We gathered in all the men we could find and set up all-round defence in the back gardens of the village. Another attack had come in on 18 Platoon while we had been down the road, and we couldn't find any of them at all. Half of Duff Dunbar's platoon had disappeared too. It was terribly difficult in the dark to know what we had and what we hadn't, but as near as we could make out about half the company was still with us.

'We stayed there about an hour, with more and more movement and shooting going on round us. Transport began milling about on the road, and we could hear Boche shouting to each other. There were plenty of them, and they were between us and the Battalion. We agreed that the sooner the C.O. knew the whole story the better it would be, but the snag was how to tell him. The wireless was *kaput*. Duff Dunbar decided to take one man with him for company and try to get back.

' ''Give me an hour,'' he said. ''If you haven't got fresh orders by then, try to bring the rest out.''

'Well, the hour went, and a bit more, and nothing happened except a lot more shooting and movement. We didn't know, but Duff Dunbar hadn't made it: he was dodging Boche until the following morning. They were all over the place. I gathered the remains of the company and led them out by the way we came in, right back to the others at the hairpin. It was a chance – the Boche were on the road fifty yards from us – but it was the only way I knew for sure and it was better than blundering about over ground we didn't know. It worked, anyway. We slipped round the Boche, tiptoed back through the mines, and that was that. We dug in on the right flank, below the hairpin.'

Now comes the fourth stage of this most complicated battle. During the night the other companies had lined the outskirts of the cemetery and the lower leg of the hairpin, peering uphill through the weird half-light of the olive trees. Trees were burning all over the slope. How they caught fire I do not know: perhaps tracer bullets were enough to touch them off, for olives were very inflammable. At any rate they were alight by scores, glowing rather than blazing. There would be a crackle, and the fire would start low down, spreading upwards slowly in red veins as it took hold of the trunk, exploding from time to time in a shower of sparks. After some hours the tree would be red to the topmost branches; and then the fire would gnaw the heart out of it, and it would topple as the sparks whirled upwards. When dawn came, the slope was covered with the smouldering ruins of trees.

Now consider the battle from the point of view of Battalion H.Q. Throughout the night the village itself and the fate of "D" Company had been a mystery, and even in daylight it was difficult to piece together an adequate picture, because the companies lying on the right flank of the hairpin position were cut off from the others by a fire-swept gap in the wall. Even shouting was difficult, because the Germans were less than a hundred yards away, and noise drew fire. As soon as daylight came, Colonel Walford climbed into his carrier (the only time I ever knew him use it: unarmoured jeeps had a curious fascination for him during battles) and charged up the hill seeking information. It was 0600 hours on July 14, and this was the situation he found. "C" and elements of "D" were barely holding their own against heavy fire on the right flank; and "A", a very weak "B" and a section of carriers were near the hairpin bend. When the Colonel knew the facts he decided on one last forlorn hope: Hugh Robertson would take the remains of his platoon on a wide sweep round by the right, and our three tanks would try to make headway up the road. Both these moves failed. The Germans had established themselves on the uphill leg of the hairpin and not only stopped the platoon by shooting it up on the flank, but knocked out the two leading tanks with sticky bombs. Then the snipers started up again.

Plainly we had shot our bolt. Everything that could be committed had been committed, and the best we could hope to do now was hang on. We pulled everyone back to the line of the road in order to give the artillery more elbow-room; and the German mobility, so effective against us in the early stages, by a happy chance recoiled on their own heads. They had many alternative positions, but they had dug in in none of them. For the rest of the day our guns, which had just arrived, pounded the village and inflicted far more casualties than we had any reason to expect. At 1700 hours the 2nd Seaforth attacked through us and, after a strenuous fight, managed at last to take the village. Their losses were about as heavy as our own, in spite of the artillery support.

We had lost four officers (including Captain George Willock) and twenty-two men killed, and four officers and fifty-seven men wounded.

THE SFERRO HILLS

(previous page) The wreckage of the German tank that reached Pt.224 during the counter-attack in the Sferro Hills.

(below) An abandoned German 88mm gun.

CHAPTER NINE

The Sferro Hills

I

SICILY HAD seemed at first sight much the same as North Africa, but now the campaign was beginning to acquire a character of its own. The differences were not obvious – the countries in appearance were similar – but small variations added up to a mental picture which made Sicily unique. In the matter of landscape, for example, the only real difference was the vines; but when it came to fighting, the vines, set thickly on their terraces, offered good cover and made us realise that the spacious days were over. No Man's Land was narrower than it had been. Ambushes were easier. The war was more cramped. Then there were small things like dress, and fruit, and rations, insignificant in themselves but all part of our background. Mosquitoes were numerous and malaria casualtiess high. and so we ate mepacrine tablets, slept under bush-nets, and wore long khaki drill slacks which we had camouflaged before the landings by boiling them in a mixture of tea, wood ash, and mud. Our shirts, too, had been the wrong colour for the volcanic soil of Sicily, and our light desert ones had been replaced by the darker pattern normally used in Britain. When we camped it was among grapes, or oranges, or almonds: we ate pounds a day towards the end of the campaign when we reached the fertile slopes of Etna. And we had compo rations for the first time.

Soldiers think a great deal about food, so compo was a landmark which must be described at length. Before it had been invented, the system of ration distribution within a battalion had been so cumbersome that in battle it had to be reduced to the simplest terms if it were to work at all. The simplest terms were usually bully beef and biscuits: no quartermaster could hope to split up a hundredweight of cheese, quarter of a ton of butter, and any of half a dozen other bulky odds and ends and then distribute them down to platoons in the heat of battle. If by any chance we did, the platoons would have been unable to cook the rations when they were delivered. Tinned foods solved this problem, but as the tins of such things as cheese, butter, and jam weighed seven pounds apiece, some dividing still had to be done at the lower levels and if a tin were not emptied it was generally filled with dust before the next meal. Compo (I like to think it was invented by the philanthropist who decided, round about 1940, that there was no real reason why the Army biscuit should be as thick as cattle-cake and proof against small-arms fire) answered all these problems. A compo box measured roughly two-and-a-half feet by one-and-a-half by one-and-a-half, and it contained a day's ration for fourteen men in a form which could easily be divided. Breakfast might be sausages and beans; lunch, biscuits (the new thin kind), jam, butter, cheese, tea; dinner, meat-and-vegetables and a steamed pudding. Also in the box were a bar of chocolate, six boiled sweets, and seven cigarettes per man; and there were packets of salt and matches. There was even a ration of toilet paper. Everything was tinned and all the tins were small, so that they could be emptied at a sitting, and heating in water was all the cooking required. The food was of the very best quality: the puddings were rich and sweet, and the strawberry jam had strawberries in it. There were seven different types of box, so that in theory there was a change of menu for each day of the week. (In practice the "A" Box – the one with the steak-and-kidney pudding and the tinned peaches in it – seldom seemed to survive its passage through Base, where it was apt to be swapped for the "F" Box, the one with the greasy pork stew and the sad date pudding.) In the Army small comforts were appreciated, and compo was more than a small comfort. We became a little tired of it before the war was out, but in Sicily a box was as good as a Christmas hamper. Its inventor has the Infantry's heart-felt thanks.

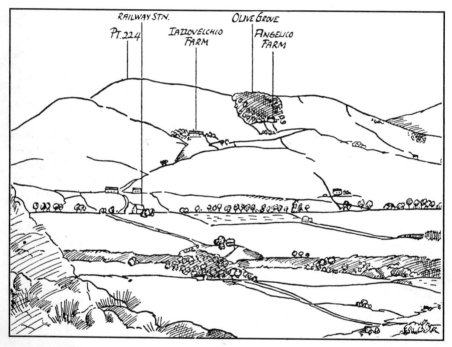

A sketch of the Sferro Hills as seen from our Observation Post.

Apart from these things we lived much as usual. The sun still blazed, water was short, cactus still had prickles, our bodies were brown and our faces black. We moved up slowly by dusty tracks and groves of unripe lemons towards the valley of the Dittaino and the Sferro Hills.

The big picture, though cheerful enough, had not developed as it had been expected to do, and the carefree dash of the early days had spent itself round Mount Etna. Messina was still a long way away. The Germans, as was their habit, had reacted quickly and, far from being cut off in the western half of the island, had now established a line behind which they were retiring northwards in order and at their leisure. This line ran from north-west to south-east, and passed near Etna. It had held several attacks. Catania, blocking the narrows between the mountain and the sea, still held out. It was decided to crack it farther west, across the valley of the Dittaino.

The valley was a wide one, steeper on the German side than on our own. The crests were manned, but the valley itself, with its road and railway line running parallel to the dried-up bed of the Dittaino, was No Man's Land, patrolled after dark by both sides but otherwise left in peace. Opposite us were the Sferro Hills, steep, grass-covered, and ending at their northern extremity in a hump called Point 224. This was our brigade objective.

Our recce parties lay on Monte Turcisi on our own side of the valley, studying it. It did not look too bad. A little white track wound up it after disentangling itself from some awkward looking hummocks near the road. Half-way up the track was a farm called Iazzovecchio where, said our patrols, the dogs still barked. Now, in daylight, there was no sign of life there. The track ended at another farm, Angelico, which lay beside a small olive grove a hundred and fifty yards below the crest. It too was peaceful. It was difficult to believe that the reverse side of the ridge must be crawling with Germans and Italians and that up there on the skyline were men with binoculars, scanning our side of the valley. The only movement in a dead world came from the far left, where the 5th Division was conscientiously raising dust in the hope that the enemy might believe our attack was going in there instead of to the north.

The Brigade plan was worked out at leisure and, as usual, seemed simple enough. The Camerons were to lead, and capture Point 224. We were to follow their axis as far as Iazzovecchio and then attack north-east and take Angelico Farm. 2nd Seaforth would be in reserve, and there would be six regiments of artillery and two companies of machine-guns in support. Away on our left, 154 Brigade were to capture the next hill on the ridge.

The Battalion plan also appeared to be simple. Colonel Walford, knowing what could happen on a single track in the dark, elected to use two routes instead of one. "A", "C", and "D" Companies, Battalion H.Q., and a few Battalion H.Q. vehicles would follow the Camerons direct to Iazzovecchio. "B" Company and the supporting weapons would cut across a cornfield to the left, and climb another track to the same farm. At Iazzovecchio the Battalion would deploy for the assault, and would, if possible, exploit over the crest of the hill to the line of a wadi on the far side after its main task of capturing the farm and the olive grove had been completed.

It was neat, but it was not going to be easy. The men on their feet, granted good route-finding, should have no more than normal difficulty in reaching the rendezvous at Iazzovecchio; but for the vehicle column the outlook was not so bright. It might look tidy on the map, but the cold truth of the matter was that the plan involved moving the carriers, mortars, machine-guns, and anti-tank guns of two battalions in single file and total darkness down a rocky mountain, across a river bed and up a steep hill against an enemy whose positions we could only guess and whose strength we did not know. Corps was talking airily about 'the Highland Division skirmish', but we had our own ideas on the subject.

The approach march was done on the night of July 30, and by dawn on the 31st the rifle companies were lying up in the narrow grassy gullies on the west side of Monte Turcisi, resting for the attack that night. The vehicles had stayed behind: they would have been heard by the enemy if they had moved up with the rest of the Battalion, and they were not due to move until the attack opened and the Cameron barrage made silence unnecessary. We lay in the sun, and sweated. Perhaps, we felt, the unexpected attack was best after all: here we had too much time to think, lying huddled in the gullies, unable to move about without being seen. Would the taping across the bed of the Dittaino be adequate, or would the vehicles lose themselves among the gorse on the banks? Was Angelico occupied or not? Would the Boche have tanks? At Alamein there had been no time: we had had only one day out of the line, and that had been a bedlam of recces and conferences. The Battle of the Hills had been a scramble. The day before Akarit had been filled with planning and marching. At Francofonte we had jumped from peace to war in a few seconds. But here we had planned for a week, and now there was nothing left to do but think.

At 2100 hours the Intelligence Section moved off to tape a route for "B" Company and the supporting weapons across the cornfield, and to post guides in the dried-up river bed. At 2200 hours the barrage opened, and the rest of the rifle companies began to move down to the river behind the Camerons. Farther back still, the vehicle column was bumping down an atrocious track, slowly gaining on the main body.

The rifle companies had a few hesitations and castings about in the dark, but they did reach Iazzovecchio without major difficulty. Not so the vehicle column. The expected snags began to arise.

I had taken over the Mortar Platoon after Francofonte, so I had a ringside seat for this part of the performance. It was a hard seat – in the front of a bren carrier, to be precise – and my chief memory of that night is of the tape, grey and indistinct in the darkness, winding endlessly under the nose of the carrier as it twisted over boulders, through minefeld gaps, and finally down into the bed of the river. We were like hens on a chalk-line, hypnotised, hating the tape for its windings and occasional breaks, but fearful of losing it. At the river voices shouted at us from the darkness. Vaguely, for our attention was held by the tape, we were conscious of the red shell-bursts spattering the hillside ahead and of the five red tracer shells which were fired over our heads every fifteen minutes to mark the direction of the advance. Gravel crunched under our tracks, gorse bushes loomed up, and the tape disappeared. We backed, and turned, and swore, and then we found it again. A few mortar bombs were bursting here and there, but apart from them little seemed to be coming back in reply to our barrage. Then, for reasons we were never able to discover, we lost the cornfield tape and wandered in a long straggling column through field after field while tracer drifted past and vague figures moved ahead, silhouetted against the shell-bursts. They were probably Camerons, but they may have been Germans. I do not know where we were. Someone flung a grenade at us. After a while we turned the column and tried to find our way back to some known point. We stumbled on a guide, and reached our track.

It was a difficult track, much more difficult than it had appeared through our binoculars from Monte Turcisi. At one point it passed through a deeply cut gully, clinging precariously to the bank about half-way between the stream-bed and the top. As we entered it, the ground rose on our left hand and dropped away sharply on our right: and in this bottleneck, at exactly the place where there was no way round, a huge portee towing a six-pounder gun had chosen to break down. The column stopped, vehicles jammed nose to tail. Infantry were milling about as well

– Camerons, I think, because I could hear Colonel Monro roaring in the darkness. We were late already, and we knew that this place, having been registered by the German artillery earlier in the day, was not healthy. A single spandau was firing wide: the red bullets were whipping along the top of the bank twenty yards to our left. The men and vehicles of two battalions were somewhere in the darkness, trying to disentangle themselves; and the portee was blocking everything. We did the only thing possible – unhitched the gun from it and tipped it over the edge. It bumped downwards and we never saw it again. The engine of the portee would not start, so we put it in gear, pressed the starter button and ran it on the battery while a dozen men pushed. As it toppled out of sight the driver jumped clear. We sorted ourselves out, drove on, and a few yards farther up the track found Battalion H.Q. at Iazzovecchio.

Meantime our attack had started. "D" Company made itself firm in Angelico Farm without much difficulty; but the olive grove beside it was still alive with the enemy, and Jack Davidson made a decision on the spot against exploitation over the ridge. "C" Company on his left was having heavy weather in the grove (for all its innocence when seen from Monte Turcisi it had turned out to be a German strong-point); and "A" Company, at that time spreading eastwards towards the end of the ridge, sent its left-hand or westerly platoon to help. "B" Company pushed towards the crest of the ridge on the far left, between the Camerons and ourselves. Over a hundred German and Italian prisoners came trooping back. By dawn, which broke dimly through mist and cordite fumes, our first task had been completed in an untidy sort of way, but there were still many loose ends to be tied up. We were digging in all over the slopes below the crest and we had guns on the crest itself, but scattered snipers still lurking on our own side of the skyline made it impossible for us to move with any freedom or to dominate the ridge as completely as we should have liked; and there were still Germans in the grove. The enemy artillery had opened up, but it was shelling the road behind us: the Boche had evidently not yet renounced his claims on the ridge.

This partial success had been achieved by very close and confused fighting in the darkness, the flanking companies making good progress against the few scattered spandau posts on the open slopes, and "C" Company edging slowly forward over the skyline and round the back of the strong-point in the olive grove. The heaviest fighting took place here. The Germans were well dug in, and though the company could move with comparative ease in the open, they met strong resistance whenever they tried to penetrate the grove itself. Furthermore, our maps of the area were inaccurate: the grove was shown as ending on the skyline, whereas in fact it continued down the far side into enemy territory, providing good cover by which the Germans could filter back into our positions. It was cleared at first light, but as soon as our men retired to consolidate on the crest, the Boche snipers wormed their way back up the hill through the olive trees.

The clearing of the grove was one of the finest individual efforts of the battle. Here is a first-hand account of it, told by Private J. Graham of "C" Company.

'During the night we'd been able to work round the rear of the place and pick up a hundred Itie prisoners, but we couldn't get inside it. When daylight came I was with the reserve platoon, lying back a bit, and I could see a section of one of the other platoons dug in on the edge of the grove and having a bad time from a breda and a spandau somewhere in the middle of it. They began shouting for a bren gun, so I ran across to them with mine. They were all private soldiers. There was a lad called McLaughlan there with a bren, and he seemed to be the boss. He was talking to his No. 2 – Kennedy was his name – and when I arrived he said: "Let's get cracking, or we'll never get this finished."

'So the three of us – McLaughlan, Kennedy, and me – went into the grove. We couldn't see anything at first. We just sprayed ahead and kept moving. After a bit Kennedy spotted the breda. We got down and let it have it with both guns at a hundred yards, and that fixed it good and proper: we killed one of the crew, and when we got up to it the other was lying wounded and shouting for aqua.

'We kept on running, and dodging, and spraying. We could see Boche nipping about among the trees by this time, and there were Ities too, but so long as we kept moving they didn't seem to be able to hit us. The others stopped and covered me, and I worked up close to the spandau and heaved a grenade into it. Four Ities came out and surrendered. I sent them back, and then another spandau outside the grove opened up on McLaughlan. It missed him, but it killed an Itie prisoner and wounded a Boche; and Sergeant Smith (he'd seen us and come up to help) got a burst along the side of his face. He was in a hell of a mess. We made the other prisoners carry him back, and then started off again. We got odd prisoners in all the doovers – there were doovers all over the place – but most of them put their hands up fast. And that was all there was to it. We got eighteen or nineteen altogether, half of them Jerries.'

Graham does not mention that he and McLaughlan also got the M.M. for their performance.

The rest of "C" Company moved in and consolidated on the crest. By 1000 hours the part of the grove which lay beyond them had been cleared for the last time and most of the mopping-up outside it had been done. The Germans had retired to their own side of the hill, leaving behind only one obstinate gentleman with a spandau who continued to spray the unwary from some point well out on the left flank until one of our tanks waddled over and persuaded him to stop.

We were able to draw breath and wash the taste of battle from our mouths, knowing that the crest was firmly in our hands. (The taste was a memorable one, peculiar to fighting in hot climates. There was a raging thirst far beyond anything mere heat could produce; the tongue was dry; and the mouth was coated with a scum which tasted equally of dust, cordite, and corpses. It was the kind of taste which stays in the mind for life.) Under the dusty olive trees on the ridge lay dirt and disorder, carbines and egg grenades, black bread, ammunition, clothing, a few dead Germans gathering flies. The eighty-eights were plastering Angelico; and Jack Davidson, mortally hit, was being carried down to the Regimental Aid Post. The sun blazed down. We felt very tired.

The Brigadier had told Colonel Walford before the battle began that once we gained the ridge we were certain to be counter-attacked. It was an odds-on chance that they would do it, he said, because they simply could not afford to lose the Sferro Hills. For a time we beleved he was wrong, because throughout the late morning odd packets of Boche could be seen pulling out from wadis beyond the crest; but soon we knew his reasoning had been sound. The Colonel and Paddy were up at the observation post with a medium-gun major from the Scottish Horse, peering hopefully down into German territory and comparing the map with what they saw. It was a magnificent panorama. Immediately below was a valley planted with a handful of squalid farms. On the right rose brown hills where Germans were still moving (the major licked his lips), and in front more hills stretched back like a wrinkled and very dusty carpet towards Etna, smoking on the horizon. A rough track emerged from the hills and disappeared below the Cameron positions on Point 224.

The gunner major was arguing with his signaller.

'I say,' said Paddy suddenly, 'are those tanks ours ?'

A dozen tanks, some motor-cyclists, and lorried infantry were driving unconcernedly along the track towards the Camerons.

'They might be,' he said doubtfully, focussing his glasses. 'But they can't be. They CAN'T ... I can see! I can see now! They're Mark IVs!'"

Slowly and happily the Scottish Horse major began to issue fire orders over the wireless.

There is something which must be said in this book, and though the Sferro counter-attack was only one of many occasions when we were saved by our artillery, this is a convenient place to say it. We in the Infantry thank the gunners for the support they gave us in every battle. Time and again we reached our objectives with negligible casualties simply because the defences had had the stuffing knocked out of them before we arrived; and for that we thank all who co-operated with us, from Brigadier Jerry Shiel down to our own particular cronies, Majors Norman Owen, Taffy Wilcox, and H.J.Decker, and Captains Arthur Stobo, John Trapnell, and Neil Millar.

(below) Panzer Grenadiers of the Hermann Göring Battle-Group receiving decorations prior to the Sferro Hills action – a print taken from a film found after the battle.

The reunion of the 2nd, 5th and 6th Battalions of the Seaforth Highlanders and the 1st Seaforth Highlanders of Canada on 25 August 1943 in a stadium in Catania, Sicily.

On this afternoon they were superb. The German tanks were dropping "fast balls" all over the hill. Heavier calibre stuff droned overhead to the Sferro road behind us. Panzer Grenadiers assaulted Point 224, and one German tank forced its way gallantly to the peak, where it was knocked out. But six gunner regiments, backed by every anti-tank gun on the slopes, put down all they had in support of the Camerons, and by 1400 hours the Herman Göring battle-group had had enough. Their attack had disappeared in a cloud of smoke from which only a few surviving tanks limped away. The shelling slackened. By 1800 hours it was just another sunny Sicilian evening. The battle was over.

We had lost three officers and three men killed, and sixteen men wounded.

II

With the Etna line broken, the campaign too was as good as over. The Germans retired slowly on Messina, blowing bridges in such numbers as they went that the Allies were never again able to force a major action upon them. By August 17 the last German had crossed the Straits to Italy, and Sicily was ours. During this period we advanced to Biancavilla on the slopes of Etna and later to Pisano, but from both places the Germans had gone before we arrived. Despite various orders and counter-orders we fell out of the chase. Other divisions took it up and we were left among the vineyards of Pisano to eat grapes and rest.

There are occasions when war may be positively pleasant, and the end of a campaign is one of them. We climbed Etna and saw the dawn, went junketing in the villages, and in Catania held a reunion of the 2nd, 5th and 6th Battalions of the Regiment and of the 1st Seaforth Highlanders of Canada, the first on such a scale since the war of 1914-18. On August 28 we moved north to Meri, a village by the sea, and there held dances, bathed, and took our ease. Eleven days later the Italians surrendered unconditionally, but the Germans in Italy fought on. Then a tremendous rumour began to take shape.

After almost every battle since Alamein this same rumour had gone the rounds. We were going to be sent home. The clerk in So-and-So's office had it positively from the batman of an officer who had dined with the General. The quartermaster had a new stock of shirts angola. A camp was prepared for us near Perth – hadn't Private Such-and-Such a brother, a carpenter, who was working on it ? We had heard all this after Tripoli, and Akarit, and the anti-tank ditch. People had sworn to its truth at Djidjelli. Now we just smiled when it came up again: it was an old one, that.

And yet.... The crossing had been made into Italy, but only one of our brigades had been called upon and it had been concerned only with the preliminaries. There was no sign of our moving. The Colonel was hedging a bit when the subject came up in Mess. Perhaps, after all....

On September 25, General Montgomery came and spoke to us. In his address he said he had come with bad tidings; but in the past we had taken the bad with the good and we could doubtless do so again. He hardly knew how to break it to us, but here it was. He was very much afraid we were going back to Britain.

The cheering was still at full blast five minutes later.

COUNT-DOWN TO D-DAY

(previous page) Officers of the 5th Seaforth at Much Hadham, Spring 1944:
Back row, left to right: Lieutenants Harrison (1), Galloway(2), Jones (3), Lisle(4),
Mackintosh(5), Cowie(6); Centre row: Donnie McCleod (7), Sutcliffe(8), Cochrane(9),
Latta(10), Angus(11), Houldsworth(12), Capt. Purgavie(13), Ferguson(14), Mair(15),
Offin(16), A.Grant(17), Wade(18), P.Grant(19), Smart(20);
Front Row: Padre Simpson (21), Capt. Perry(22), Capt. Watt(23), Capt. H.Macrae
(Quartermaster)(24), Maj. Green(25). Lt.Col. Walford(26), Lt.General Sir W.Thompson
KCMG, CB, MC, Colonel of the Regiment(27), Maj. Fleming(28), Capt. Forshaw-
Wilson(29), Capt. H.A.C.Mackenzie(30), Capt. Rutherford(31), Capt. F.Macrae
(RAMC)(32). Absent: Maj. Findlay-Shirras, Maj. Robertson McIsaac, Capt.
D.J.M.Robertson, Capt. H.S.Robertson, Lt. Borthwick, and others.

CHAPTER TEN

Count-down to D-Day

I

WE LEANED OVER the bulwark, and each of us was using the word 'green' every second sentence. Yet the green fields of Ayrshire and the Cumbraes were not the most striking feature of our homecoming. The first glimpse of them was spectacular enough (the colour was so deep it seemed almost blue), but after all we had expected it. We had talked about it for a thousand miles. 'Green fields, and the wife, and a half-pint,' we had said, and thought we had summed up most of the things we had missed for two long years. What no one had consciously missed was the air.

Now it was blowing sweet in our faces from the land, and we marvelled that we had not missed it. It was cold, and clean, and... what is the word? 'Moist' does not quite hit it off, though moisture lay somewhere at the root of it. 'Soft' is too vague. There is no single word in the language to describe it, since the need for one is known only to returning travellers. They, and they only, know that the air of Britain is so mellowed by just the right proportion of moisture that when it is met after long absence the skin is conscious of and grateful for the change. The air of Africa and Sicily had been hard and brittle. In the desert, no matter how fresh it might have been, it was brittle, and there was no smell. Near an Arab village it had still been brittle, and there was much smell. But this wind that came to us from Scotland was more than sweet: it had an enfolding softness.

Our lives had been changed, and we still carried Africa with us. It was inconceivable that other people's lives had remained unaltered, that while, for example, we had lived on one waterbottle a day it could have been raining in Glasgow. Reason told us that our circumstances had changed, but for two years the evidence of our senses had told us that the world had changed. Rain in Glasgow? With all this sand about? Glasgow was something out of Hans Andersen. Any fool knew the world was bone dry.

When we landed at Gourock on November 4, the gable-ends contained only references to such homely things as beef extract and savings certificates, and for some reason did not say: *'Un seul but, la victoire - Giraud'* on one side of the street and: *'Vive De Gaulle'* on the other. No hoarding said that Mussolini was 'Always Right' or even suggested that Churchill was 'Frequently Right' or 'Very Right' or anything like that. No one above the age of ten seemed to write on the walls at all. People went shopping in real shops with glass windows, crowds and crowds of them, and their clothes were all drab browns and blues and blacks. The men wore trousers. Children had shoes and stockings on their feet. And, crowning felicity, as we passed through the outskirts of Glasgow on our way to Hertford and leave there were tram-cars, great, ugly, unbelievable tram-cars bearing offhandedly the names of destinations which to us were still five thousand miles away. It must not be assumed that all these wonderful things could be digested on the spot. We had fourteen days of disembarkation leave for that. No one can believe a tram-car, just like that. We had been fooled by mirages too often, seen too many Promised Lands melt into squalor when we approached them. Behind that sooty public house there obviously lurked a bootblack. True, all the prickly-pear hedges seemed to have disappeared, but at any moment we should be importuned to buy a fly-swat or visit the Blue Mosque. Soon a donkey must appear between the tram-lines, carrying well back over its rump a dirty old gentleman with an umbrella and followed at a decent interval by the dirty old gentleman's wife, on foot, with no umbrella but a great deal of luggage. Surely all these puddles bred mosquitoes.

We began to realise how good toast was. We had not been able to make toast on Benghazis. We knew again the sound, solid, honest feel of a half-crown after months of messing about with piastres and dirty notes worth fivepence. We turned on taps, and just sat, gloating. We contemplated the infinite beauty of baths.

The reality of these things came to us slowly, after many days. There were also personal matters of which one does not talk; but, these apart, it was the unexpected thing which still makes our homecoming memorable – not the green fields and the smoky chimneys, but a breath of fresh air on "A" Deck at dawn.

II

When our leave was behind us there was a period of training and taking stock as we made ready for the invasion of Western Europe. Reinforcements came in, and we began to handle assault boats, practise the advance to contact, train snipers, and think in terms of water and close country instead of the distances of Africa. New faces appeared. Major Richard Fleming had "D" Company, and Leslie Forshaw-Wilson was Adjutant. Major David Blair, M.B.E., newly escaped from Italy, had "B". Of the old officers who had sailed to Suez in the *Bergensfjord* only a handful remained – Colonel Walford, George Green, Hector Macrae, Hugh Robertson, Farquhar Macrae, and a few others. Of the old Territorials in the ranks only about a third were left. Still, the Battalion retained its identity, calmly swallowing the newcomers and passing on to them its language and its customs: Yorkshiremen forgot 'champion' and said 'just the job' instead; and the Padre was 'Padrone' to scores who had never seen Sicily. The individuality of battalions is not, as might be imagined, a sentimental fiction: in war they can consume twice their own weight in recruits and yet remain unmistakably themselves. Our losses had been grievous and the soft vowels of the North were salted with many alien twangs; but we were, strangely enough, still very much a Highland battalion.

During this calm between two storms we were first at Much Hadham in Hertfordshire, and later at Wimbish, Essex. Tension throughout the country was probably greater than it had been at any time since the opening days of the war. The Second Front in Europe, once only a wistful dream, had passed through the stage of pious hope to immediate certainty. The handful of ill-equipped battalions which had manned our coasts in 1940 was now an Allied army prepared to attack in overwhelming strength, and the only matters which were in doubt were the date and the place. By the beginning of May, 1944, the masses of troops and equipment concentrating on the south and south-east coasts of England could only mean that the curtain was about to go up; and throughout the land the double question of where and when was being argued wherever two people met and talked.

That the secret of D-Day was kept, considering the number of people who must have been concerned in the planning, was one of the miracles of the war; but it was a miracle not achieved by chance. The lengths gone to maintain secrecy were extraordinary. Of the higher levels I know nothing; but I do know that when the security arrangements had spread downwards through the chain of command, taking in increasing numbers of men at each stage until the battalion level had been reached, the precautions were staggering.

On May 17 we left Wimbish, spent the night in Southend-on-Sea, and two days later went to S.6., one of the many camps strung out along the Southend/London road. These camps had not been used before. They had been erected purely for the marshalling of the invasion army and for maintaining secrecy throughout the complicated process of embarkation. Each consisted of a barbed wire perimeter, a few huts for washing, and tents. Each, when the gaps in the wire were closed, could become a prison. All lay in an area of hundreds of square miles where movement of civilians was either checked by the police or barred altogether. Most of south-east England had become a honeycomb of which each cell could be sealed at will.

At first the camps were not sealed. One-day leaves to London continued until the marshalling was completed and all the camps were full; and then, on May 28, the gaps in the wire were closed. After that, no one left except under escort, and then only to another sealed camp. There were even special sealed hospitals for the sick. At this stage, so far as we were concerned, only Colonel Walford had any inkling of the plan, and he did not know a great deal. On the day the gaps were closed the Battalion officers were briefed.

The spell of good weather which was to help us so much in Normandy had begun, and the day was sunny and hot. We climbed into trucks and drove in convoy to another camp, passed a red-cap at the gate who checked our identity cards and admitted us through the wire, and left our trucks in a park inside. Ahead of us was a second belt of wire manned by sentries. Again we produced our cards, and again passed through. There was a third wire barrier, this time set in a circle one hundred yards in diameter. In the centre of it, fifty yards from the nearest sentries, was a big black hut. We went in.

The entire wall facing the door was covered by a gigantic map (the men who had drawn it had already been in sealed camps for six weeks), and as soon as we saw it we knew that for us the denouement was still to come. It was the same old story. Our marshalling area across the Channel was called Edinburgh, or Chicago, or some such name, and all we knew of the beach on which we were expected to land was that it was called Nan. Still, we heard the plan. The vital questions of when and where were still unanswered – no date was given; and the map, though huge, was on a big scale and covered too small an area of ground to offer any clue as to its whereabouts – but we did at least have something to chew on. We were told that we should not land in the first wave. We should go ashore on D+2 into a bridgehead which had already been formed, march to a marshalling area, and remain there in reserve until a task should be found for us. The routes from the beach to the marshalling area were gone into in great detail. Apart from these domestic points we had the plan only in general terms. The Canadians, who were landing before us, were going to exploit as far as possible, perhaps even as far as

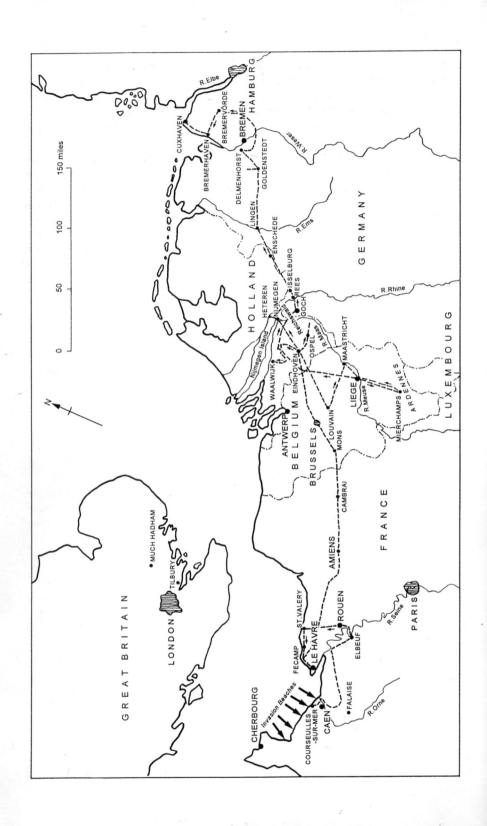

the big town which lay ten miles inland. They might capture the town in the first flush of surprise; but that was not, on the whole, likely. If they did not reach it, we might be launched to help them. On the other hand we might.... It was all very vague. We knew in what order we should land, the routes we should follow, and an outline of the bigger picture. The rest was in the lap of the gods. We returned to our camp, and waited.

The stages by which the various parts of the Battalion travelled from S.6. to the Thames Estuary need not be discussed here. It is sufficient to say that the parties travelled at different times according to their embarkation priorities, and staged at an intermediate camp where rations were issued and our money was changed into francs, this last to the immense excitement of our more argumentative armchair strategists. By the evening of June 5 most of us were lying in ships below Tilbury. At 0700 hours on June 6, the B.B.C. announced that British parachutists had been dropped near the Seine Estuary, and that the German radio reported British and American landings all along the coast of Normandy.

NORMANDY BRIDGEHEAD

(previous page) *In the woods to the east of Caen.*

CHAPTER ELEVEN

Normandy Bridgehead

I

THE MORNING was dull and grey. We edged down the river past Thameshaven and Southend, past the anti-aircraft platforms rising on stilts from the estuary, and out into the North Sea. Once the boom was passed the convoy took shape, stringing fore and aft from horizon to horizon. England lay grey and low to starboard.

We were all excited, but our excitement had nothing fresh on which to feed. The radio reports which were coming hourly to our people at home did not reach us, because the enemy U-boats had devices which enabled them to detect not only transmitting sets but receiving sets. After the one brief announcement we had heard before sailing, wireless silence had been imposed, so that even after we had landed in Normandy we knew a good deal less about the war than anyone in Britain with a penny to spend on a newspaper.

Briefing was carried out as we approached Dover, but we heard little we did not know already. The only novelties were maps which showed that the big town mentioned at the original briefing was Caen, and that our landing-place was to be Courseulles-sur-Mer. However, this morsel was sufficient to set the armchair strategists talking, and arguments were still raging when someone rushed in and said we were being shelled by the French coastal batteries.

This was the only excitement of the voyage and was a minor one. Our destroyers were charging up and down the convoy laying a smoke-screen, but we felt they need hardly have bothered because the only signs of life from the much-vaunted German Long Toms, at any rate in our convoy, were a few small splashes not less than two miles from the nearest ship. We soon grew tired of watching, and went below again to win the war on paper. By evening the housie-housie schools were in full cry, the canteen was open, and card games were going on in corners. It was not at all the kind of invasion we had expected.

We had to disembark next morning at 0700 hours, so reveille was at 0430. As was customary on such occasions, we did in fact disembark at 1430, after hanging about on crowded decks for hours; but for once no one grumbled. It was not a day for boredom. No one who saw the Normandy beaches that morning will ever forget them. It was an even more impressive sight than the Sicilian landing. We came gently in to landfall and dropped anchor four miles offshore. Ahead was a low ridge with a small town below it, fat farming country, neat and peaceful, like the coast of Devon before the war. Only on the sea did the picture fit our preconceived ideas of D-Day. Ships were everywhere. None of us had ever seen so many ships. The whole sea crawled. There were battleships and tiny landing craft, channel packets and ocean-going liners, ducks and hippos and all the other contrivances designed for this day, some going, some coming, some anchored; and this monstrous regatta, this mass of some five hundred vessels, was spread over only seven miles of a bridgehead already more than fifty miles long. Beyond, out of sight, were thousands more. As close as the next bay, a bare five miles away, was a tangle of masts and funnels which must have represented a fleet as great as the one we could see spread out before Courseulles; and astern of us the sky was black with the smoke of more and still more convoys creeping over the horizon.

We transferred into a tank landing ship which was acting as a ferry, and at last we were off, threading our way in the sunshine through the maze of shipping towards "Nan" beach at Courseulles. Half-an-hour later we grounded in three feet of water thirty yards off-shore. We put on our waders.

The Jock, as he prepared to go ashore, was a sadly burdened creature. First, as a basis, he wore boots, battledress, and a steel helmet. Next came his web equipment, to which were attached ammunition pouches, two waterbottles, a small and bulging haversack slung at the side, a bayonet, and an enormous pack round which a blanket had been bound with pieces of string. Next, on top of all that had gone before, were a respirator and a lifebelt. If he were lucky, he carried a rifle: if unlucky, a bren gun, a two-inch mortar, or a load of two-inch mortar bombs done up in sacking and worn round his neck like a horse-collar. If any man had gone overboard he would have sunk like a brick, lifebelt and all. And to all this was added the invasion wader, a garment of repulsive design and doubtful utility, elephant-waisted and duck-footed, made of green oiled cotton, and (we found) extremely liable to split. As the seat was so cut as to admit the small haversack and the two waterbottles as well as other necessary portions of the wearer, the invasion wader must go down as the least becoming garment in history.

We struggled ashore through the fast-receding tide and dropped our waders and lifebelts on the beach, which, again contrary to expectations, was a reasonably leisurely place. There was no confusion, no shellfire, and no great hurry, despite the fact that the first landings had been made only thirty-six hours before. A few wrecked landing-craft lay about, but there was no real sign of warfare except some buildings which the Navy had shelled at dawn to evict snipers. Our landing could not have been more peaceful; which fact, bearing in mind the waders and the amount of gear we were carrying, was a very good thing. We sorted ourselves out, marched up the beach past a long line of German prisoners, set our pipers at our head, and trudged inland to the assembly area at Rivières, woefully overloaded, very hot, but still far from the battle.

II

During the following two days the rest of the Battalion came ashore in varying degrees of comfort and joined the others at Rivières, where we were complete with all men and vehicles by June 9. Rivières was a quiet little backwater untouched by the war, and as the weather was sunny and warm it was no hardship to sleep in the fields round the village. We dug ourselves in, opened our twenty-four-hour packs, and made ourselves at home.

The twenty-four-hour pack may be of some historical interest and is worth mentioning here. It was a waterproof cardboard box, six inches by five by two-and-a-half, and it contained enough to keep one man's body and soul together for one day. The backbone of the diet was porridge and stew, each compressed into a small iron-hard brick which, when whittled down with a penknife and heated with water, blossomed miraculously into something very like a real meal. Round them were blocks of tea-milk-and-sugar, chocolate, and meat extract; and there were besides boiled sweets, packets of chewing gum, soft unsweetened biscuits, lump sugar, and salt. Each man carried two of these packs and one tin of bully beef; and although some of us were landed a day ahead of schedule and consequently had to exist on the packs for three days instead of two, nearly all of us had some food left by the end of the third day.

There was little to do during these days of waiting for the Battalion to assemble except lie in the sun or visit the hill behind our area where German corpses and a few derelict anti-aircraft guns proved that there actually had been a war in Rivières. During daylight the war seemed remote or impossible; but at night the German bombers were over the beaches and we were glad of our slit trenches. Sometimes anti-personnel bombs fell near us, but no one was hurt. It was difficult to believe that men were fighting barely seven miles to the south.

This state of affairs continued until June 10. At 2200 hours on that date we were ordered to move to St. Aubin d'Arquenay, and the move took place at 0300 hours on the following morning. This was only a staging area. At 1300 hours on the 11th, after a short air raid which produced our first casualty, we crossed the Orne.

Though we did not know it then, the Orne was a milestone. Beyond it, in the tiny bridgehead within a bridgehead, were names none of us will forget – the Bois de Bavent, Escoville, the Triangle, St. Honorine, the Butte de la Hogue – places upon whose capture or loss were to depend the plans not only of our Division but of the Army. At this time the Allies occupied a strip of the Normandy coast seventy miles long by about ten deep, with the left flank anchored on the River Orne. Running north and south three miles beyond the river was a long hog-backed ridge, densely wooded, overlooking the Orne valley. In German hands it meant a constant source of observation over our flank; and moreover, though we did not know it, our Higher Command had a use for the gently undulating plain of cornland which lay between the ridge and the river. Knowing the plan as it unfolded later, it is easy to appreciate the importance of the Orne plain and the ridge: then it seemed just a bridgehead without much future, and an uncommonly small bridgehead at that. At St. Aubin we had come under command of Brigadier 'Nap' Murray of 153 Brigade, and were ordered to take up a defensive position near the road intersection south-east of Escoville, a nameless place later to become famous as the Triangle.

'You'll be all right for the first mile or so,' said the Staff Captain, 'but watch your step in the woods. Both sides have paratroops there, and it's damned nearly impossible to tell which is which. Don't stop for anyone. Look what happened yesterday. Convoy driving down the road, all nice and peaceful ... Boche steps out in front of the last truck and holds up his hand ... driver brakes instinctively ... one burst of schmeiser, and he's had it. Most unpleasant. They tried the same dodge on the Brigade Major this morning. He trod on the gas for all he was worth and tried to run the fellow down; but he got a bullet in the leg just the same. I tell you, it's no picnic in the woods.'

With this cheerful farewell to ponder upon, we crossed the twin bridges at Bénouville, every truck bristling with small-arms. The journey was uneventful but not without interest. The 6th Airborne Division, as cheerful a band of cut-throats as ever handled a hunting-knife or a slab of guncotton, had dropped over the Orne on D-Day and for five days had been fighting a little war of its own in the woods and down on the plain. The signs were there for all to see along the road-side – burned-out trucks and tanks, bodies lying unburied in the ditches, houses roofless and gaping; and in the fields dead cows, the trade-mark of the war in Europe. They were in every field, those cows, swollen, legs stiff and straddling, grotesque, all placidity gone. There can have been no more vulnerable creature in this war. They died in thousands all the way from the Orne to Bremen.

Some of our transport was on loan to the 2nd Seaforth, so all our companies but one had to march. It was 1645 hours before our last troops arrived at the Triangle and our relief of the 5/7 Gordons was complete. We dug shallow trenches and settled in for the night. They were the last shallow trenches we were ever to dig.

Our position was an interesting one. The British bridgehead over the Orne was not the tidy semicircle beloved of the strategists, but a sprawling, irregular pattern as full of possibilities for the Germans as it was for ourselves. It ran from Longueval on the bank of the Orne north-east to le Bas de Ranville, then south-east through le Mariquet and Herouvillette to the Triangle and on to the brickworks above Touffreville. Then it doubled back north and followed the main road to Sallenelles, via le Mesnil, Bréville, and Amfréville. Its length was four miles, and its greatest depth three-and-a-half miles. The northern half was held by 6th Airborne and Special Service troops, the southern half by the Highland Division; and it was essential that we should hold on until the build-up of ammunition and stores and men on the beaches was far enough advanced for a break-out to be attempted, a probable period of two months. The various moves which are recorded in the rest of this chapter may seem confusing and pointless, but they all had this one end in view – to hold the Orne bridgehead, and while doing so to share the heavy work as fairly as possible among the units of the Division. During this period the Battalion relieved or was relieved by every other battalion in the Division.

Two facts were painfully obvious when we studied the maps of the area. The first was that although we held Longueval, Herouvillette, and the Triangle, the Germans held St. Honorine and no one at all held Escoville, which meant that there was nothing to stop the Germans swanning north to Ranville if they felt so inclined. The second was that the Germans were in the Bois de Bavent, Touffreville, and Troarn, which meant that anyone sitting in the Triangle or the brickworks would be surrounded on three sides. Added together, these two facts meant that (a) roughly speaking we held the bank of the Orne and the road on the ridge, while the Germans held the plain between: and (b) our new home, the Triangle, was nearly as far out into the blue as it was possible to be. Our headquarters were in a small field at the base of the Triangle, and the companies were disposed to the west and south, downhill, covering the approaches from the plain. A mile down the main road at the brickworks, similarly disposed, was another battalion; and below them on the plain was the small village of Touffreville. On the evening we relieved them, the 5th Gordons captured Touffreville without opposition.

This explanation is tedious, but as the Orne bridgehead filled most of our thoughts for seven long weeks it is as well to understand at the beginning how the land lay. Whoever held the ridge commanded the plain, and the Triangle was the key to the ridge. There were to be many comings and goings before our general advance swept forward and the place became once more what it always had been in the past, a simple junction of roads.

This, our first visit, lasted only two days. There were excitements but few casualties. A self-propelled gun lobbed some shells unpleasantly close; the Gordons were counter-attacked three hours after taking Touffreville, but held easily; at 2200 hours "B" Company counted eight tanks milling about on their front, but nothing came of it. Only once, on the morning of the 12th, did we seem likely to see action, but nothing came of that either: the Gordons were counter-attacked again, this time from the rear, and at half-past six we were ordered to have one company standing by to help them. It was not needed. On the 13th our mortars gave support while the Camerons, out on the plain, made an abortive and bloody attack on St. Honorine.

'At first it looked thoroughly bad country for observation posts,' wrote Richard Fleming, then commanding "D" Company at Pre Baron Farm on the edge of the plain. 'It was quite flat, and the high hedges and thick woods screened all but the immediate foreground. As Ian Houldsworth and I were making for the farm to see if a convenient stack might give a view, we were suddenly halted by Corporal Galleitch of the Intelligence Section from the branches of an enormous elm above our heads. After a certain amount of heaving and hoisting we found ourselves in the most wonderful leafy perch looking right down the plain to the outskirts of Caen – a perfect observation post. Furthermore, we had arrived just in time to see the Germans put in their counter-attack on Touffreville....

'The next morning trouble brewed up on our left, again directed on Touffreville; but by this time Donald Munro had a mortar O.P. established in our trees and it was very satisfactory to be able to hurry up the unsuspecting groups of Jerry infantry who were plodding about the plain, pulling their mortars along in blissful ignorance that they were under observation. Drivers started up their trucks and drove off very hurriedly; the gallant grenadiers scuttled off with their overcoats flapping; and even an S.P., disguised very ineffectively as a haystack, decided that discretion was the better part of valour and pulled out back to the Démouville woods. We had a certain gruesome satisfaction as we climbed down to our breakfast to notice that the only sign of life was an ambulance touring the scene of our shoot.

'The fame of our O.P. spread quickly, and before mid-day our line of elms was like a rookery, with a different O.P. in each. We had the Intelligence Section, the Company snipers, a forward observation officer from 127 Field Regiment, the Mortar Platoon, and even a naval gunner from H.M.S. *Arethusa*. The sailor was anxious to be shown at least one German because, as he pathetically explained, life was becoming intolerable for him on board through lack of targets. He was soon able to gratify his wish, and an unfortunate patrol of some half-dozen Herrenvolk skulking cautiously over the Butte de la Hogue were the astonished recipients of a couple of broadsides from the cruiser, the shells passing over sounding very much like so many tube trains on the Inner Circle. The patrol was not seen again....

'The doings of the last day at Pre Baron must be told by an abler person. How Ian Houldsworth and his fellow O.P.'s perched in their trees were almost knocked out of their perches by a flight of Typhoons rocketing the village of Escoville only five hundred yards away. How some over-keen member of the Brigade Intelligence Staff magnified an enemy patrol of eight into a force of eight hundred attacking our Company positions. Of the unfortunate artillery S.O.S. called for into Escoville which, unregistered, came down fair and square on our positions, wounding "The Greek" (our popular Company Sergeant Major Gordon) and McLean, the Company barber. And finally of the weary march back to an equally unhealthy area. Little did we think as we marched away that warm June night that we should be back in a month's time, and that our old positions would be in enemy hands.'

The 'equally unhealthy area' was le Bas de Ranville. We took it over from airborne troops in the middle of an air-raid at the horrible hour of half-past two on the morning of June 14.

III

Le Bas de Ranville was not so lonely as the Triangle, but lay close to the Bénouville bridges beside the Orne. It was a solidly built little village of mellow stone, not much knocked about; but the Devons, our predecessors, had dug deep and assured us that there was no temptation to live in any of the houses. There were no set times for shelling, they said. Any hour of the day or night was good enough for Jerry.

We were in Brigade reserve, but at this time everyone occupied tactical positions and there was little difference between being in the line and out of it. The situation was so unstable that in some places only a few hundred yards from us it had not even been possible to bury the dead.

We discovered one particularly grim spot when "A" Company's positions were pushed forward a short distance on the right flank. They lay as they had fallen eight days before. The gliders had landed near the bridge and the airborne men had fanned out beyond le Bas de Ranville. The Boche had counter-attacked, and the line had fallen back and stabilised with our men in the village and the enemy somewhere to the south. This place we found was the highwater mark of the airborne advance. The whole story was there on the ground – the little hand-carts full of ammunition and stores, hidden in a hedge; the German armoured car, brewed-up, with its crew dead around it; the sixty corpses, German and British, in the corn between the hedge where the fight began and the outskirts of the village where it had ended. There was a pond near the hedge. One airborne man had dragged his helpless comrade there for shelter and, fearing he would drown, had tied him by the arm to a tree which grew on the bank, so that he lay half in the water and half out of it. Then he himself had been killed, barely a yard away. They lay there still. We went out that night and buried them.

We were in le Bas de Ranville three days, during which the shelling and mortaring grew steadily worse. At first the Boche seemed to be concerned mainly with the bridge, and we soon learned not to duck when the big 150's and 210's came rumbling across the sky and crumped down into the river behind us. A few shells landed in our area on the 14th, but there were no casualties. On the 15th we were mortared steadily and, as the bombs were exploding in the treetops and we were as yet only imperfectly aware of the need for trenches with stout roofs on them, we had five casualties. Lieutenant A.F.S.Hector joined the Battalion that morning and was dead within the hour. On the 16th between 0430 and 0615 hours we had the father and mother of all stonks put down about our ears and had six men killed and seven wounded. It was accurate fire – four were killed by direct hits on slit trenches – and it came from weapons of all calibres. No one was sorry when, on the evening of the 16th, we were ordered to move into the line proper and relieve the 5th Camerons at Longueval.

We were in Longueval from the evening of June 16 until the evening of June 26. During that period little of note occurred on our immediate front, though on the far side of the plain the Germans recaptured the Triangle. Most of us will remember it as a rather lonely little village perched on the high east bank of the Orne, a village not too frequently bombarded but liable to be so at any time, where the chief activity was night patrols out over the plain and Battalion H.Q. lived in the most jerrybuilt and least shellproof chateau in the entire north-west of France.

The chief event of those days concerned the Camerons, though we became embroiled in it. On June 23 they made another attempt on St. Honorine, this time a successful one. Casualties were heavy, however. An S.O.S. went out, and as Longueval was not much more than a thousand yards away across the cornfields, two platoons of our ''A'' Company were sent across and put under their command. Later the 2nd Seaforth also moved in. On that day, seventeen tanks were destroyed on our Brigade front.

One hour before midnight on the 26th we relieved the 2nd Seaforth, who had been left to defend St. Honorine while the Camerons came out for a rest.

IV

This was the first time we had seen what war could do to a village. It must have been a douce little place once, with its seven or eight big farms and huddle of smaller buildings round them, lying snug behind its fringe of trees like a mediaeval town within a wall. It was well out in the plain. At sunset it looked like a small green island.

It was not quite dark when we went in. We waded waist-deep through the corn, following the white tape; and every now and then there was a bald patch in the corn, perfectly symmetrical, with the flattened stalks radiating precisely from the centre where a mortar bomb had fallen. The standing corn hid the dead, but the smell of death lay in little pools along the way. The craters grew thicker. The tape swung round by a wall, and we were under trees, picking our way through broken branches. Some trees were blown in half. Others were split down the centre. Nearly all had lost something. It was dark now, and muddy, and we were heavily laden. We went slithering along the track, not knowing where we were but following the muddy tape, until it brought us to a sea of mud, and dim trenches, and sandbags, and corrugated iron. The 2nd Battalion was suspiciously glad to see us.

St. Honorine (its full name was St. Honorine la Chardonerette) was an altogether beastly place. We were to occupy villages where the shelling was heavier and the material damage even greater, but never one which had to such a degree the power to depress. The French were good at hanging on, but this had been too much for them. There were no housewives drawing water under fire, or men ploughing among the minefields. The village had been abandoned completely, and fast. The walls were down and the windows in, and the contents of the houses were ragged heaps where pigs rooted. Dust from the shell-bursts lay thickly over half-finished meals and burst mattresses. In those days a bombing meant a crowd of helpers, but this place was dead.

Nothing lived among the ruins except cattle and hundreds of hens. As many more had died: the Germans had been firing airburst, and that is a terrible thing for cattle. There were nineteen dead cows in one farmyard and eleven in another, all killed by shrapnel.

They had lain there in the sun for twelve days. The less fortunate ones had been wounded, and these we shot. Hens were plastered on to the walls like pats of mud. The place was a shambles. In the end they sent us a bulldozer, and we scooped forty-seven beasts and countless hens into three gigantic graves.

There were men to bury too, but most of that had been done before we came.

The Germans were sensitive about St. Honorine and seemed to be unusually resentful at being thrown out of it. Instead of following their normal practice of either shelling or counter-attacking immediately after the capture of the village and then easing off, they did not seem to be able to leave the place alone. It was a nagging sort of warfare. There was nothing big or decisive about it; but every night their patrols were prodding at our defences and every day they shelled us. On the night of our arrival, a man in ''A'' Company was wounded by a grenade thrown into his trench and was being dragged away by three Germans when he was rescued by the rest of the platoon. Next day the odd airburst or fast-bowling eighty-eight came over from time to time, and later we had our first taste of Minnie.

Minnie is worth a paragraph to herself. Moaning Minnie, the six-barrelled rocket-propelled mortar, was a weapon more noisy than dangerous; but as we had not met her before we were not to know that. The scene in and around Battalion H.Q. that evening will serve as well as any to illustrate her activities. We lived in a damp, ill-smelling tunnel under the road and were dining there when pig-like squeals came from the south. We were puzzled and stopped eating to listen; but Bobby McIsaac's dog, a notably bomb-happy bitch, dived under the nearest bed without even pausing to yelp. A few seconds later a howling and wailing grew until it filled the sky, rising in pitch as it approached, and ending in a series of shattering explosions all round us. Blast swept in past the baffle-wall at the end of the tunnel and blew us sideways. There was a pause. We congregated in the centre of the tunnel. Then more squeals, the same horrible wail, and another batch of thirty-six bombs exploded astride us, so that the pressure came first from one side, then from the other, then from both at once. There was silence. We breathed again. The dog whimpered under the bed. The signallers prepared resignedly to go out and repair all the lines which had been cut. And from the Intelligence Section trenches came lamentations from Private Harrison whose illegal fresh pork dinner, tended lovingly over a petrol fire for three hours, had received a direct hit.

Colonel Walford was returning from Brigade when the stonk came down, and saw it all from the crest of a nearby hill. He said the whole village disappeared in smoke and it was difficult to believe that anyone could live under it. In actual fact, one man was killed and eleven injured, including Captain I.G.H.Houldsworth who, though caught in the open by a bomb which burst three feet away, escaped with wounds.

The perimeter was long and difficult to defend with a single battalion. We mined ourselves in and tried to cover the gaps by which enemy patrols might penetrate at night, but we were too thin on the ground to cover everything and the strain on the men was, in consequence, great. We slept during the day when we slept at all, and stood-to at night. Even so, ''A'' Company was raided three nights running.

Although St. Honorine will remain in our minds as a place of desolation and all-pervading stench, it was remarkable how quickly we settled down in it. In surroundings where all civilised usages had gone by the board we found new interests. Our job was hardly a dull one; and then, of course, there were eggs.

Egg-hunting was the only sport possible in St. Honorine, and it was pursued so diligently by the garrison that some claimed eggs were snatched before they even touched the straw. All the hens certainly had a harassed look. The great thing was to find half a dozen which habitually laid away from the others in some odd corner, and then visit them three or four times every morning. This would bring you three eggs a day. Failing that, you had to follow the hen into the hen-house and sit staring it out of countenance until it had laid, because if you took your eyes off it for a second someone came in and robbed you. So we poked about the ruins, foraging here and there, and were absurdly delighted when we added to our store. There were strawberries in the garden of M.le Maire, too, for early risers. In these small ways we made ourselves at home. Looking back now, it seems we were in St. Honorine for a long time. In actual fact we were there only five days and never returned; but when the 5th Black Watch relieved us on the night of 1/2 July, it was a tired Battalion that marched back over the hill to the comparative peace of Ranville le Mariquet.

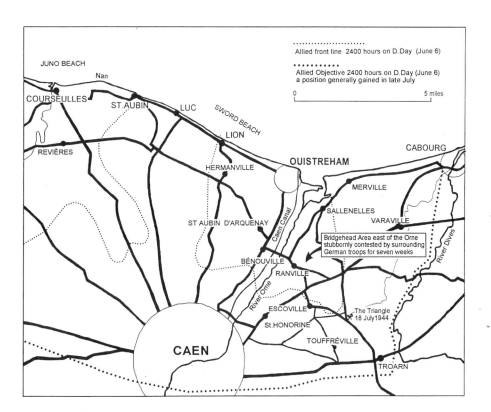

THE TRIANGLE

(previous page) German soldiers, who surrendered in the fight for the Triangle, are frisked by Seaforth Highlanders.

CHAPTER TWELVE

The Triangle

I

LIVING FROM from day to day in the bridgehead, there seemed little change in the pattern of the war. If you kept a diary, you wrote in it: 'July 7. Rested. Hedge-hopper dropped A. P. bombs. One wounded. July 8. Quiet day. Had bath in biscuit tin,' and could see nothing behind or before but the same routine of slit trenches and patrols and moving from village to village. Yet, looking back over the diary to-day, a story emerges whose chapters are of almost exactly equal length. The length is one month. Whether this was due to chance or to orderly planning I cannot say; but it is a fact that the Battalion's movements so marched with the calendar that, however settled the situation might appear to be at any time, one could be tolerably certain that the next thirty days would tell a new tale which was complete in itself.

June was the invasion month, the month of landing, exploiting a little, and hanging on. When July came there was no apparent change in our situation – after all, one slit trench looked very much like another – yet the difference was there. When, after a week of resting and patrolling at Ranville le Mariquet, we went back to the Triangle on July 9, it seemed to be just one more stage in our pilgrimage through the Orne villages. Few of us could have foreseen that our first defensive period was over, and that we were going to attack.

We took over from the 7th Black Watch, who had dug themselves clean out of sight in the wooded fringes of the plain. The Command Post was a pit seven feet deep, roofed with logs and earth; and everything else was dug to scale. All doovers were roofed and revetted; and no one, we noticed, strayed far from them. This was scarcely surprising when one considered that the Boche were practically in the next field.

Since the Germans had captured the Triangle on the summit of the ridge, one battalion or another had been hanging on below them with a second battalion in reserve five hundred yards to the rear. The 5th Camerons now took over the rear position. Our own defences were in a tight square in country where the fields were so small and the trees in the hedgerows so numerous that it was almost a continuous wood. Visibility, except westwards out into the plain, was nowhere more than fifty yards, and to cover every gap in country so close the Battalion had to be concentrated into an area less than four hundred yards square. One corner of the square was barely two hundred yards from the nearest angle of the Triangle.

Our opposite numbers, the 858th Grenadier Regiment, were by all accounts low in manpower, weapons, and spirits, a fact we could readily believe after hearing their evening serenade. Every night at dusk they appeared to become convinced that they were being attacked by the entire British Army, and loosed off countless rounds of spandau and rifle fire at the empty air. No one was ever hit by these bullets. No one ever found out what they were aimed at. We just used to sit outside our doovers, watch the verey lights climbing frantically into the sky, hear the odd bullet clip through the trees thirty feet above us, and shake our heads.

Their artillery, however, was a different matter. They had a great deal of it, and it was accurate. When it opened up (which it did several times a day, sometimes for hours on end) no one lingered, but dived into the deepest recesses of his doover and stayed there.

We came to know the 858th Regiment quite well. Deserters used to drop in to see us nearly every morning, always (to my annoyance, because I was now Intelligence Officer and had to interrogate them) at stand-down. Before long we knew almost as much about the German positions as we did about our own, because deserters as a class are talkative persons and in any case no one in the German Army then or later had the least idea of security. These men who came in were all Poles or Russians, each protesting that he was in the Wehrmacht against his will, and anxious to prove his good faith by giving his friends away down to the last detail. The Russians were unable to do this, because no Russian ever learned to speak anything but Russian; but the Poles were better linguists. They gave our gunners some beautiful targets.

The enemy strength was between 300 and 350, of which 60% were German, 25% Polish, and 15% Russian; and all the Poles and Russians, said our prisoners, were anxious to desert. In light of later events, this was probably true.

From the 9th until the 16th July our routine was the same. During the night, two sentries per section were on watch, with the others on immediate call. At 0430 hours we stood-to, peering miserably from our trenches into the gloomy hedgerows, feeling too bleary and cold to care whether the Germans appeared or not. At some time between 0530 and 0600, depending on visibility, we went back to whatever we happened to be calling our bed, wrapped the dew-damp blankets around us, and slept until 0900 hours. Then the petrol fires were started and the compo rations were cooked for breakfast. In theory, one made good during the rest of the morning the sleep lost during sentry-go at night, but I never met anyone who claimed to have been able to do so. There was always some job to do, or some conference to attend, or a shell to be dodged; and then it was evening again, with the serenade going full blast. If it had rained it would have been a loathsome existence: as it was, the sun shone and life was tolerable.

There may be some who will quarrel with this. 'Tolerable', it may be felt, is too strong a word to apply to any scheme of things which included the Triangle mosquito. This insect, once described by Farquhar Macrae as a tough variety with H.D.'s on its shoulders, was far bigger and more inquisitive than any we had encountered in Africa, and its powers of penetration were phenomenal. Battledress was no bar: if a mosquito decided it would dine off your knees, then dine it did, battledress or no battledress; and as it sucked, its friends would be wriggling happily inside your gaiters to nibble your ankles while others clamped down in hordes upon your wrists and face. Dougie Cochrane, now Pioneer Officer, was so goaded one night that he sprinkled his doover with petrol in an effort to keep them at bay: he was found an hour later nearly unconscious, overcome by the fumes – and still being stung by mosquitoes. If this general state of affairs is thought to be exaggerated, consider facts. We used to count the stings. On the average, each of us had twenty on the back of a single hand at any one time. Before the day had healed the itch, darkness brought fresh multitudes. They caused more discomfort and loss of sleep in the Orne bridgehead than ever shelling did.

So much for the background. Here, in one paragraph, are the chief events of that period. Brigadier Harvey Haugh handed over our Brigade to Brigadier Jim Cassels, a tremendous man who led us with unvarying success until the end of the war. On July 10 a raid was carried out north of us by the 6th Airborne at 1530 hours; but as no one, British or German, had any warning of it there was a tendency over the whole area to fire whatever weapons came to hand, and the result was three most unpleasant hours of shelling and mortaring. On this day the north half of Caen fell. On the 11th, 153 Brigade made an unsuccessful attack on Colombelles factory, south-west of us on the far side of the plain, and our positions had a share of the German counter-battery fire during the attack. On the 12th, the enemy guns began to lay shells systematically all over our area, beginning at 0300 hours and working up to a crescendo at 0500 hours. It was more than a casual shelling, and we stood-to expecting an attack. However, the shelling began to taper off, and by 0530 the woods were peaceful again. On the night of the 15th we were bombed, and on the 16th Colonel Walford planned our first attack of the campaign.

II

The big plan began far above our level. Away to the west the Americans were massing for the breakthrough which, in a few weeks, was to carry them hundreds of miles through France. Meantime it was the object of the High Command to lure as many German divisions as possible eastwards on to our front, so that the Americans would have a clear run through once the gap had been made. The enemy was already heavily committed west and north-west of Caen, and now an attack on the grand scale down the Orne plain was planned to harass him still further. We might even achieve a breakthrough. That was in the lap of the Gods: but even if a breakthrough were not possible, more German divisions would be tied down in opposing us and fewer would be left to face the Americans in the west.

The curtain-raiser for this offensive was the battle of the Triangle, which was to drive the enemy from the high ground and deny him observation of the plain. Until we were firmly planted there, no one else could move.

It is now necessary to consider the geography of the Triangle in detail. The Triangle itself was formed by the junction of the Escoville road with the road running north and south along the crest of the ridge, and by the intersection of both of these by the minor road running east from Pre Baron. The apex pointed south. The base, which was three hundred yards long, faced north; and the other two sides were five hundred yards long. The three roads enclosed fields and orchards and the whole Triangle was surrounded by woods.

So far as was known, the German defences lay along the roads, with the two crossroads on the base firmly held. We had an excellent set of air photographs, and from them it was apparent that once these crossroads were in our hands it should not be too difficult to advance from them to the apex and clear the whole area. Obviously a simultaneous attack on the two crossroads was indicated. Equally obviously, tanks would be a help. The trouble was going to be in getting them there. A simultaneous attack could only come from the north, and there the woods were dense and, to all appearances, tank-proof.

Two patrols were therefore sent out on the night 15/16 July to recce the approaches. The first reported that the east crossroads were guarded by a dense wood and a steep bank, and that tanks could not get through. The second, aiming for a point midway along the base of the Triangle from which tanks could turn left or right to the two objectives, was blocked by spandau posts long before it got there, and could make no report. This patrol was sent out again after dawn. It had a stroke of luck. The Boche, methodical as ever, had stuck rigidly to his policy of manning outlying posts at night only; and where a few hours earlier it had been impossible to make any headway was now silence and total peace. Our men followed a little track which ran parallel to the base of the Triangle and after a few twists and turns took them to a field, the other end of which touched the road forming the Triangle base. They found many empty spandau posts on the way, and several booby-traps. Beyond the road the smoke of fires rose gently as the Boche cooked his breakfast. The approach problem was solved.

The following day was spent in recces and briefings, while rumours spread of entire divisions and vast numbers of tanks and guns pouring across the Bénouville bridges. For once rumour did not exaggerate. Our days in the wilderness were over. Our bridgehead was crammed with men and material, ready for the offensive.

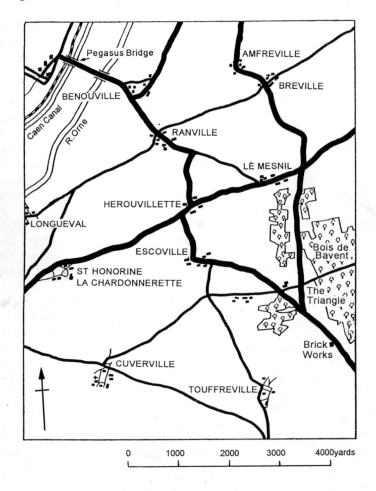

III

The battle of the Triangle was fought on July 18, 1944, and was completely successful. All objectives were taken according to plan. We took eighty prisoners and killed between sixty and seventy. Our own losses were eleven killed and fifty-one wounded.

The curtain went up at 0545 hours, when the heavy bombers came over to prepare the way for the main body of the attack, then waiting on the plain. They came lounging across the sky, scattered, leisurely, indifferent. The first ones crossed our lines, and the earth began to shake to a continuous rumble of falling bombs. There were no individual explosions, just a continuous rumble which lasted for three-quarters of an hour; and at no time during that period were fewer than fifty 'planes visible. The din was tremendous. We could see the bombs leaving the 'planes and drifting down almost gently, like milt from a salmon, and as they disappeared behind the trees the rumble rose a little and then sank to its old level again. The Jocks were all standing grinning at the sky. After weeks of skulking in trenches, here was action; action on a bigger scale than any of them had dreamed was possible.

At 0645 the artillery started with a tremendous crash which merged into a steady roar. The 4.2 mortars were slamming away in the field behind us (they got rid of 2,500 bombs in that one field alone), and from the Triangle we could hear their deep "Crrrump" above the crack of the twenty-five-pounder shells and the heavier crack of the mediums. I remember a flight of pigeons going up as the guns started. The sky was blue and clear and sharp, contrasting with the hedgerows, where cordite fumes were beginning to hang like cigarette smoke in a crowded room. Later (the guns still firing) the rocket-firing Typhoons sailed in to blast Touffreville and Sannerville and Demouville and all the other Villes which had faced us for so many weeks. All sounds were merged now, but the squeal of the rockets came through the din as the 'planes went over us in tight formation, more determined and busy-looking than the bombers. There had never been anything like it in Africa. The sky was full of 'planes. The Typhoons kept low and headed due south, all of them. High above, the fighters cut across at many angles, very fast. The clear blue of the sky was dotted with dirty black flak bursts. One Typhoon was hit. Its wing glowed, then the 'plane exploded in flames and dropped down the sky, orange against the blue. Miraculously, half-way down, a tiny parachute emerged. The flight carried on. Tremendous screams of rockets followed.

H-hour was 0745. Before this the forward companies had withdrawn to give the barrage elbow-room. The barrage opened dead on time, and the attack began.

The start-line was the track running parallel to the base of the Triangle and two hundred yards north of it. On the right was "C" company (Major Douglas Findlay-Shirras, M.C.), and on the left "B" Company (Captain Hugh Robertson, M.C.). Both companies crossed the forming-up line on time, but almost immediately ran into heavy shelling. They had to advance through extremely dense woods which had not been noticeably improved by the barrage; and an orderly advance was still further complicated by uneven resistance on the part of the enemy. Fourteen Platoon (Lieutenant Alan Wade) on the extreme right of "C" Company bumped trouble on the start-line itself, where thirty or forty Boche were dug in along a hedge, pouring fire into the right flank of the platoon. While this was being cleared up, the rest of the company continued to advance (taking the left-hand half of 14 Platoon with it) until it met similar resistance along the base of the Triangle. These two pockets of Boche put up the biggest fight of the day; but a certain amount of dash by "C" Company and the appearance of three crocodiles so impressed them that the survivors gave themselves up or went flat out for the woods. Twenty of them were killed. Finally, 15 Platoon (led, with much invective, by Lieutenant Bob Galloway) took the western crossroads and continued forward to consolidate. The wood was dense. Bob edged off too much to the right and overshot the mark, fetching up in another wood containing both Hun and booby-traps. By the time he had extricated himself from this, he was wounded and 13 Platoon had been sent on to his consolidation line. The other platoon was also in position. So much for "C" Company.

"B" Company on the left did not meet so many Germans, but the going in their wood was even worse than in the one on the right. Originally a tight-packed plantation of young spruce, it was now a mass of broken timber firmly interlaced, and it was only with the greatest difficulty that they managed to force a way through it. However, they met no fire, and 12 Platoon (Lieutenant Russell Ferguson) reached the consolidation line two fields beyond the base of the Triangle in fifteen minutes flat. The other two platoons switched left, 11 (Lieutenant Pat Grant) to cover the east crossroads, and 10 (Sergeant Lockie) to take them. Eight determined men in a hedge gave 11 Platoon a hard fight and had to be winkled out with grenades at close range. Meanwhile 10 Platoon had fallen foul of a party retiring into the Bois de Bures and were being fired on by three spandaus. Two crocodiles came up to help, but both were knocked out. The platoon dealt with the retreating Germans unassisted, tidied up the position, and consolidated.

Both the crossroads at the base of the Triangle were now firmly in our hands and the way was clear for the second phase of the attack. On the right was "D" Company (Major Richard Fleming) and on the left "A" Company (Captain Hector Mackenzie). "A" Company met no opposition of any kind, and their attack passed off sweetly according to plan. They walked on to their objective a hundred yards east of the apex, and dug in.

"D" Company, advancing outside the Triangle on the right, had more difficulty. Visibility in the woods was only a few yards; and 18 Platoon (Lieutenant Fraser Gingold) on the right followed Bob Galloway's example and had several casualties in the jungle before regaining contact. On the left, 16 Platoon (Lieutenant 'Sammy' Hall) had easier going and took the small wood inside the Triangle without much difficulty. Seventeen Platoon (Lieutenant John Mair) took 18 Platoon's objective, a timber mill near the apex which the crocodiles had breathed upon and was blazing hard, and lost most of his men in the undergrowth while reaching it. He took the mill with only eight men, followed through beyond it, captured a 75mm. anti-tank gun, and killed two of the crew. There was no sign of "A" Company on the left, so 16 Platoon took the apex, which was part of "A" Company's task, and consolidated forward. Some obstinate spandaus held out in the copse west of the mill until the afternoon, but were mopped up in the end by crocodiles. All "D" Company's objectives were taken by 0950 hours. Shelling fell off towards evening and was not resumed that day.

That is the bare bones of the battle. The flesh – the sights and sounds and emotions which remain in our minds today – must vary from individual to individual and cannot be recorded: the only battle I am qualified to draw in detail is my own battle, and this is not the place for it. However, I think it is true to say that most of us were impressed principally by two things: first, the crocodiles; and second, the enemy morale. Crocodiles, which were Churchill tanks with flame-throwers, were beyond doubt among the more hellish contrivances of the war. I watched them operating on "D" Company's copse. The spandaus were blazing away cheerfully enough, and then one of these horrors came waddling up. It gave them a burst of machine-gun fire and then quietly breathed on them. It was all very methodical and businesslike, just a thin jet of flame which fanned out as it shot along, low to the ground, until it arrived on the target as a great blazing cloud. Bushes caught fire everywhere. There was a pause. Again the jet of flame, the spread, the billowing cloud. The spandaus stopped. Men ran out, burning.

Before our attack, the Poles and Russians had been deserting so enthusiastically that the rest had been sent to work in the transport lines and their places taken by Germans. Even so, the morale was low. Apart from the few tough pockets mentioned there was little fight shown, and it is probable that half the enemy did not fight at all. During the battle Hugh Robertson and his batman collected five prisoners, one of them an officer, by the simple expedient of lifting the ground-sheets they had spread over the doors of their doovers and explaining to the occupants that they would not be shot if they took their heads out from under the blankets and came upstairs. Whole sections had taken to earth in this way, convinced that the British shot their prisoners. The Padre had a harrowing time trying to explain to two weeping members of the Master Race, hands filled with rosaries, crucifixes, and photographs of their wives and children, that he was not going to murder them. In the end he drew himself up, thumped his chest, and bellowed: 'Ich bin Pastor, you silly men, Ich bin Pastor.' They went like lambs. Two more Germans sat with a spandau and a full box of ammunition within a hundred yards of Battalion H.Q. for three hours without firing a round: after that they walked over and asked if someone would please take them prisoner. They dug us an excellent command post.

Last, there was the man in the field behind "B" Company. The field was pitted all over by our barrage, and the trees behind were scarred by shellfire. Across the grass ran crocodile tracks. He was sitting outside his doover, a corpse at his feet and a towel in his hand, oblivious to the bullets and shell splinters which still spattered around. He was waving the towel aimlessly and howling like an animal. The crocodiles had been too much for him. He was raving mad.

We took one 75mm. anti-tank gun, one 50mm. anti-tank gun, forty-eight rifles, fourteen spandaus, eight bazookas, and many smaller pieces of equipment.

IV

As soon as we were firm, the Camerons and 2nd Seaforth passed through and established themselves south of the Triangle astride the Troarn road. Then the divisions on the plain were loosed, and by evening Cuverville, Démouville and the rest were in our hands and our armour was two miles south of the Caen/Troarn railway. There, however, it stopped. The plain was good tank country, open and rolling; but it was also good anti-tank country and the Germans had massed their

(above) The heavy machine-gun teams of the Middlesex Regiment that supported our actions in the Triangle, the Ardennes and in many other critical situations.
(below) Officers at the H.Q. party after seven weeks in the line: (l to r) Lt. Col. Jack Walford, Capt. H.A.C.Mackenzie, Lieut. Jack Latta, Capt. Hugh Robertson, Maj. Robertson-McIsaac, Maj. George Green, Maj. Douglas Findlay-Shirras, Capt. Leslie Forshaw-Wilson

guns well back. For a few more days large-scale fighting continued, and then the attack bogged down. The bridgehead had been expanded and attention was diverted from the Americans, but there had been no breakthrough.

A miserable eleven days followed. The Germans we had chased from the Triangle were now hanging on along the edge of the Bois de Bures, two hundred and fifty yards to the east; and, as the flank of the bridgehead still had to be protected, we were doomed to yet another period of digging deep and waiting. Worse still, the Germans knew exactly where we were.

However, we had another trial in store before they made use of their knowledge and the shelling began. The weather broke. It had seemed so easy all these weeks since D-Day to make ourselves comfortable below ground, adding one refinement to another as we moved from place to place and our skill grew. The firm clay of Normandy made good digging, and we soon learned to make ourselves snug. Although the basic model was only a pit six feet long by two-and-a-half wide by four or five feet deep with a sheet of corrugated iron and a heap of earth on top, there were many things a man could do to improve it. There were doovers lined with parachute silk, doovers with electric light, mosquito-proof doovers with face-veils over the entrances. Doors were lifted from their hinges and used to strengthen roofs (though some preferred earth-filled wardrobes), and few houses had a shutter left five minutes after the Battalion moved into an area. Then the weather broke.

The thunderstorm burst upon us on the afternoon of July 20, and by evening the whole place was a shambles. Nothing that human ingenuity could devise would keep the tide at bay. We baled. We made roofs with gas-capes. We piled compo boxes into the mud and lay on them, only to be wakened as the water lapped over the top. By morning all our trenches had three feet of water in them and we were driven into the open, soaking and without hope, with the rain falling.

Strangely enough, it was not until 1700 hours on the 21st that the Boche artillery decided to make use of this opportunity. Possibly they had been too busy baling out their own trenches earlier in the day to do anything about it. At any rate, it was not until the evening that they began to shell us, and even then not heavily. We took refuge in the drier ditches and escaped with three casualties. Next day the tide receded and the sun came through; but, although we were established well below ground by evening, it was many days before we regained our former comfort.

The week which followed made heavy demands on the spirit of the Battalion. We had been in the line for a long time, continuously under fire, and doing (as it must have seemed to many) absolutely nothing; and yet here we were, still in the same old doover, getting nowhere. The enemy mortars had our range, and casualties were mounting. We were all bone-tired. When a man sees his friend killed in an attack he can understand the need for it and accepts it; but bridgeheads and build ups and Army plans are abstractions too vague to be comprehended when he is sitting in a trench and seeing, day after day, five or six of his mates being carried off or buried. It is to the credit of the men that none of them ever did ask why, that they did accept the situation even if they did not understand it, and held on uncomplainingly until the end.

On July 29, after eleven days in the Triangle being shelled and mortared and eaten alive by mosquitoes, we were relieved by the 7th Argyll and Sutherland Highlanders and went back to the rest area at Gazelle. We had been in the line for seven weeks.

BREAKOUT

(previous page) British troops, in   Kangeroo   tank transporters, moving up to their start lines ready for the   breakout   south of Caen in August, 1944..

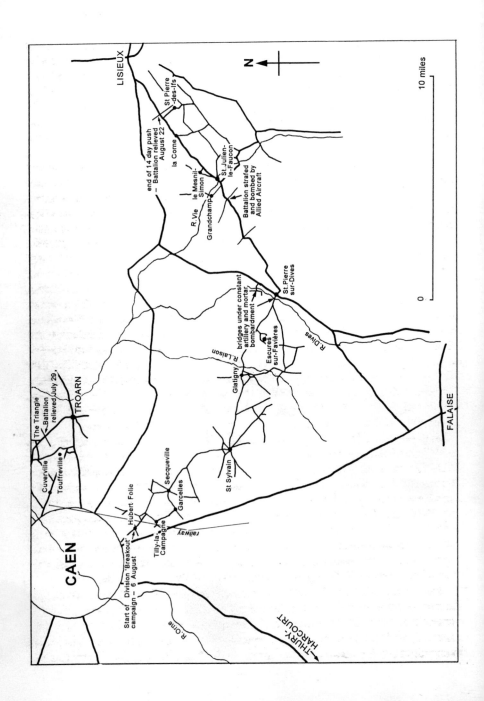

CHAPTER THIRTEEN

Breakout

I

WE HAD NOT consciously lived under strain at the Triangle, so seemingly normal had our abnormal existence become. The cluster of mortar bombs falling on the crossroads every twenty minutes was as commonplace and as little noticed as a striking clock at home. The routine of mosquitoes, stand-to, shells, and night bombers was like any other routine, a background no one thought about. Yet the moment we left the place, relief bubbled up. The grass was greener and the roads less dusty. The world was bigger than just one field. There were cinemas and ENSA shows back there – shows with women! The NAAFI beer was in. There was to be a rum ration. It was true, wasn't it, that they'd no stand-to at the new place? Sure it was true, sure, and the C.O.'s batman said reveille wasn't until nine o'clock the first morning. It was heady stuff, this feeling that life was not such a cramped and mole-like thing as we had imagined it to be. We hung out of the trucks, shouting and singing, feeling as we had not felt since we were ten years old and on holiday.

Anyone who was there will remember his own particular party that night. We had a very fine one in the officers' mess. For the first time since landing we were all together, and not only had the month's whisky ration arrived but the Padre had liberated a cheese factory. It was camembert cheese, rich and creamy, and there was plenty of fresh butter to go with it. We had all had biscuit-tin baths in the sunshine during the afternoon and changed our clothes for the first time in a fortnight. Colonel Walford sat at the head of the table beaming from ear to ear, his face bright scarlet with sunburn, leaning back from time to time and loosing his own peculiar 'Hah!' at the company. It was a good party and a short one. By nine o'clock we were all in our beds, sleeping the clock round. Pyjamas never felt better.

At this time Major Robertson-McIsaac, who had been second-in-command of the Battalion since the Sferro battle, left us to join the 7th Seaforth and was succeeded by Richard Fleming. Grant Murray took over "D" Company.

Before long, rumours began to circulate. By August 3 they were a certainty, by the 4th the company commanders had been briefed, and on the 5th the Battalion "O" Group was off to recce a place called Hubert Folie. Another operation was in the wind. The time for the breakout had arrived. The Americans had cut the Cherbourg peninsula, swung inland, and were fanning out over France in the drive which was to take them to Paris and beyond. One arm of this drive was pointing at Falaise, seventeen miles south of us, making a wide encircling movement to scoop up into a pocket most of the remaining German divisions in France. If we could reach Falaise, the trap would be closed. The advance would be made by the Canadian Army, under whose command would be the Highland Division.

Our Division's first objective was the high ground at Garcelles Secqueville, at that time approximately three miles behind the German lines; and the plan was an unorthodox one. The Germans had two defence lines, the forward one fully manned, and the rear one dug, prepared, and for use only if the first were penetrated and the men in it were forced to fall back. As our objective was a key point in the rear line, it seemed to us (as it certainly seemed to the Germans) that we should have to fight two battles in order to capture it, by which time the Boche no doubt hoped to have a third line prepared still farther to the rear. It must have occurred to the Corps Commander that it would be pleasant to capture the second line first and forestall all this nonsense from the start; nor was the idea so fanciful as it sounds. A way was found. A new animal had lately been added to our zoo. We already had wasps, crocodiles, dingos, ducks and hippos: now came the kangaroo, the device which was already making possible the tremendous American advances farther west. It was a Sherman tank without a turret. Into the 'pouch' where the gun, the ammunition, and two of the crew should have been, it was possible to pop ten fully equipped infantrymen and carry them safely (eighty-eights and mines permitting) wherever one wanted to go.

The plan was to line up two columns of kangaroos (one filled with our 154 Brigade and the other with a brigade of Canadians) with tanks in front, set off in darkness, and drive straight through the German defences. The Germans would hear hundreds of armoured vehicles clanking around but would not be able to see what was happening; and when dawn came the two brigades would be comfortably dug in miles behind them.

The plan was complicated in detail (one problem alone, that of keeping the columns on their courses, was solved by using compass, fixed searchlight beams, tracer anti-aircraft shells, and radar); but the details need not concern us, as 152 Brigade was not involved. Our task appeared to be simpler, though it turned out in the end to be much more difficult.

For reasons which need not be gone into here, it was necessary for the armoured columns to breach the first German line near a village called Tilly-la-Campagne. One column was to pass on each side of it. This was well enough in the dark when the defenders could not see to shoot properly; but it would be disastrous for our supply convoys if this strong-point were left in the middle of our lines of communication for long after daylight came. Not, it was felt, that the nut would take much cracking. With hundreds of British tanks and kangaroos to their rear, the defenders would pack and go as soon as an assault on their position began – if, indeed, they had not gone sooner. One battalion, the 2nd Seaforth, would make the assault, with the two other battalions of the Brigade remaining in reserve in or near Hubert Folie. All this was perfectly reasonable. The only snag was that the Boche in Tilly decided to stay and fight.

We took over Hubert Folie from the Algolquin Regiment at midnight on August 6, and lay there all next day. At 2300 hours the R.A.F. bombed and the gunners shelled on the scale we had come to expect, the armoured columns went through successfully, and 2nd Seaforth opened their assault on Tilly. One hour passed, two hours, and then came news that matters were not going too well with the 2nd. Tilly was strongly held. Casualties were heavy. They could make no headway. Their reserve company, which so far had been firm-basing at a level-crossing eight hundred yards north of the village, must be thrown in. At 0215 hours Brigadier Cassels ordered Colonel Walford to send our "D" Company (Captain Grant Murray) to take over the level-crossing.

Another uneasy hour followed, during which messages coming in over the rear-link set made it increasingly apparent that 2nd Seaforth were in an awkward situation. Casualties, heavy fire, and almost total darkness are serious handicaps in an action which is being fought, as this one was, on a wide front. The 2nd were coming in on the village from two sides simultaneously; and by this time, the original plan of a quick assault having failed, neither half knew exactly what the other half was doing. Moreover one company had lost direction in the dark and had arrived at the wrong place. At this stage (0310 hours) the Brigadier asked Colonel Walford whether or not he could launch his battalion to speed up the attack. Colonel Walford considered that the situation was hopelessly confused and would remain so until daylight. The Battalion had not been briefed, and would have to advance into the confusion over strange ground. Until a daylight recce was possible, he advised against attack. The Brigadier saw the force of this and agreed to postpone the assault; but in the meantime our "D" Company was to go forward to reinforce the fighting companies of the 2nd Battalion, and the rest of us were to go down and firm-base at the level-crossing. This was done.

"D" Company, now under command of 2nd Seaforth, advanced in the dark eight hundred yards down the railway to the south-west, with orders to attack a strip of trees south-east of a second level-crossing which lay on the immediate outskirts of the village. "D" Company of the 2nd Seaforth was said to be on their right, but this was the company which had lost direction, and it was in fact held up beside "B" Company, 2nd Seaforth, one hundred yards short of the level-crossing. Thus, instead of attacking from between these two companies, Grant Murray found himself on the right flank.

17 Platoon (Sergeant Barnes) attacked the strip of trees, 18 Platoon (Lieutenant Jerry Dawson) held the flank, and 16 Platoon (Sergeant McLeod) made a firm base on the level-crossing. The attack failed with heavy casualties. Grant himself was killed. When daylight came, mist reduced visibility to a hundred yards; but later it cleared, tanks arrived, and 16 Platoon mopped up the trees behind them. Of the forty men in "D" Company (we were badly under strength at the time) one officer and ten men were killed, and ten wounded.

Meanwhile, the rest of us were plodding towards the first level-crossing, praying that the mist would not lift until we had reached some sort of cover. Even in the mist it was sufficiently unpleasant. The Germans had spandaus firing up the track on fixed lines, whipping splinters and pieces of bark from the trees in the hedgerow on our left; and we could not wander from the track for fear of losing direction. The sun was up by this time, but we could not see more than fifty yards; and neither, praise be, could the Boche. We reached the level-crossing, dug in, and waited for the mist to clear.

Colonel Walford made his customary recce-cum-deep-penetration-patrol, accompanied by the faithful Private Miller; but no amount of imagination could penetrate the mist, and it was not until 0900 hours that he had the information he needed. By 0930 an attack with full artillery support had been laid on, H-hour to be 1000 hours; and all was set when, ten minutes before the attack was due to begin, the story took an unexpected turn.

The force which had broken both the German lines during the night was pushing on towards Falaise; but when news of trouble at Tilly reached it, one squadron of tanks was sent back to attack the village from the rear. The mist which had so hampered our movements allowed the tanks to approach unmolested) and when the mist lifted they rolled through the village twice, on the second occasion picking up the only surviving officer there, a lieutenant of the 1055 Infantry

Regiment. He said his garrison of seventy men, all that was left of a much larger force, had had enough and was prepared to surrender. This news reached us at 0950 hours. The tanks were sent in again at the request of Colonel Walford to tell the Germans that a major attack was prepared and would undoubtedly take place if they did not come out. The lieutenant asked for half an hour in which to collect his men, and at 1050 hours they marched out and surrendered.

It was good to see them coming through the stubble, unarmed, a little ragged column, dirty and red-eyed. It was the first organised surrender we had seen in France, and it was heartening to know that such things did sometimes happen, even with first-class troops who had fought so well as these had done. We were a little thoughtful, too, when we counted the prisoners and found there were only thirty. The 1055 Infantry Regiment, it appeared, had not been entirely licked. The lieutenant had given his strength as seventy ... just in case.

II

Once again a month had passed, and once again our situation had changed radically. There were to be no more days of waiting. The whole line was on the move, and it was not to stop until it had liberated two capitals and entered Holland. The policy of our Higher Command was to attack without respite, never giving the Germans a chance to re-organise or build a solid line, but hustling them along until disorganisation became rout and rout total collapse. The Canadian divisions and ourselves advanced not as lines, but as columns. The moment the leading brigade had attacked and consolidated, the next brigade passed through, then the third brigade, then the first one again. In this way, working on a narrow front, a division could mount two or three brigade attacks in one day, each with the full weight of the divisional artillery behind it.

The rest of this chapter, which is a long one, tells of the fourteen-day running fight which followed. Shape it has none, unless it be the shape of a string of sausages, each incident the same size as its neighbours, strung out in a long line to an end we could not see. The background was sleeplessness, exhaustion, and hands blistered with digging. No single event can be emphasised, for none stands out in our minds more than another. It just went on and on, day after day, until the Germans broke utterly and we could sleep.

The general direction of the Highland Division's advance during the first few days after Tilly was southeast, aiming at a point a few miles north of Falaise. Before reaching this point we swung left and headed north-east for the Seine.

We did not begin this advance immediately. When Tilly had been declared clear at mid-day on August 8, we returned to our positions at the first level-crossing and spent the night there. On the 9th, a very hot day, we marched to a wood two miles east of Secqueville la Campagne, and dug in. At 1630 hours, just as the last spadeful of clay was coming to the surface and we were beginning to spread heather for camouflage, we were ordered to take over from the 5/7 Gordons on the outskirts of another wood, this time a mile south of Secqueville. Once again we marched. Once again we dug. Long after midnight we were still hacking away at the ground, which was villainously hard.

We stayed beside the wood for four days, but little real rest was possible because all the time we were at one hour's notice to counter-attack any enemy penetrations which might be made into the 7th Black Watch positions to the south of us. The mosquitoes, too, were deadly.

On the morning of the fifth day, August 14, the Division attacked in the general direction of St.Sylvain; and at 1200 hours we were on the move again, on foot. It was a blazing hot day, close and windless. A whole army was using the network of roads and cart-tracks which led south and east from the Secqueville high ground; and behind each truck, no matter how slowly and carefully it was driven, rose a great plume of dust. The plain in which St. Sylvain lay was criss-crossed everywhere by columns of dust, some of them miles long, where the convoys crawled southwards. Wherever two columns intersected, the German gunners laid shells. Occasionally there was a burning vehicle by the roadside, or something covered with a blanket. Although normally one saw only one's own small part of an advance or a battle, on this day we had an impression of something vast and irresistible rumbling down by a multitude of routes towards Falaise.

Our task was to move to an assembly area near la Bu sur Rouvres and attack an elongated wood fifteen hundred yards due west of Glatigny; but as the sole desire of such Germans as remained in the area appeared to be to find someone willing to accept their surrender, the day remains notable only for the amount of sweat lost by the rifle companies, which were on foot from midday until midnight, most of the time being sprayed with dust by passing vehicles. Before the attack Colonel Walford recced forward to within two hundred yards of our objective, taking seven prisoners on the way ('Most awkward. Didn't know what on *earth* to do with them. Hah!'), and shook our tank commander to the very foundations by embarking on a second and equally hazardous recce in a jeep. "A" Company (right) and "B" Company (left) crossed the start-line at 2030 hours with one squadron of tanks in support. They met little opposition except shelling. "C" Company followed, and all dug in. At this stage we had no "D" Company: after the Tilly battle its remnants had been used to reinforce the other companies.

The next day, again one of great heat, seemed likely to be another of unopposed advance. During that period of fast movement, plans changed so frequently that we were seldom able to guess what we should be doing in two hours' time; but on this day everything was cut and dried and the information was precise. We were to march three-and-a-half miles south-east to a big wood on a plateau, and in the wood we should find several villages, the principal one of which was called Favières. We were not to worry about the size of the wood or the number of the villages: that had all been buttoned up. The Recce Corps people had put their infantry through it with tanks in support, and although the infantry had had to move on afterwards, the tanks would be waiting for us on the outskirts. We were to occupy the wood and winkle out any Boche who might be lurking in doovers too frightened to emerge.

We marched down in the sunshine to the valley of the Laison, past orchards and small woods and pleasant villages, and followed the river to le Hamel where a blown bridge held us up for a time. A way round was found for the transport echelons following us, and by 1530 hours we were plodding uphill out of the valley along the track which led across the cornfields from le Hamel to the Favières woods. The route was poorly marked and difficult to follow, so I went on ahead on a motor-bike and posted guides where tracks branched off. By the time I was half a mile from the woods I had only one man left, so I dumped him down beside a hedge, pointed out the way the companies should go, and went back down the road to tell the Colonel that everything was fixed. On the way I met the leading company with Padre Simpson padding happily along in his usual place at the head.

'What's it like?' he shouted.

'Just the job!' I said, 'not a sign of anything,' and carried on to report to the Colonel. About ten minutes later I drove back up the column, thinking I might as well lead the companies in. A motor-bike was a bad vehicle to drive because it was impossible to hear anything above the noise of the engine, but on this occasion it was not necessary to hear anything. When I was fifty yards from the head of the column, the Padre and the whole company behind him dived as one man for the ditch. The battle of Favières had begun.

Our first impression, naturally enough, was that one or two bloody-minded Germans had been overlooked by the Recce Corps when the woods were swept earlier in the day; but when at least six spandaus had opened up from various places over half a mile of front the situation seemed a little more serious. Perhaps, we thought, a platoon or even a company had been overlooked. "B" and "A" Companies pushed on and disappeared into the first trees. "C" Company followed. Shooting broke out and died. David Purgavie took the Carrier Platoon to deal with an objectionable spandau post firing from the far left. A few prisoners came back. Nothing at all was to be seen from the woods.

The prisoners, a dirty unshaven lot, sat in a ditch near Battalion H.Q. looking apprehensively back the way they had come. How many comrades had they in the woods? Three hundred. Nonsense. Surely they meant thirty. No, they did not mean thirty: they meant three hundred. Or maybe four hundred.

'They say they have three or four hundred pals in the woods, sir,' I said to the Colonel, 'but it can't be true.'

'It might be.' He looked worried. 'Something is very far wrong. The tanks aren't here. Not one. I'm beginning to wonder if they ever were here, or the Recce Corps either.'

A battle seemed to be boiling up in the woods, and judging by the noise of grenades, spandaus and brens, it was being fought at close quarters. "B" Company, which was leading, wirelessed that it was held up by a strong enemy position astride the main road running east from the village. The plan had been for "B" to follow this road to Escures sur Favières, with "A" advancing parallel up the left-hand road to Bas d'Eseures. "C" Company was to be in reserve in the village itself, near the little square from which both these roads branched.

The situation was rapidly becoming very complicated indeed. "A" Company's wireless had died, and no one knew where they were. Colonel Walford was trying desperately to raise some tank support (by this time Brigade had discovered that our tanks were miles away, and that the alleged clearing of the woods by the Recce Corps had in fact been the clearing of one small orchard by thirty men), and went so far as to tour the countryside in his jeep begging or stealing stray tanks as he went. In this way he raised six. Meanwhile a confusion had arisen over maps. It happened that we were fighting the battle on the junction of two maps, which made them difficult to read; and furthermore an error had been made in the interpretation of a conventional sign. On all the maps we had used at home the sign for a church had been a small white circle with a cross on top. In the village of Favières was, on the map, a small *black* circle with a cross. Throughout the preliminary planning this had been referred to as 'the church' ('"A" Company will turn left at the church, and 'B' will go straight on.'), none of us realising that the French had a habit of scattering calvaries or crucifixes about the countryside and that the sign for a calvary was a black circle and cross.

In normal circumstances, this mistake would have been obvious the moment the leading troops entered the village; but the circumstances were not normal. They were, in fact, thoroughly unpleasant. The companies were left with a deep sense of grievance over the shortage of churches in Favières ignored the calvary, and (as the non-existent church was the landmark round which the whole operation had been based) were quite unable to say where they were. The artillery, mortars, and machine-guns were therefore unable for a time to fire a single round in their support for fear of hitting them.

By the time this muddle had been sorted out it was 2000 hours, darkness was approaching, and a further complication had arisen. Although "B" and "C" Companies were still pinned down on the outskirts of Favrières, barely holding their own and with little prospect of making any more ground that night, "A" Company had met only light opposition and had reached its objective, a farm to our left front fully a thousand yards ahead of everyone else. They had no anti-tank guns and no tanks, and they were very lonely. Between them and the other companies were thick woods and orchards which were known to be full of Boche.

Anti-tank guns and four of the six tanks were rushed up to them just as darkness fell. The remaining two tanks, having a shorter distance to go, reached "C" Company (now supporting "B" on the right) in the half-light and were knocked out by an S.P. gun at point-blank range within two minutes of their arrival. It grew dark. We dug in, and hoped, without a great deal of conviction, for the best. During the night, 2nd Seaforth moved up and covered our right flank.

When daylight came, the enemy had gone.

III

We found our first ripe apples that morning. After breakfast we lay in the orchards and ate them, basking in the sun and marvelling that a place so grim in the darkness should be so pleasant in the day. Many times during the months that followed, the battle was to pass on and leave us high and dry like this; but to the end we never became used to it. The change was always too sudden: battlefields became peaceful country gardens within an hour, and the slit trench which had been one's dearest possession was a meaningless hole in the ground. Nor could one comfort oneself when the shells were flying and the outlook as bad, with the thought that in a few hours the fighting would move on and the usual miracle happen, because it was always unbelievable until it did happen Battles were too vivid to be dismissed from the mind so lightly.

So the day seemed marvellously bright and silent as we lay in our orchards on the morning of August 16 and ate apples, and drank cider, and searched for eggs, and had rain- water baths from the spouts of the tubs which stood below the cottage eaves; but it did not last. At mid-day we moved on again.

Two miles to the south-east was the River Dives and the town of St. Pierre-sur-Dives. The bridges in the town were blown, but one had been found intact a thousand yards to the north, and across this bridge the 49th Division was to pass.

"A" Company went immediately to hold it until the 49th arrived. They were strafed by our own Spitfires while doing so, but neither seriously nor for long. The rest of the Battalion lay up during the afternoon in an assembly area outside the town, and later took up positions protecting the northern outskirts. The town itself was held by the 5th Camerons. Nothing of any tactical interest took place, because the enemy were falling back all along the front and were more interested in small delaying actions than in counter-attacks; but it was nevertheless a night not easily forgotten. Some of us remember queuing up with the transport echelons to cross the north bridge, jammed tight and moving a yard a minute, while the German eighty-eights laid salvos all round. The rifle companies remember the long, straight, cobbled street through the town, with the broken bridge half-way up it, and how they scrambled across the wreckage of the bridge and hoped they would reach the other side before the next mortar stonk came down. Battalion H.Q. will certainly never forget the field they chose for a headquarters: before they had dug in, shells were falling in it ten at a time and they had to up sticks and move across the road into a field less obviously part of the German harassing programme. It was a black, cloudy night lit only by the fires which blazed behind us in the town and by the flare dropped from time to time by German bombers intent on the one remaining bridge. Somewhere up the road a German tank kept cracking armour-piercing shells over the heads of "B" Company and into the houses on the edge of the town. No one slept very much.

The advance of 49 Division on our left drew the battle with it, and once again we found ourselves in total peace when morning came. At 1600 hours we moved forward a thousand yards into clean, untouched orchard country beside the main road from St. Pierre to Lisieux, and dug in wearily but well content.

That night we had undisturbed sleep, our first and last for a long time. At 1920 hours next day, the 18th, we moved off in troop-carrying vehicles along the Lisieux road to a lying-up area in a valley two thousand yards short of the River Vie, ready for an attack across the Vie next day.

We had hardly driven our vehicles off the road before disquieting rumours began to circulate, and on hearing them most of us began to dig. It was said that the close support provided by the R.A.F. had become much too close ('What did we tell you!' said "A" Company), and that enthusiastic pilots had been flying around pranging anything and everything forward of the River Dives, which was five miles behind us. The marksmanship of these pilots had certainly been admirable, whatever might be said of their map reading, because the 5th Camerons had had to abandon their attack across the Vie that afternoon because the Spitfires had knocked out every wireless vehicle they possessed and they were unable to communicate with Brigade, their companies, or the gunners. Against such an emergency we had each been provided with a triangle of bright yellow silk, the idea being that the forward troops should lay them out and draw attention to themselves. The triangles, however, were by no means foolproof, because the man who was being shot up was usually much too busy taking cover to have time to display one; whereas all the troops a mile behind him, fearing that they would be the next victims, immediately rushed to display theirs. The pilot then took these triangles to be the front line and continued to harry those in front – if he saw the triangles at all, which in many cases was doubtful.

Why communication between ground and air broke down so tragically that day we never discovered. All we know is that at 2215 hours, before any of us had had time to dig in, we were surprised to see streams of bright red objects shooting into the ground around us. Some Lightnings had been circling overhead, but no one had paid much attention. After a day of disasters, we thought, they must surely have been warned of our position. I do not think that for the first split second (which on these occasions seems to last so long) many of us connected the 'planes with the strange red objects. Then we heard the cannon blazing, and looked up. The 'planes were diving straight towards us, and the streams of half-inch tracer shells were snaking down the sky in long, wavy, parallel lines and clipping through the apple trees. There was no cover. One man ran and saw a stream of tracer two yards ahead. He turned, ran the other way, and found himself almost under the stream from the 'plane's other wing. He stood between them, staring upwards, paralysed. He was unhurt. Others tried to hide behind six-inch trees. Some just lay in the open with their faces buried in the ground. There were men under every carrier and every truck. A bomb dropped in the field behind us, and the wave passed.

They came round again, jockeying for position. A woman in the farm fifty yards away began to scream. The shells came again, and after that most of us lost count. I do not know how many times they strafed us. I do know that in the middle of it there came a great whistling, and a bomb demolished the farm, and after that there was no more screaming because the woman was dead, and her husband and two children with her. Then the 'planes went away and we came out. The farm had almost disappeared; and in it, as well as the French family, had been Brigade Headquarters. All we could see of Jimmy Watt was his head sticking out of the ruins; but he was smiling. John Thornton, the Brigade Major, was dead; and so was Douglas McCrone, one of the Liaison Officers. Lieutenant-Colonel Andrews of the 2nd Seaforth was wounded, Brigadier Cassels had had a crack on the head and was buried with the two other L.O.s, also wounded. We dug for what seemed like hours. It was a bad night.

When the mess was cleared we returned to dig our trenches, thankful that our own casualties had been light; but the night was not yet over. At 2325 hours the Luftwaffe started where the R.A.F. had left off, pouring down incendiary, butterfly, and high explosive bombs on a scale far greater than any we had experienced before or, indeed, were ever to experience again. Most of us, thanks to the earlier affair, were still not properly dug in; and the Germans were right on the target. We had casualties – two killed and four wounded, with six vehicles damaged or totally destroyed – but we were lucky to escape so lightly.

For a long time most of us looked upon that night as the worst of the war; and, although there were unfortunately many worse ones in store, there are still men who claim that the strafing by the Lightnings was the most terrifying single experience they have ever undergone. There was a helplessness and a hopelessness about it which gave it a quality all its own; and somehow the fact that our own 'planes were doing it made it ten times worse. For days afterwards we had one eye cocked at the sky.

IV

Next day we fought the battle of la Butte. In terms of bloodshed it was hardly a battle at all; but then (as every infantryman and no staff officer knows) nervous strain cannot be assessed by counting casualties, and nervous strain is what matters at the end of the day. The Germans were still withdrawing, and their plan was to make a series of small stands with their rear-guards, forcing us to deploy and stage an attack every few miles. Sometimes our assaulting troops found them waiting in strength, sometimes in only small numbers, and sometimes they withdrew before we reached them; but from our point of view each attack was identical until the moment when the leading company discovered the true state of the enemy's strength. Until that moment, the attack could be a walk-over or another Favières; and somehow the pit of one's stomach always expected a Favières.

The ground ahead was admirably suited to defence. Our road (the St. Pierre-Lisieux road which we had followed for two days and were to follow for many more) climbed over a low crest and dropped down to the River Vie, which it crossed at a village called St.Julien-le-Faucon. On the other side of the river it disappeared into steep and rugged hills which were continuous along the far side of the valley and gave the Germans magnificent observation of our movements on the near bank. If they chose to contest the crossing at St. Julien (and it was difficult to see why they should not), everything was in their favour.

It was decided to outflank the place. Twelve hundred yards to the north-west a minor road, less heavily defended, crossed the Vie at Grandchamp and wandered off aimlessly into the hills on the far side, where it spent itself in a maze of farm tracks. If it could be followed for a mile it would take our troops on to the opposite crest, and it would then be possible to attack south-east and cut the original main road behind St. Julien, forcing the Germans there to withdraw or surrender. The bridge was blown, but the Sappers built a new one during the night of August 18/19, and on the morning of the 19th the 5th Black Watch crossed and took a farm near la Butte, high on the far hillside. We moved off at 1300 hours on foot; and, using the Black Watch as a firm base, attacked south-west.

The plan was for us to go down into a minor valley, secure Min de la Varonne and le Mesnil Simon on the valley floor, and for the 2nd Seaforth to pass through us, climb the far side, and cut the road. This was done. Little resistance was met, we had no casualties, and all the companies were on their objectives forty minutes after crossing the start-line. We took thirty prisoners on the spot, and another seventy came in next morning.

Yet it had been a bad day. The Grandchamp bridge and crossroads were in full view of the German gunners, and the whole Battalion had to cross them before even the assembly area was reached. David Purgavie was killed there. Then the assembly area itself was under mortar fire from time to time; and, as it had been fought for by the 5/7 Gordons before we arrived, it was strewn with corpses and the smell of death was everywhere. On the way to the start-line we had to pass through the 5th Black Watch, and they too were still being mortared. The actual attack was the easiest part of the day. As soon as it was over, a heavy mortar stonk came down on "B" Company as they were digging in and caused casualties; and far into the night stray shots and occasional streams of tracer bullets were coming from all directions, including the rear. It was certainly not a day to ease the strain of long and continuous campaigning.

We were tired and dirty and footsore, but there was to be no respite. Next evening, just as it seemed we might be left in peace for the night, we were ordered to attack again and pinch out yet another stretch of the Lisieux road. Two miles north-east of us, at a small village called la Corne, there was a crossroads. We had to capture it. As the main road was almost certainly stiff with German rear-guards, another flank attack was decided upon, this time from the right. The 5th Camerons would lead for the first mile and a half up a side road, then we should pass through, swing left-handed, and take la Corne from the south.

To help us we had a squadron of tanks from the East Riding Yeomanry under Major Humphrey Philips – an early stage in a very useful partnership. They were to fight beside us many times. We established a tremendous liaison with them, and before the war ended "Humphrey's Boys" had practically been adopted into the Battalion. On this occasion we were going to need them badly.

We moved off at 1930 hours with the rifle companies in front, the leading two with half a troop of tanks each, followed by all "A" Echelon transport – a self-contained force which could go into action at any time without delay. The lane we followed was atrocious. The surface was dirt and gravel, the angle was steep, and for one long stretch it was so narrow that the trees met overhead and the tanks filled it with only inches to spare. Most of the roads and lanes in the district were so sunk between high banks that they were almost tunnels, and this one was worse than the average: in places the fields on either side were level with the tank turrets. Even when less precipitous stretches were reached, the hedges were so thick that visibility was never more than a hundred yards or so. Still, it was possible, and we had passed through the Camerons and reached a point only five hundred yards south of la Corne before we met serious resistance. Here the leading tank was brewed up by an eighty-eight.

An attack on a two-company front was laid on, with "B" Company advancing up the right-hand side of the road and "A" Company on the left. The attack went in at last light. There was no artillery: we did not want to give warning of our approach. The only sounds were the whispers of the men as they lined up in the fields, and the explosions from the road where the tank, still blazing fiercely, was broadcasting its ammunition in all directions. The attack was successful. The companies crept on to their objectives and met no opposition, except from one German work-party which wandered into "A" Company's area, unaware that it was in our hands. They fired only one burst of schmeiser, and fled. By villainously bad luck, the one burst killed C.S.M. McLeod and three others. We dug in.

Now, the Germans were thoroughly beaten and were running as hard as they could for the Seine. The Falaise Gap had seen one of the greatest slaughters of the war and the remnants were being harried without mercy. Even on our own front, which was north of the main break-through and still retained some semblance of order, the retreat was on in full force and the prisoners we had been taking for days past had been the most woeful specimens imaginable. Infantry, pioneers, gunners, signallers, cooks, renegade Poles and Russians, and even Mongolian horse-holders were being flung together under a lieutenant or a sergeant and told to hold a stretch of road to the last. They were short of everything, from food and ammunition downwards, and their morale had touched zero. This being so, the Germans still lurking around la Corne should, by all the rules of the game, have run away in the darkness while the going was good. But of course, war being war and Germans being Germans, they did no such thing. They waited until dawn, and then they counter-attacked.

At this stage we were not in particularly good shape ourselves. True, we had had a diet of unrelieved victory; but it had been taken neat and no one could remember when he had slept last, or changed his socks, or seen a clean shirt. Furthermore, the brilliant weather had broken, and all night the rain had poured down, flooding the trenches and making everyone miserable. When daylight came there were no Boche to be seen: obviously they had moved off towards Lisieux. ''B'' Company, who were in an orchard in the northern angle of the crossroads, posted sentries and disappeared into houses to cook breakfast and dry off.

At 0730 hours, with the water coming to the boil and the soya-link sausages warming up nicely, sounds of strife and shouts of warning were heard outside, and from the windows of the houses ''B'' Company saw the better part of a hundred Germans filtering down the hedges from the north-east. Some of them were less than two hundred yards away. Breakfast stopped abruptly. Our men bolted for the trenches, sped on their way by brisk fire from the Germans, who seemed to be much more determined than those of their friends we had met recently. Our brens replied, and within two minutes of the alarm being given a small battle was raging. Two parties of Germans established themselves in houses and covered the others as they continued to filter along the hedgerows, more slowly now but still with determination. Both sides began to take casualties.

Meanwhile, the left flank of the attack had crossed the Lisieux road and was approaching the positions east of the crossroads. Sergeant Lachlan Mackintosh, then attached to ''C'' Company, said: 'We were trying to do something about keeping the rain out of our doovers when eight mortar bombs came down. They weren't close, but they were close enough. I looked up and saw a section of Jerries sneaking along a hedge over ''B'' Company way, and just as I gave the alarm I heard ''B'' Company opening up. They began coming down our way. I don't know how many there were – you just saw one or two helmets here and another two or three there, in among the hedges – but they *sounded* like a lot. They were yelling their heads off, as if they were half-crazy or drunk. I never heard the like of it ....'

The hedges by which the Boche were approaching were few and obvious, so Donnie Sutherland, the Company Sergeant Major, set up all the company two-inch mortars and laid sixty rounds of high explosive into the middle of them. Screams began to mix with the shouts, but still they came on. Suddenly they broke cover only fifty yards from ''C'' Company's trenches and came charging across the open. The two forward platoons, 13 and 15, gave them everything they had (the company had to indent for 8000 fresh rounds of ammunition that night) and the German line wavered, broke, and ran. A few minutes later, while the attackers, now thoroughly disorganised, were trying to escape up the hedgerows, the East Riding Yeomanry tanks came up, waddled after them, and completed the rout with their seventeen-pounders and machine-guns.

More tanks were at the crossroads, meeting O.C. ''B'' Company, Hugh Robertson. The main weight of the attack had fallen on him, and he was glad to see them. He climbed on the turret of the leader and guided the column up to the platoons.

'These are my chaps there,' he said to the troop commander, 'and there are Boche in that house.'

'Hold on,' said the troop commander.

The house disappeared in a cloud of smoke, bricks, and slates. Germans scampered from the back door and hit out for home.

'And ...?' said the troop commander.

'That house in the next field,' said Hugh, 'and the others are in that hedge.'

The tanks put a few rounds through the second house and machine-gunned the hedges; and the attack was over. The prisoners taken included two officers. How many were killed cannot be said for certain, as we moved soon afterwards and had no chance to search the hedges; but it is estimated that between thirty and forty were killed. Some of them lay within thirty yards of our trenches.

V

There was no respite. By noon another attack was being planned, and by 1615 hours we were off on our daily routine, stealing another two kilometres of the Lisieux road from the Germans. Again we attacked on the right flank, first sending out a patrol to recce the route almost as far as the objective, then advancing by tracks and minor roads through Lieu Hardi and then swinging northwards near St. Pierre des Ifs and cutting the main road. There was some resistance, but it was quickly dealt with and the Battalion was digging in on its objectives by 1845 hours. We had no casualties. It was not a particularly interesting action, though no doubt most of us still have our memories of it. I have two. One is of lying full-length in an orchard, with a machine-gun firing through the trees overhead and showers of apples falling all round. The other is of the magnificent old brigand who led our patrol almost into St. Pierre des Ifs – Monsieur Fernand, the local butcher. Much wine had given him a radiant face and a bottle-nose. He was seventy if he was a day. He stood there in his blue denims and cloth cap, clutching with one arm the three wet loaves we had given him, and with the other making imperial gestures.

'I say to you there is nothing, nothing, nothing,' he roared. 'Have I not come the way this hour? Nowhere are there machine-guns, nowhere dirty Germans. I can show. I can demonstrate.' He tapped the side of his nose with a forefinger. 'I take you the secret way. Give me two men with the little machine-guns, and I assault the village myself.'

We gave him six men with the little machine-guns, and he led them by an excellent covered route to the outskirts of the village. He was broken-hearted when he was not allowed to advance at their head and capture the place.

That night, August 21, we were left in peace and slept well; and in the War Diary for August 21 appear the blessed words: 'The Battalion rested.'

Could we have gone farther? Probably we could if we had been called upon to do so; but it would have been a dying spurt. The Battalion was never more exhausted. After fourteen days of continuous advance and attack, broken only by the uneasy halt near Secqueville; after bombings by night and strafings by day and shelling or the threat of shelling all the time; after miles of marching, and digging without end; and above all after a long succession of sleepless and anxious nights, the men were fit to drop. They slept as they stood. They leaned against trucks and slept.

They went about heavy-eyed, seeking roofs for their doovers, and when the doovers were complete they lay on the hard flints and slept the clock round. We were not called upon again. Lisieux fell on the 22nd, and the whole front loosened up. We rested for four days; and, although hitherto our progress had been just two miles a day, when we moved on we had to drive fifty miles to find the front line.

LE HAVRE

(previous page) The Seaforths fought a night battle at Le Havre against defensive fire which had been prepared over years. Artillery, rocket and mortar casualties were heavy.

(below) Farquhar Macrae (right) with his team of medical orderlies. They played a central role during battles often working in dangerously exposed positions.

CHAPTER FOURTEEN

Le Havre

I

AT THE BEGINNING of September, 1944, the German General Staff decided to cut their losses in France and the Low Countries and withdraw behind the Siegfried Line, abandoning everything as far east as the German frontier and as far north as Holland. They could establish a secure line nowhere else. The British were closing up on the lower reaches of the Seine, and the Americans were across it east and west of Paris. Neither the Marne nor the Somme was wide enough or long enough to form an effective barrier with the few troops they had available to man them; and in any case the American armoured columns were cracking about almost at will and only prepared defences would stop them. The sole means of delaying us now left to the Germans was to hold the Channel ports, thus forcing us to feed and maintain ourselves through the Normandy bridgehead and stretch our lines of communication to the utmost. Suicide garrisons were left in the ports, and the rest pulled back to Germany.

When our rest was over we advanced to the Seine. It is sufficient to say that our advance was unopposed and took place in a gentlemanly manner in troop-carrying vehicles, and that we arrived on the south bank near le Landin on August 30. The fields were full of horses abandoned by the Germans as they fled; and many of us, with Colonel Walford well to the fore, enjoyed excellent riding for the next two days.

On September 1 we crossed the Seine. At first the plan was a cautious one. The Highland Division would advance to St. Valery-en-Caux, and so cut off the whole of the le Havre peninsula; but it would do so by stages, a brigade at a time, one foot on the ground and no nonsense. For all we knew, the Germans might be prepared to fight delaying actions all the way to Berlin; and until definite information to the contrary was available, we were not to go too far. 152 Brigade would lead, cross the river at Elboeuf, advance in tactical formation through Rouen, and establish a firm base in the Barentan/Pavilly area until such time as the rest of the Division should arrive and pass through.

This we did. However, the Derby Yeomanry armoured cars were scouting on ahead and claimed that the civilians they met had seen no Germans for the past two days. This was a chance worth taking. We pushed on, and by evening our Battalion was established on the coast at Veules-les-Roses, the rest of the Brigade was ten miles inland, and the le Havre peninsula was cut. We had covered nearly eighty miles in a day.

None of us will ever live such a day again. Though we live to be ninety we will never do it. During their first hours of freedom after four years of German occupation, the French went mad. On any public occasion in Britain when masses of people are enjoying themselves, there is an easy-going mood behind it all: there may be excitement, as at a football match, but at heart they are out for pleasure. The game, or the procession, or whatever it may be, is good fun; and on that basis the emotion of the crowd is built. This was different, something much deeper. These people who crowded the village streets and walked for miles across the fields to line the roads for us were happy and excited, but behind the flag-waving and the cheering and the singing was a profound thankfulness. It was an impressive thing to see.

I had the luck to be a little way ahead of the column with my sergeant, Hugh McLeod of Ullapool. We were mobbed in every village. Gigantic streamers announced: *WELCOME TO OUR BRAVE LIBERATORS*. Others said *GOD SAVE THE KING* in letters three feet high. There were flags in every window and in every hand, speeches of welcome to be made and cognac to be offered; and everywhere there were flowers. We left each village with bouquets piled on the tanks of our motor-bikes and had to throw them away once we were out of sight for fear of hurting the feelings of the next village. It was a tremendous day. Always we tried to ask if there were mines on the road or enemy in the neighbourhood; and always we failed. The crowd surged round and engulfed us, Monsieur le Maire made his speech, the little girl in her best frock was pushed forward to present yet another bouquet. Breathless, our steel helmets tipped over our eyes and lipstick behind our ears, we would say: 'But are there any mines ?' and the crowd would howl: 'Mines? None, none. They are all gone, the Boche.' Then the head of the Battalion column would appear round the corner, and in the confusion we would escape and roar on ahead to the next village.

In most places they boasted of the prisoners they had taken. There was much rivalry in this matter. As in our villages before the war you might be told of the prize onions at the flower-show, or the champion bull, so here it was the prisoners taken by the young men of the resistance. 'We have taken five, five in the woods!' they would say. 'At Beau Soleil – a village of no importance, monsieur – are three only, very small.' And then an old woman would be led forward, and she would take our hands and try to speak; but instead would break down and turn away abruptly into the crowd.

It was almost as great a day for us as it was for the French, because not only were we seeing the results of our weeks of fighting in the bridgehead, but we were approaching, much more quickly than any of us had expected, a district of peculiar interest to our Division. St. Valery was the place where the original Highland Division, pinned against the sea by the German advance, had been forced to lay down its arms in 1940; and next day it was our luck to be the first to enter it. We slept that night at Veules-les-Roses, and at first light Jerry Dawson took his platoon, with a troop of tanks in support, and disappeared down the coast road. Two hours later he reported St. Valery clear of the enemy.

Colonel Walford was in tremendous form that morning. He had been at St. Valery as a company commander and had been one of the few to get away at the time of the surrender. At dawn he went as usual round the company positions, and then his jeep was seen whistling off down the road at top speed. It was not very difficult to imagine where he was going. Already we had come across vehicles of the old 51st Division lying by the roadside, still with the stags' heads and Highland Brigade colours visible on their mudguards; and that morning he was to find his old company shield and sign in a farmhouse.

A few hours later we moved to Ingouville, on the far side of St. Valery, and settled down to rest. The Germans had all gone three days before, leaving nothing but unhappy memories and empty Benedictine bottles ('The bandits! For a week they drank more than they ate,' said the local people), so we were able to relax completely for the first time since D-Day. Next day (September 3) the massed bands of the Division beat retreat at Cailleville, which had been General Fortune's last H.Q. in 1940: several thousand of the Division were present, and St. Valery turned out in force, vastly excited to see us back again. On the 4th we moved on once more, along the coast through Fécamp and Éntretat to a small village called Beaumesnil a dozen miles north of le Havre, and there we stayed for a week. On the 11th we attacked le Havre.

<h1 style="text-align:center">II</h1>

The Germans had been sitting in le Havre for four years, well knowing that if we ever regained a foothold in France, the port must inevitably be attacked. For four years they had dug, and tunnelled, and mined, looked at their handiwork and dug again. Everything that modern engineering and unlimited slave labour could do to make the place impregnable had been done, and done at leisure. All the guns and most of the infantry were under concrete. The minefields were hundreds of yards deep. Anti-tank ditches, dug with who knows how much expenditure of human sweat, cut precise zig-zag lines across the countryside in the path of any route by which tanks could possibly approach. In the end, the defenders must have been satisfied when they studied their defence maps and saw what they had done. The sea approaches were all covered, and the whole tip of the peninsula was cut off from the rest of France by defence-works which stretched from the Seine estuary to the sea in an unbroken semi-circle two-and-a-half miles from the city. The defences varied in depth from one thousand yards to more than a mile.

However, the best defences lose half their value when their position is known to the attacking force; and in this respect we could not have been better served. As usual, our air cover had been excellent and had supplied us with photographs of all our objectives. We had maps over-printed with all enemy diggings and emplacements. But in addition we had the help of the French resistance movement, whose spies were able to fill in details which no aerial photograph could supply. Many of them had been forced to help in building the defences, and all had been in le Havre recently. They knew which sites were occupied and which were not. They knew how many Germans were in each strongpoint, and the exact layout of the minefields. They had stolen the German defensive fire-plan. Before our attack began, the Divisional Intelligence staff had examined and sorted reports from hundreds of civilians and had built up an excellent picture of the state of the defences. Even at the Triangle we had not had such precise information on which to base our plan.

Still, le Havre was a hard nut to crack. The defences are most easily imagined as a square (this is not accurate, but it is sufficient to allow the main outline of the plan to be understood) with the bottom, or south, side representing the estuary of the Seine, and the left-hand vertical side representing the sea. The other two sides were the land defences. The port of le Havre itself filled the bottom third of the square; at the top right-hand corner was the town of Montevilliers; and at the top left-hand corner, where the land defences met the sea, was Octeville.

Now the plan. There were two divisions available to make the attack, the 49th and ourselves. The 49th were to breach the defences near Montevilliers and turn south. We were to go through later and turn west. Both divisions would then be advancing *behind* the German defences and could mop them up from the rear at leisure. As a final touch, a fake attack was to be staged on Octeville to divert the enemy's attention while the real attack went in.

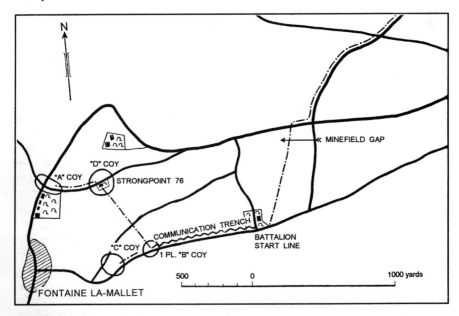

Our own part in this operation seemed straightforward. One set of minefield gaps big enough to carry the 49th Division would certainly not be big enough to pass through the Highland Division when its turn came. By that time the 49th would be evacuating casualties and bringing up rear echelon and supply vehicles. The Highland Division would need gaps of its own; but the most convenient place for them was covered by a German strong-point. The plan was for the 5th Seaforth to use the 49th Division gaps on the night of September 10, turn west, attack the strongpoint, and hold on until new gaps could be made behind it and the rest of the Division pass through on the morning of the 11th. Our objective was on the high ground east of Fontaine-la-Mallet, and was known to the Germans as Strongpoint 76. The general lay-out of this area is shown in the diagram above.

The attack was due to open on the 9th, but heavy rain so softened the ground that it was doubtful if the tanks and flails could operate. Everything was postponed for a day. The sun came out, the bombers had one last crack at le Havre (they had been pounding the defences for a week; and, as we discovered later, had had a profound effect on the Boche morale), and off we went in troop-carrying vehicles to our assembly area north of the 49th Division gaps. We lay there until 2345 hours and then plodded off towards the start-line.

The attack divides itself conveniently into three parts – the first approach march, the second approach march, and the assault. The Battalion had been lying-up outside the enemy defences and was not going to break new ground until it had followed the 49th Division through the gaps and reached the small wood occupied by the South Wales Borderers. This wood was the Battalion start-line, the parting of the ways where the 49th continued southwards and we swung west. The distance between the Brigade start-line which we had just crossed and the Battalion start-line in the wood was twelve hundred yards. This was the first approach march. The distance from the wood to our first objective was five hundred yards. This was the second approach march. The assault will be dealt with in its proper place.

These things are always a matter of opinion, but as we dropped down from the Brigade start-line towards the gaps it seemed to me that this march was the most melodramatic one we had ever done. The foreground was normal enough, just the usual column trudging along resignedly in the darkness as it had done so many times before, heads down, steel helmets and rifle muzzles making a frieze against the night sky, the occasional longer gap between two men where a stretcher was being carried, the wireless operators stooping forward against the weight of their sets – a column immensely patient, almost apathetic, storing up nervous energy for the demands of the night. There was nothing new in that. The melodrama was in the background. It was a black night of low cloud and no wind. Three searchlights were up to light us on our way, but the landscape was so vast that they made little impression on it: the ploughed fields soaked up what little light was reflected back from the clouds. We were dropping down into a wide, shallow valley, so that we seemed to be in the centre of a great saucer; and all round the rim villages burned. There were eight big fires, so widely spaced that one could not see them all without turning one's head. The distant ones were orange-red glows on the horizon, but there were three within a radius of a mile where the skeletons of farms were visible in the flames. These farms were in woods, and the trees showed up black in silhouette. Some of the trees were burning too. The nearest wood was our start-line.

Down in the saucer there was, for the moment, silence. There was just enough light to enable us to distinguish the black of the tank tracks from the near black of the fields. The ground was still very soft after the rain and most of the flail tanks had bogged or blown up, but somehow the mines had been cleared and one gap made. There should have been three, but the failure of the flails had put the Sappers hours behind schedule, and the other two were still incomplete. The single gap was in a horrible state. For seven hundred yards it wound over the fields, churned up by tanks, flails, AVRE's and similar devices to such an extent that it was impossible to expect any wheeled vehicle to cross it. Carriers would only manage it with luck, and even the infantry would be slowed down. The ground was like a peat-bog. The tank ruts were two feet deep all the way.

The column began to go through, the more expert casting approving eyes on the ruts. They were right: the ruts saved many lives before dawn. The Germans had over a hundred guns in le Havre and, since the 49th's attack had been made in daylight, their gunners knew exactly where the gap was. They also knew which woods the 49th occupied, and no great amount of imagination was required to guess which other woods and strong-points would be attacked before morning. These gunners were sitting on top of ammunition dumps built up over a period of

years, and a gunner in a concrete bunker six thousand yards from the target does
not need to be a very brave man to do his job efficiently. There were far too many
efficient Germans in le Havre that night. They shelled the gap, they shelled the
road beyond it, and most of all they shelled our start-line at the little wood. The
wood was only two hundred yards square, but it had three hundred shells between
midnight and dawn.

The gap met the road a hundred yards east of the wood, first crossing an anti-
tank ditch. When the 49th had gone over, an AVRE had come up and dropped a
bridge; but it was damaged and insecure. None of our carriers could cross it, and so
until dawn both the heavy wireless sets and all casualties had to be manhandled –
a desperate situation so far as the casualties were concerned, because the long carry
back through the churned-up gap was so exhausting and slow that most of the
wounded could not be evacuated before first light. Until then, most of them lay in a
deep concrete shelter in the wood. Some of them died there.

The companies reached the wood and lay up in a ditch until H-hour. The
shelling was intense. There had been some scattered shells in the gap, but now they
were concentrated and terribly accurate. The Germans were using dug-in rockets,
too. Shells were landing all round us, not in ones or twos, but by the score; and the
casualties began to mount – beastly, heavy-shell casualties, men losing arms, and
worse. We were glad when, at 0040 hours, "C" Company began the second
advance.

This, thanks to the Germans, was unexpectedly easy. The first objective was a
pill-box five hundred yards west along the road, and the Germans, who throughout
the war never seemed to be happy unless they were digging something, had seen fit
to connect it to our start-line by a continuous zig-zag communication trench
running along the roadside. "C" Company followed it gratefully, and before long
had collected most heartening proof that, however cheerful the German artillery
might be feeling, the infantry morale was low. The Boche knew that the South
Wales Borderers were in the little wood. They knew that the trench was a perfect
approach to their position. Yet "C" Company found in it only one lonely Pole who
had obviously remained there in the hope of deserting. He was an obliging
creature. When Alan Wade, who was leading the column, doubted his tale that the
pill-box was a dummy one, he proved his statement by leading the company up to
it. At this point "C" Company was supposed to breach the perimeter wire so that
the others could follow through unimpeded and attack the heart of the position, but
the wire had already been flattened by our artillery. They scrambled through and
dug in.

Here the real difficulties began. No amount of foresight can overcome the fact
that a map-maker or an aerial photographer can only portray the ground as it
appeared when he surveyed it; and that in modern war ground can change
drastically inside an hour or two. This ground had changed very much indeed.
Every landmark had been bombed and shelled out of existence. The road disappeared
into a mass of craters and fallen trees. A wood shown clearly on our photographs
had vanished overnight. It was possible that the darkness might be hiding the row
of houses in the valley, but it was much more likely that there were now no houses
in the valley at all; and finally, there was the difficulty of the valley itself.

How this difficulty arose it is impossible to say. Even to-day, wise after the event, I cannot see that the map indicates anything more than a shallow valley at the point where we crossed it; nor do the aerial photographs give any clue to the true nature of the ground even when examined through a stereoscope. The fact remains that when "D" Company passed through "C" and turned right-handed to take the strong-point proper they found, not the shallow valley and gentle slope they had expected, but what Hamish Paterson described as a ruddy precipice. It was not quite so bad as that, but it was extraordinarily steep, and both hands and feet were needed to climb it. Added to the other confusions of the night, it might well have led "D" Company astray. It required a great deal of faith and self-confidence to lead a company up that slope under shellfire and in almost total darkness without imagining that some monstrous error had been made and that they were heading in the wrong direction. However, it was done. In my opinion, it was the best job of route-finding we did in France.

The strong-point was a network of communication trenches, concrete pill-boxes, and bunkers. There were two 88mm. guns and a 75mm. in it. There was a 50mm., the dug-in turret of a Czech tank with a 45mm., two 20mm. flak guns, half-a-dozen banks of rockets still unfired, and eighty men. There were mines, and wire.

One German threw a phosphorous grenade. The rest came out with their hands up.

It was a night when we could do no wrong. Even when the Padre trod on an S-mine and the primary charge knocked his glasses off his nose, not only did the main charge fail to explode but his glasses were unbroken. The company's luck continued to hold. It was a bald, naked place, and the digging was hard. When the men had dug down only a few inches a spandau opened up from the north, attracted by the clinking of picks and shovels; but at that moment Hamish Paterson found the main communication trench system and bundled the company inside. No sooner had he done so than one of the biggest stonks we ever experienced came down on top of them. Even in the trench there were casualties: without the trench it would have been slaughter.

The Padre says: 'It was so bad that there was no cursing. In the lulls there was no sound at all. We just lay flat on our faces, hardly breathing, waiting for the next lot to come over.'

"A" Company now began to pass through, heading downhill to take the road-junction on the northern outskirts of Fontaine-la-Mallet. How Hector Mackenzie or his company found their way it is difficult to say. Lieutenant E.S.Collins had orders to send one section down each side of the road. He could find no road. After hunting about in the dark for a time he noticed a slight change in the feel of the ground, which had been completely shattered by bombing. He stooped, and scraped at the earth. Two inches down he came on concrete. It was the road.

The company took its objectives unopposed and dug in at 0300 hours. They too were heavily shelled, and in addition had a few small encounters with enemy who were still in the village itself. Most of these Germans came out later and gave themselves up, including four who had been hiding within half-a-dozen yards of our trenches. The slope where the company dug in was an exposed one, and later in the day the C.O. pulled them back a little to a less prominent position.

"B" Company, which has not been mentioned so far, had three tasks. One platoon protected "C" Company's left flank while the gap in the perimeter wire was being passed, another was in readiness to exploit northwards from "D" Company's objective (this was unnecessary, as "D" carried out the exploitation unaided), and the third platoon remained in reserve.

When daylight came it uncovered much that would have been best left covered. What had once been a peaceful stretch of farmland was totally devastated. The farms were burned-out shells, deprived even of the vividness which the darkness had lent their flames. Haystacks smouldered. Cattle and men lay dead in the fields, where the tank-tracks crawled and curved for miles and the earth was pocked by shelling. The woods had been thinned by the bombardment and looked as if they had been gone through with a gigantic broken-toothed comb. The village of Fontaine-la-Mallet, pounded by artillery after the heavy bombers had done their work, was simply tragic. Even the woods round it were worse than any we had seen before. The trees had not just lost a few branches: they were stripped of everything, even their bark, and most of them were shattered stumps. There were trees like them in the last war, but they had been reduced to ruin by months of shelling. These trees had been wrecked by two bombing raids of a few minutes each. The houses in the village had disappeared, so smashed to rubble that bulldozers had to clear the street. The stench of buried bodies was everywhere. The survivors had fled, leaving only the priest, whom we found wandering distractedly in search of help for the seventy people still under the ruins. We were still fighting, and could not give him the help.

He said: 'We hated the Germans, and we prayed that they would go. But we did not know it would cost so much.'

The shelling continued during the morning, and only eased after the rest of the Division had passed through us and its transport was following through the new minefield gaps. Then the battle moved on, and we lay in the sun and slept. It had been a successful night but a bitter one. We had lost twenty killed and thirty wounded, almost all by shelling. Among the dead was Major Douglas Findlay-Shirras, M.C., as fine an officer as ever fought with the Battalion.

III

The German defences collapsed so quickly once the initial breakthrough had been made that the other battalions of the Division had hardly any casualties and were able to advance rapidly throughout the late morning and the early afternoon. They were overrunning guns as they went, and the shelling had dropped off almost to nothing. Prisoners began to come back down the road in thousands, and the sound of German demolitions from the direction of the docks was a good omen. At 1900 hours, just as we had hopes of settling down for the night, the inevitable order to move came through and soon we were in troop-carrying vehicles heading for Mont Trotin, a village one mile to the west where we were to take over from the 2nd Seaforth. There was the usual moan about having to dig in for the second time in one day but when we saw Mont Trotin we changed our tune and decided that perhaps this was not such a bad war after all. We approved of Mont Trotin. The industrious Hun had been burrowing there for years, and the results far exceeded anything in the doover class we had ever had the luck to see. Near the lip of a wooded valley was a small steel door. Beyond it was a tunnel, concrete-lined. It went straight on under the ground for a distance of a hundred-and-fifty yards, at which point it divided, each branch continuing for another twenty or thirty yards. Throughout its length it was flanked by dormitories and store-rooms containing anything from ammunition to such desirable commodities as fresh butter and champagne. The two branches ended in spiral staircases which led to small and carefully camouflaged cupolas in the middle of a potato field. In each cupola was a periscope. That was all. It was an artillery command post, and the incredible labour of driving and lining the tunnel had been directed purely towards establishing the two periscopes. The dormitories and stores were incidental: they could have been built just as safely and with much less labour elsewhere. When we looked through the periscopes we thanked our stars we had attacked in the dark: our start-line, Strongpoint 76, and all our route between them were in full view.

There is a great deal to be said for a shellproof billet on the night after a battle, even without champagne. We filed in and made ourselves at home. The commandant's bed, with its spring mattress and clean white sheets, remains one of my happiest memories of the war.

Next day le Havre capitulated.

CANALS, DYKES AND SNIPERS

(previous page) Smoke covers a canal crossing by collapsible boat, Each boat carried sixteen men.

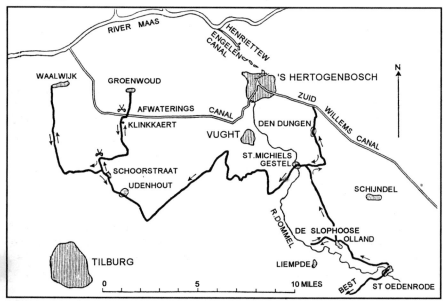

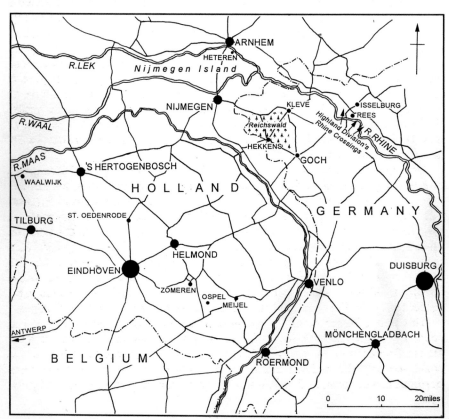

CHAPTER FIFTEEN

S.W.Holland: Canals, Dykes and Snipers

I

ON SEPTEMBER 13, after a second night in the tunnel, we returned to Beaumesnil, where they gave us a conquering hero's reception. We were right out of the war in a peaceful backwater far behind the fighting line. Our armies were on the Dutch frontier two hundred miles away, and the problem of maintaining them was so acute that no transport could be spared to carry us north to join them. This arrangement broke no hearts at Beaumesnil. We were, as the Jocks said, cushy. We had good billets, the hens were laying furiously, butter and cream were unrationed, there was a hall in Étretat where company dances could be held, and the Benedictine distillery was at Fécamp. What more could the tired warrior ask ? It was a good rest, and we felt we had earned it. "A" Company spent a few days garrisoning le Havre and guarding food stores there, but there was nothing else for us to do until the 30th. Then we moved up into Holland, a three-day journey. On October 3 we took over from the 2nd Glasgow Highlanders in the village of Best, a few miles north of Eindhoven.

The war by this time was almost at a standstill. The Germans had established a line again. The parachute landing at Arnhem, intended to carry us at one swoop over the Maas, the Waal, and the Leck, and so into the North German Plain, had failed; but we still held a fat corridor from Eindhoven to Nijmegen. The swanning days were over. The winter campaign in Holland was designed to consolidate our gains, open the port of Antwerp, and prepare the ground for the spring offensive. It involved a series of minor campaigns all aimed at enlarging the Eindhoven-Nijmegen corridor until all Holland south and west of the Maas was in our hands. We were about to take part in the first of these elbowing movements -- the south-west Holland push, which was to capture 's Hertogenbosch, advance westwards, and mop up everything south of the Maas.

Not much can be said of Best. We were there only three days, and during that time nothing happened but patrols, counter-patrols, and flying visits by the officers to the big white house we had acquired in Eindhoven. (It was the home of Sergeant Sinclair, the P.R.I. Sergeant, and of Private Goldberg, the Battalion Tailor; and it had the only real bath we had seen since D-Day.) Best may have been a prosperous place once, but when we were there it was tumble-down and depressing and liable to sudden outbursts of shelling and mortaring. We were glad to leave it. On the 6th we took over another section of the line between St.Oedenrode and Olland from the 7th Royal Welsh Fusiliers, and there we were rejoined by Paddy Nairne, who succeeded Leslie Wilson as adjutant. Leslie, now a major, took over "D" Company.

This was to be our home for a long time. Olland was in German hands. The country was flat and well wooded; and though our right flank was open for a thousand yards or more, our left, where Olland lay, was screened by trees and we could see only the outlying houses of the village. On this flank the German positions and our own, both astride the Olland road, were only four hundred yards apart.

Immediately after the take-over, Colonel Walford (who had just been awarded a bar to his D.S.O.) made it clear to the Germans where their place was: it was below ground, and they were to stay there. When they tried to move about, they were sniped; and when it grew too dark for sniping we sent out patrols to annoy them, an average of five a night. The Boche were impressed, and left us in peace. They gave us trouble only once during the fortnight we stayed there.

Patrolling apart, we sat in our trenches and left the war to the snipers; and as they were at their best during those sixteen days at Olland, this is as good a place as any to tell their story from the beginning.

Sniping had been a neglected art during the first years of the war, and as often as not in those days a sniper was an untrained infantryman with telescopic sights on his rifle. The African campaign, with its huge distances and lack of cover, did not improve this situation, and few battalions can have left the desert with a trained team on its strength or even with properly zeroed rifles. The Germans had other ideas. Our armies in Italy suddenly found themselves in close country being sniped by experts.

Schools were started, the establishment of snipers was doubled, and the training of snipers became a priority job. By the time we reached Normandy we had a good team, and we had someone who would direct their operations with imagination. When Major Richard Fleming, M.C., became second-in-command of the Battalion at the time of Tilly-la-Campagne he spent half his time in No Man's Land with a telescope and the other half going into a huddle with the snipers and hatching plots. His planning and the snipers' skill made a deadly combination.

'The snipers, of course, are a law unto themselves,' he wrote at the time. 'They submit to the fatherly will of C.S.M. Davidson, M.M.; but apart from that they go their own ways regardless of what the rest of the Battalion does, what Standing Orders say, or what three brigades, the Divisional Artillery, and the machine-gunners think they are doing. You can easily spot them when the Battalion is settling down for the night. In quite the most comfortable corner, but at the same time at a discreet distance from the Regimental Sergeant Major's habitation, you will see a bundle of shapeless figures in a variety of dress gathered like tinkers round a blazing fire which has clearly been made up regardless either of black-out or of petrol scarcity. A savoury sizzling smell rises from the centre of the group, and a cloud of white feathers eddies in the evening breeze. In the background a murder is being committed. The shrieks of the victim die away in an ominous gurgling, and a red-headed figure smoking a pipe appears out of the gloom carrying the corpse – a fat young porker.

'To call this independent band a problem is understating it. They are a menace to all order-loving sergeant-majors whenever we are out of the line. Luckily they are even more of a menace to the enemy at anything under four hundred yards when we are in contact.'

They had several kills at the Triangle and elsewhere, but it was only when we reached Olland that the full reward came for their patience and planning.

Everything was right. There was cover, but not too much cover: the approaches were good, but the target was clear. The Boche, at first, were careless. Our front lines were a convenient distance apart. The snipers rubbed their hands.

The Game Book entries soon showed results: 'October 7, Fraser killed two.

October 8, Fraser killed one. October 11, Fraser killed two, and Ostergard one. October 12, Lance-Corporal Matchwick killed two. October 13, Fraser killed one. October 14, Douglas killed one. October 15, Mackenzie killed two...."

We did not lose a single man by sniping, and by the end of the campaign our total bag was thirty-eight. So great was our ascendancy at Olland that the redoubtable Fraser was seen one evening disappearing into No Man's Land on a bicycle. It was also a time when the snipers, never a particularly self-effacing crew outside working hours, developed an even more than usually vivid turn of phrase in describing their exploits. Fraser's best contribution was: 'I got him through the head. How did I know ? Och, he just curled up and twitched his toes like a rabbit'; but I prefer the two gems by Mackenzie, a small stocky man with a mobile face and a wicked grin. Of one encounter at Best he said: 'They chust gave twa-three grunts, and scattered,' and of an Olland kill he said, with immense relish: 'Aall we heard wass the shot, and the dying gurrrrgle.'

It is perhaps unfair to describe any one of these adventures fully, at the expense of the others, because all the members of the team put up a very fine show and many of the stalks which produced no results at all were as daring as those which did; but the story of Lance-Corporal Matchwick's Military Medal must be told, and one of Fraser's kills at Olland was so spectacular that I cannot resist the temptation to record it. The Fraser incident happened first. As I remember it, he was out where he had no right to be. The artillery had been warned to give him elbow-room north of the Olland road; but Fraser, a tall, raw-boned man with red hair, a remarkably short and foul-smelling pipe, and no crease in his trousers, was allergic to discipline and saw something that interested him on the south side of the road. He lay up there in a midden for a long time, watching a group of houses three hundred yards away. Nothing moved there, but he had a feeling that something might if he waited long enough. We were watching him from the Battalion Observation Post, which was in an attic in "D" Company's area beside the road; and as we watched, a mortar bomb landed without any kind of warning right between the two forward sections and wounded Sergeant Tommy Downs. It was a perfect shot, and could mean only one thing – without any more time being wasted on ranging, another dozen bombs would follow immediately. Everyone dived for cover. But no bombs came. Instead we heard the crack of a rifle. There was a slight pause, and then from the roof of one of Fraser's houses a German rolled slowly over and fell two storeys to the ground. There were no more bombs after that. The man had been invisible so long as he remained motionless, but Fraser had seen him when he signalled up the first bomb.

Matchwick's big day was hardly a sniping expedition, but it was a magnificent example of what could be done by a few determined men against an enemy whose morale was beginning to wear thin. After hours of watching, the Intelligence Section had pinpointed a German observation post in a tree twelve hundred yards in front of our positions, and had nicknamed it Tarzan's Tree. It was well to the north of Olland village in an area we did not know a great deal about, and it was decided to investigate it. Sergeant Urquhart and Privates Mackintosh and Clanachan were briefed for the job, and Matchwick and Mackenzie were sent out ahead to cover them. The patrol was to go out in darkness, lie up, see what they could see when daylight came, and then make their way back along the hedgerows. It was no easy task: twelve hundred yards under the enemy's nose in broad daylight was not exactly a picnic.

When they had foregathered and seen the ground at close quarters, Sergeant Urquhart and Matchwick decided that the idea of the snipers making a firm base and covering the others on to their objective from it was not feasible: the cover was too thick to give an uninterrupted field of fire. The snipers and the patrol therefore joined forces and carried on towards Tarzan's Tree together.

Here is Mackenzie's version of what happened: 'Matchwick and myself had been lying up in a ditch for a while before Danny Urquhart arrived, and two Jerries came along the road and stood jabbering at each other fifteen yards from us. We couldn't have missed. I was for shooting them and getting out, but Matchwick says if we do that Danny would never get his job done. So we let them go. They walked on up the road towards Tarzan's Tree. When Danny arrived, the whole lot of us got into the ditch and started off after them. We'd a bonny time of it. The damn ditch was full of wire; but we'd wire-cutters with us, so we kept on cutting the stuff and laying it outside, and crawling on a bit, and cutting some more. It was awful slow work, but after a while we heard voices. Now, the Jerries were in a doover. That was how we got things wrong. The ground sort of muffled their voices, and although they were only ten feet away from us they sounded as if they were about a hundred yards away. Matchwick whispers to me to get hold of Mackintosh and the bren gun, and go out to the right to cover them; so the pair of us wriggles back down the ditch for a bit, crosses the road, and gets into a good position – thinking all the time, of course, that the Boche were a hundred yards away. And then the fun starts.

'Matchwick poked his head out of the ditch, and at exactly the same moment a Jerry poked *his* head out of the doover, and only the width of the road between the two of them! The Jerry squawked like a hen. Matchwick had a grenade ready in his hand, but instead of lobbing it into the doover the way he should have done he threw it straight at the Jerry's face. Of course the Jerry ducked, and the grenade went past him and burst outside. Matchwick went right after it. There was a spandau and three rifles lying at the door of the doover. He dived across the road, kicked them out of the way, and got down behind the spandau. There was shooting all over the place. The woods were fair hotching with Jerries, and what with all the smoke and the shouting I couldn't see what to shoot and what to leave alone. I ran back to join Matchwick. He was lying outside the doover with the spandau, and a dozen Boche were coming at him through the trees. He gave them a burst with the spandau and killed the first one.

I took a running jump into the doover and landed on the chest of one of the Jerries, who was just coming out to see what was happening. He crawled away into the back of the doover after that and sat there whimpering with two others.

'Clanachan in the other ditch couldn't get his sten to work, Mackintosh was frightened to fire the bren in case he hit us, Danny had only a revolver, and after the one burst the spandau stopped and neither Matchwick nor myself knew how to get it started again. Anyway, we got going with our rifles and killed four of them, and Danny was pitching grenades out of the ditch for all he was worth, and after a bit the Germans sort of lost heart and went away. It seemed about time to get out. Clanachan's sten was working by this time, so he and Matchwick stayed behind to cover us as we got back down the ditch through all the wire. It was a bit difficult with the prisoners, you see: we'd howked the three Jerries out of the doover and taken them with us, and they were half dead with fright and not very good at crawling, especially the one I'd jumped on. When we were clear, the other two followed. Matchwick brought the spandau with him. We all got back O.K.'

Matchwick was awarded the Military Medal. Four months later, a full corporal by this time and with a bar to his M.M., he was killed after crossing the Rhine.

It is always interesting to hear the customer's point of view, so it is fitting that the final tribute to the work of the snipers at Olland should come from the platoon sergeant of a German parachute battalion who deserted to us on the night of October 14. His platoon faced "D" Company, on our left flank. He said: 'Last week I had thirty-one men. Now I have twenty-one. Four have been shot. The others have gone sick – our trenches are flooded, and we haven't been able to leave them for a week.'

He wore the Iron Cross, had five years' service, and had fought in two Russian winter campaigns.

The one occasion on which the Germans showed any sign of offensive action was marked by a singular lack of planning. Possibly their habit of using odd battle-groups to plug holes in the line may have made co-ordination difficult for them; but even so it is hard to understand why their arrangements, normally so thorough, should have been so slap-dash on this occasion. Apparently the paratroopers who faced us were employed only to hold the line, and when patrols were required they were demanded from troops well to the rear. The Germans decided to put in a raid to find the lay-out of our right flank (about which they knew nothing at all) and at first light on October 13 they launched an officer and forty men out into the blue. These men had not been properly briefed. They had been marched up from the rear overnight and had never seen the ground before. Most of them had little or no idea of the plan. They just plodded on after their leader along a ditch well out on our right front.

Meanwhile some other German unit had wanted the same information and had sent out a sergeant and two men to collect it. They had not seen the ground either, but were quite happy about it because, as the sergeant explained to me later, they had been able to steer a good course by watching the church steeple in Olland. The only flaw in this piece of navigation was that Olland church steeple had been totally demolished a week before.

The two parties met six hundred yards in front of "A" Company on our right flank. Possibly they argued about precedence. Almost certainly they argued about church steeples. In any case, they were seen by us; and as luck would have it they were right under one of our artillery defensive fire tasks. The task number was telephoned to the gunners and within two minutes a full-scale stonk came down, personally controlled by Brigadier Jerry Shiel (Commander Royal Artillery), who happened to be visiting our Observation Post at the time. The sentry who had spotted the Boche was standing near our 5/7 Middlesex machine-gun detachment, at that time smarting under an alleged failure to hit Tarzan's Tree while Tarzan was in residence. Seizing the chance to redeem their reputation, they opened up with every gun they had and telephoned their 4.2 mortar company to weigh in as well. This, naturally, touched the pride of our own 3-inch mortar representative in the O.P., so he too busied himself on the telephone. The German raid disappeared in a cloud of smoke and was seen no more. Two fighting patrols we sent out to collect the remnants returned with eight prisoners, two of them platoon sergeants. There were no more raids after that.

During this period David Blair, who had been injured just before D-Day, rejoined us and took over command of his old company, "B".

"Operation Collin," the clearing of south-west Holland up to the Maas, began on October 23. Our own immediate task was to take Olland and mop up as far west as the intersection of the railway with the River Dommel; but as the Germans withdrew nine hours before our attack began, there is no point in going into the detailed plan. We walked on to our objectives unopposed, and the only shelling was our own. By evening we were disposed in the angle between the railway and the Dommel, and Battalion H.Q. was established in De Slophoose, a broken-down cafe smelling strongly of Germans and stale schnapps. (Why *did* the Germans smell so abominably? Farquhar Macrae blamed it on their anti-louse powder. Whatever the reason, it is a fact that throughout the war every German soldier, and every billet used by a German soldier, had a sour, rancid smell which was unmistakable and could not have been generated by mere lack of soap and water. It hung about for days after they left.)

Here, for a time, the war degenerated into comedy, starting with the arrival of a civilian who hobbled in on a stick, held out his hand, and said: 'My name's Joe. I'm glad to know you.' He was a crashed Dakota pilot, hidden by a farmer for five weeks while his leg healed; and he was a mine of inaccurate information. However, he told us of a priest ('Biggest goddamned thief I ever met: lookit the passport he stole me.') who ran the local resistance movement from a village across the Dommel, was game for anything, and would certainly know all there was to know about the Germans. If we wanted hot news, said Joe, he was our man.

(below) The Dutch Resistance priests at De Slophoose describing the German dispositions to Brigadier Cassels(right) and Lt. Colonel Walford.

The night was quiet, and in the morning there was still no sign of the enemy. We sent a patrol across the Dommel to collect the priest, a tall thin man who arrived beaming from ear to ear, delighted as a small boy with his first ride in a jeep, and accompanied by another priest who was extremely fat and dumpy and wore, in addition to his cassock, a Dutch steel helmet. Both these gentlemen were very excited and were voluble in three languages; but they did talk sound sense when we could understand them. The Germans had been gone twenty-four hours. They had left a few mines, but the priests knew where they were buried. Their own village of Liempde was clear. They did not know how far back the Germans had gone, but they could soon find out. How? The tall priest had a motor-bike, and all he needed was some of our petrol.

'But look here,' we said, 'It's extremely good of you; but you do realise, don't you, that you'll be shot if you're caught?'

He thought this was a great joke. Three hours later he came back on his motor-bike (not, incidentally, the ideal vehicle for a man in a cas

Piet van Osch

sock), and reported everything clear as far west as the Bokstel road on a front of seven miles. He had used one litre of his own petrol. Could we replace so much? We filled his tank, and he overwhelmed us with gratitude.

At 1830 hours we were switched northwards in the general direction of 's Hertogenbosch and ordered to move in troop-carrying vehicles to a point two-and-a-half kilometres south of Den Dungen, in readiness to take over there on the morning of the 25th from the Derby Yeomanry. The Boche went in the night, and next day we entered Den Dungen without difficulty. The road was clear right up to the Zuid Willems Vaart, where the bridge was found blown.

Since this chapter is already untidy, and since no real action is due for several days yet, this is a convenient place to tell another story. Den Dungen was the town where Peter had a personal triumph.

His name was Piet van Osch, and he came to us as an interpreter when we first arrived near Olland. He was eighteen years old, a sturdy youngster, stocky and broad in the shoulder, with a round face and by far the broadest grin in the Battalion. This grin became almost painful to watch when we rigged him out in battledress and a bonnet: his only regret was that Schijndel, his village, was five kilometres behind the German lines and his friends couldn't see him. The Intelligence Section took him unto its bosom, protected him from the worst buffetings of Army life, expanded its Dutch vocabulary from three words to six, and put on airs. They were round the fire till all hours of the night, with their heads together and Peter in their midst, thick as thieves. Soon he was working with Hughie McLeod, out questioning the farmers who still worked on the fringes of No Man's Land.

We promised him that the moment Schijndel was free he would be taken to see his people. Five kilometres was not a great distance: he could even see the steeple from the O.P. He used to tell us of the hospitality we should receive there, and how glad his father would be to see us.

'He will be two feet higher when he sees my uniform,' he used to say. 'You must all come. It will be a great day in my village.'

When we reached De Slophoose, we knew Schijndel must be free.

'Come on, Peter,' said Sergeant McLeod, 'hop on the pillion and we'll see this village of yours.'

They returned three hours later. Hughie was looking grim. Peter was pink, and his eyes were shining.

'It was hellish,' said Hughie, 'the whole place was flat. Ay, our artillery. His folk aren't hurt, but ... och, they're in a cellar with half a roof to it. Their house is gone. They've lost everything.'

'It was necessary,' said Peter, almost defensively.

Hughie looked bleakly at the ground. 'Flat it was, absolutely flat. The house and everything.'

Nobody knew what to say.

'His mother wasn't for letting him back,' said Hughie, 'but his father says: "Peter, what do you want to do?" and Peter says: "I want to go with them, father," and the old man says: "That is good. I am proud." So he came back with me.'

'There were only fifty Germans in the village,' said Peter wistfully. 'It was much damage for fifty Germans. But it was necessary. I say to you, it was necessary.'

That was why the Intelligence Section was so pleased about what happened when we went into Den Dungen. The people there were celebrating their liberty as noisily as they knew how. The streets were crowded and orange streamers and banners were everywhere; but the biggest crowd was crammed into the square opposite the Townhouse, cheering Allied pilots and paratroopers who had been kept in hiding until that morning and were now smiling self-consciously from the Townhouse balcony. When we were still a hundred yards from this place, someone in the crowd suddenly saw a known face among the khaki, shouted: 'Piet! Piet van Osch!' and before young Peter knew what had happened to himself he was being carried shoulder-high through the square and up on to the balcony, where he stood, pink with emotion and far beyond speech, while the crowd cheered its head off. It is not known how many feet higher his father was that night.

We stayed the night in Den Dungen, where the people could not do enough for us and the celebrations extended far into the morning. Inevitably it was too good to last, and on the following evening, the 26th, we had our sense of proportion restored by marching to the woods south of the Tilburg road near Vught and spending the night there, after an uneasy afternoon in an assembly area four kilometres west of St. Michielsgestel. The Germans were falling back all along the line but had been holding on to Vught, which was a road centre whose loss would sever all communication westwards from 's Hertogenbosch. The 5th Camerons were ahead of us and put in an attack which cut the Vught/Tilburg road during the evening. They met some resistance but soon dealt with it, so that we, who were waiting in reserve, were not called upon to fight. Next day we left at 1400 hours to take over Udenhout from the 7th Armoured Division, far to the west. It seemed they were going to forge ahead. When we arrived two hours later we discovered that the 7th Armoured were so far from forging on anywhere that we had to go outside the town to find billets. The advance to Tilburg was moving slowly, thanks to waterlogged fields and flat polder country which made the defence of the roads relatively easy for the enemy. They were falling back, but they were still doing it in their own time. We moved into positions astride the road at Schoorstraat, two thousand yards north-west of Udenhout.

Next morning four patrols were sent out northwards to examine the woods which lay between us and the Afwaterings Canal, but before they had gone more than a thousand yards all four were fired on from widely spaced points along the edge of the woods between De Knijperij and De Rustende Jager. Similar reports came in from the 2nd Seaforth on our left, so our patrolling programme was cancelled and a full-scale Brigade attack was laid on. The number of enemy in the woods was not thought to be great, and it was reckoned that one really good fright would send them scuttling back over the canal, leaving our Corps with a firm flank when it continued its advance westwards.

Our orders were to capture the road junction four hundred yards north of Molenstraat and the intersection of three tracks four hundred yards farther north still ("D" Company); and the junction where the main road north from Schoorstraat met the edge of the wood ("A" Company). Exploitation ("C" Company) was to be as far east as Brand, more than two thousand yards away along the edge of the wood. The 2nd Seaforth had a similar task on our left. H-hour was 1530 hours. The companies went in under a barrage that would have done justice to a whole division and so demoralised the Boche that, although they were still in their trenches when our men arrived, they did not offer serious resistance. Fifteen regiments of artillery, two battalions of infantry, and two squadrons of the East Riding Yeomanry tanks, all concentrated on a front of about a mile, were enough to make any German think twice and certainly were not conducive to a last-man stand. There was some shooting but no shelling from their side, and before dark the position was consolidated. Long after that, however, Hamish Paterson was still leading "C" Company unopposed to Brand. We had captured two 75mm. anti-tank guns and eighty men. Our own losses were two men slightly wounded, and Company Sergeant Major Doull who had been killed on patrol during the morning.

Next day was October 29, the seventh day of our curious, near-bloodless advance. In spite of the ground we had covered, our frequent approaches to the enemy, and the attack of the previous night, not one shell had landed in our area. On this day the same state of affairs continued. There was a mild brush with some Germans who had attacked and wounded two overambitious scroungers from "C" Company beyond Brand; but otherwise there was peace. Patrols sent out across the sand-dunes in the direction of the canal reported nothing.

On the 30th we moved north-west to Waalwijk on the edge of the Maas. There were no Germans there and, so far as we could see, no further place for us to advance to. A few shells came sailing over the river, but we were prepared to settle down and make ourselves comfortable. The advance was over. We had cleared up to the Maas and could afford to rest for a little.

It was a neat village, very clean, sitting strung-out along the top of a dyke. Its single cobbled street was filled with people who wanted only to make us comfortable. It was undamaged. Here, we thought, was the kind of Dutch village we used to read about in books, built among the polders and the windmills, perched high to keep its feet dry. We looked forward to a long stay; but of course that was fatal. On November 1 we were on the move again, concentrating for a crossing of the Afwaterings Canal.

II

The main advance had gone well and the Germans were almost cleared from south-west Holland. The British push westwards was linking with the Canadian thrust northwards from Antwerp and the Scheldt and it was obviously only a matter of time before that corner of the country was free. There was, however, an untidiness on our own immediate front. The High Command was most anxious that we should be established cleanly on the Maas once and for all, so that when our attention was turned to Germany proper we should have the river between us and any diversionary attack which might brew up from north Holland. The Germans, naturally, were equally eager to retain some sort of bridgehead south of the river, and this they had managed to do behind the Afwaterings Canal. The canal was not a big one (it was about thirty yards wide) but all the bridges were blown and it was a continuous obstacle. It left the Maas near 's Hertogenbosch, ran south, then west, then north again, and rejoined the Maas near Waalwijk, thus forming an island six miles long and four miles wide. The Germans were holding it in unknown strength, but some guesses put the number of battalions on it as high as six.

While the planning was going on we moved back near Udenhout to a village called, of all things, Winkel; while "A" Company was sent to the canal bank where we intended to cross, near the more easterly of the two blown bridges south of Drunen. Their orders were to lie low and simply see that our future assembly area remained clear of the enemy. We attacked on the 4th, and in the intervening three days our snipers got to work on the enemy morale. They killed nine Germans in two days, five of whom were dead drunk on looted schnapps.

Now let us consider the ground. The Afwaterings Canal, as has already been pointed out was approximately thirty yards wide. It ran behind high dykes, the tops of which were ninety yards apart. Only from vantage points far to the rear could either side see over them at all, and then, naturally, only the distant ground on the far side. Either the Germans or ourselves could have hidden a division close under the lee of our dykes without the other knowing anything about it. This fact was to be our chief consideration when we came to make our plan.

The canal ran east and west here, and was absolutely straight. Any German allowed to remain on top of or inside the dyke would be able to fire down the whole length of it. All Germans must somehow be encouraged to leave.

Two thousand yards to the north, on the German side, a road ran parallel to the canal; and on this road was the town of Drunen, the objective of the 5th Camerons. Also on the road, and a thousand yards east of Drunen, was Groenwoud, our objective. The country was dead flat, and on our front there were only two other landmarks – the ten-foot-high Drunensche Dyke midway between the canal and the road and parallel to both, and the small village of Sempke which lay roughly midway between the dyke and the road. The only conclusion to be drawn from this was that the main German defences might be based on either the road or the Drunensche Dyke.

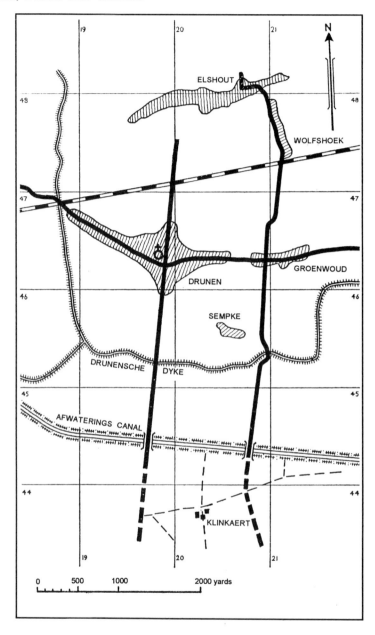

The blown bridge on our front had served Groenwoud, and a road ran due north from it to the village. All our Battalion crossings were made between this bridge and a point five hundred yards west of it.

So there was the problem – first, the canal; second, the Drunensche Dyke; third, Groenwoud, with Sempke to be tidied up on the way.

This was our first assault crossing, and the planning for it went on day and night. Life was one long conference. Who would supply the assault boats; who would dump them, and where; who would carry them to the canal; who would ferry them? Who would supply, erect, and operate the block-and-tackle which would haul the anti-tank guns up the dyke and down the other side to the rafts? How soon would the bridges be built? How would we eat until they were built? How soon could the tanks cross ? As we should have only rafts at first, and as rafting was a slow job, which vehicles would be taken over and which left behind? In what order would they be taken? How would casualties be evacuated?

As the answers to all these questions and many more filled five closely-typed foolscap pages in the Battalion Operation Order, no more than a summary of them can be given here.* In broad outline, the plan was for 153 Brigade to attack on our right and capture the villages of Neeuwkuik, Vlijmen, and Haarsteeg, starting their assault forty minutes after we had crossed. At 's Hertogenbosch, miles away at the east end of the canal, 154 Brigade was to stage a diversionary attack; and 131 Brigade was to do likewise at the west end of the canal near Waalwijk. The Camerons and ourselves were to cross simultaneously in the centre, form a bridgehead, and take Drunen and Groenwoud. Second Seaforth would then pass through and take Wolfshoek and Elshout a mile to the north.

The critical part of the operation, so far as we were concerned, was the actual crossing of the canal; and the technique which was evolved for it was so successful that we never varied it much afterwards. It was, simply, to make life impossible for any German on the opposite bank. The tanks and crocodiles could not cross until the heavy bridges had been erected, but there was nothing to prevent them shooting from the near bank. Every twenty-five yards along the front, a tank or a crocodile lay hidden behind the dyke. The barrage was to open up, blanket everything beyond the canal except the immediate bank; and then the tanks were to charge up the dyke, balance on top, and blast the Germans out of the ground at ninety yards' range. The idea appealed to us. It seemed to us, rightly as it happened, that anyone who had just met a crocodile face to face would not be there to meet us when we crossed.

H-hour was 1645 hours on November 4; and the orders were headed "Operation Guy Fawkes," presumably just to confuse the enemy. During the previous night the assault boats, collapsible canvas affairs capable of carrying sixteen men each, had been brought up by lorry under cover of darkness and dumped by "A" Company's H.Q. at Klinkkaert. From there they had been manhandled five hundred yards down to the canal. The men were lying behind the dyke, ready to cross.

We lay in the usual nervous silence, waiting for the drumfire of the guns to break out behind us. I remember a Jock lying in the ditch beside me. He was biting his lip, and his hands were shaking. Then the first shells came over, and somehow the strain was broken: he snapped the chin-strap of his helmet into place, gave me a quick grin, and jerked his head towards the pandemonium on the German side of the canal. 'Just the job!' he said. The barrage was tremendous; and, since very close support was needed, most of it seemed to be landing almost on top of us. Instead of the usual whine of our shells passing overhead, there was a deep 'whuzz,' short and clipped, as they dived for the ground two hundred yards ahead. The gunners were firing both smoke and high explosive. The air seemed to be filled

* This Operation Order is reproduced in full in Appendix III, partly for its military interest, but mainly because it may demonstrate to the general reader how much planning had to be done behind the scenes before even a small battalion attack could be considered watertight.

with shells. The tanks charged, and all along the crest of the dyke was noise, and great orange jets of flame. The winter reeds beside the canal caught fire. A little pumping station stood a few rounds of armour-piercing and then went up in smoke. The whole of the far bank as far as the eye could see was being scorched and hammered. Then "B" and "D" Companies struggled over the home dyke, first heads, then men, then boats, and swarmed down to the water. The straight, receding lines of the canal disappeared into clouds of oily black smoke; and the water was crawling with boats, going and coming and going again. Two hundred men were there, each in his ordained place, little black jerky figures against the smooth grey of the canal. The barrage lifted. They were over without a casualty in seven minutes flat.

The defenders of the German dyke – those that were left of them – were running back across the open fields. Our men lay down and picked them off as they ran.

So far, so good. The next objective was the Drunensche Dyke, a thousand yards away. "B" and "D" Companies continued, "B" aiming for the area where the road to Groenwoud cut the Dyke, and "D" to link up with the Camerons where the Drunen road cut it. When they were firm, "C" passed through and took Sempke. There might have been trouble here, because it soon became evident that the Germans had intended the Drunensche Dyke to be their main defence line; but they had been badly shaken by the barrage, and "B" Company caught a whole platoon of them in enfilade, crouching in the lee of the Dyke and still peering anxiously across the fields to the canal. It was a sitting target. Pat Grant's platoon set up a bren gun very carefully, and let drive into the middle of them. The few survivors fled, leaving a pile of dead and wounded behind them. Phase Three of the attack, the advance to Groenwoud, turned out to be a canter with "B" Company under David Blair going up the road like scalded cats in the lead. We were unmolested, and found the village empty when we arrived there at 2200 hours. We had taken eighty prisoners for the loss of three men slightly wounded, and the only part of the Battalion to be shelled seriously had been Battalion H.Q. – a very reasonable battle, according to the rifle companies.

"A" Company, having supplied most of the ferrymen, was now protecting the Sappers while they built the bridges. These were not expected to be complete until 0700 hours next morning, which meant that we should have neither blankets nor hot food until then; but the Germans solved half this problem for us by failing to keep their "B" Echelon in the picture. At midnight, unaware that we were in residence or that they were about to qualify for the manna-and-quail class, a German regimental quarter-master sergeant and one of his henchmen drove into the village with the company mail, the laundry, two enormous cans of hot soup, hot-boxes full of rissoles and sausages, and baskets of fresh farm butter, cigarettes, and cigars. We fed two hundred men on the soup alone, while the Germans looked disconsolately on.

When daylight came, the enemy had pulled back over the Maas and blown their bridges behind them. In addition to our prisoners, the final count included twelve dead and twenty wounded, one 20mm. A.A. gun, two 81mm. mortars, seven bazookas, ten spandaus and (from a weapon-pit on the Drunensche Dyke) one medieval crossbow. Once again we hoped for a rest, and once again we were disappointed. On the afternoon of the 5th we were on our way back to Winkel, and on the 7th began our long trek to take part in a completely new operation.

THE VENLO PUSH

(previous page) Kangeroos and Tanks in South-West Holland.

(below) A game of Quoits during a lull near Olland.

CHAPTER SIXTEEN

The Venlo Push

I

THE RIVER MEUSE flows north through Belgium, changes its name to Maas as it crosses the Dutch frontier, and continues on until it reaches a point a few miles south of Nijmegen. There it swings to the left and flows west to the sea. The original corridor held by us before south-west Holland was cleared actually crossed the Maas on a narrow front and included Nijmegen; but neither to the west nor to the east had we closed up to the river. To do that we had to push in two directions. As the previous chapter tells, the first of these tasks had been completed and we now held the river throughout its east-west course; but this had been done at some cost to the other flank. The Germans had always held a bridgehead there, and once our assault to the west was fairly launched and our backs were turned, they put in an offensive from the general direction of Venlo and Roermond, aimed at Eindhoven. This attack had been held before serious damage was done; but the Germans had overrun so large an area that any further attacks from that direction must inevitably threaten Eindhoven, through which nearly all the supplies for the Army in Holland passed. Our next job was to push them back across the Maas on this front as well.

We arrived in Ospel, fourteen miles south-east of Eindhoven, at 0400 hours on November 8, a time of day when no village looks its best even if it has not been shelled sideways beforehand. It was a sad village. The Americans had taken it, dropping a few shells in the process, when they first came to Holland. The Germans had retaken it, dropping a few more shells, while we were at Udenhout. Then the Americans had pushed them out again, with the assistance of several regiments of artillery, and what was left of the place the Americans now occupied. They told dismal stories of mines, and particularly of schumines. When they had gone and daylight came, we liked it even less than we had done in the dark. No house was undamaged. It was a muddy, grubby little hole full of slates, and broken glass, and tattered curtains, with a badly chipped church at the crossroads and a number of outlying farms which, though for the most part undamaged, lay in countryside so flat and waterlogged that they were every bit as depressing as the village itself. A thin drizzle fell over everything, and the mud on the road was ankle-deep.

A thousand yards south of the village, the Nederwert Canal (on some maps called the Canal du Nord) ran across our front; and as we were to be in Ospel for only a day and a half and would have to cross the canal when we returned there after a short rest, patrols were sent out by all companies that evening to investigate it. One was fired on, and a man was wounded. Next morning at 0600 hours patrols went out again, so that when we were relieved in the afternoon by the 7th Black Watch and moved back a few miles to Zomeren, we had a fair idea of the task which lay ahead of us.

The canal was much narrower than our previous one, not more than fifteen yards across; but unlike the Afwaterings it had no convenient dyke to cover our approach. In fact, the whole area lacked cover (the Division seemed to be trying to huddle into two or three villages and push all its vehicles down the few muddy tracks where concealment was possible) and the last four hundred yards to the canal were devoid of cover of any kind. The country was flat as a billiard table as far as the horizon in every direction. Along the far bank of the canal ran a strip of trees where signs of enemy movement had been seen, and beyond that again were a few woods. We had not yet had our orders, but we expected that when the attack came we should be first across.

We remained in Zomeren from the evening of November 9 until the morning of November 14, when we returned to Ospel and lay up in readiness for the attack.

As will be seen from the map, two canals intersected near Ospel – the Nederwert, running north-east and south-west; and the Bois le Duc, running north-west and south-east. The more easterly arms of both these canals joined the Maas twelve miles away, and everything inside the triangle thus formed was in German hands.

The plan was for the 53rd Division to attack due east across the Bois le Duc and for the Highland Division to attack due south across the Nederwert. Once across, we also were to swing east, so that the two divisions would advance side by side, we to Venlo and they to Roermond. In reserve behind us would be the 49th Division. Our own part in this was to be the assault crossing, the Camerons again going over simultaneously on our left.

The technique which had been employed so successfully on the Afwaterings crossing was adapted to suit the new circumstances. The enemy, mostly young paratroopers, were known to have all their goods in the shop window, strung out along the far bank of the canal without much behind them; and once again the idea was to blanket the bank, using tanks and crocodiles. The variations were dictated by the ground. We were forced through lack of cover to lie four hundred yards back from the canal; but this was not altogether a bad thing, as it allowed our artillery to fire directly on to the bank without running the risk of hitting us. The artillery would therefore plaster the bank with high explosive, then change to smoke, and under cover of the smoke the tanks and crocodiles would advance ahead of the infantry, take up their positions on the home bank, and cover us while we crossed.

The second variation also depended on the open four-hundred-yard stretch. On the previous crossing we had been able to carry the assault boats down to the canal at leisure, covered by the dyke. Here some quicker means would have to be found. Many methods were discussed, and in the end it was decided to try three different ones, one for each of the assaulting companies. "B" Company was to carry its boats, assembled and ready for action, on bren carriers. "A" was to pile its boats on to sledges, which would be towed by the tanks. "C" was to travel in buffaloes.

On the night before the Afwaterings crossing, Brigadier Cassels had said: 'I've just been promised a new beast called a buffalo. I haven't seen one, and I don't know how it works, but I gather it's an amphibious tank affair. You let down a door, and drive in a bren carrier, or a truck, or a couple of anti-tank guns, and it whistles them across in no time. Or so they say. We're taking no chances, so the rafts we've already laid on will stand. I'm just warning you that your vehicles and guns *may* get across much faster than you think.'

The buffaloes on that occasion had been a great success: in spite of the steep dykes they had crossed the canal many times and had saved hours of tedious rafting. It seemed to Colonel Walford that if they could carry vehicles they could carry men. "C" Company would embark behind cover, waddle across the four hundred yards of open fields under the smokescreen, cross, and be ready for action on the far bank. Each buffalo was capable of carrying twenty fully equipped men.

We crossed on a seven-hundred-yard front, with our right flank on the road running south from Waatskamp, and our left where a small track to the east met the canal bank. H-hour was 1600 hours on November 14. It was a very big barrage. Even the super-heavies were firing in it. One moment the canal bank was a peaceful line of trees and a few houses, with the decks of some barges just showing below them: the next it erupted. Fountains of earth and stones and branches shot into the air, and the fumes rose in clouds. Then the smoke canisters went over. The bank disappeared. The buffaloes, huge ungainly brutes like armoured barges with tracks, came sailing down the road with "C" Company aboard; then the tanks with the sledges; then the carriers. "A" and "B" Companies spread out and began to advance across the fields. After a few minutes the tanks opened up, invisible now in the smoke. The evening was calm and misty and everything was in grey silhouette. The din was terrific, with that deep grumbling from the heavies

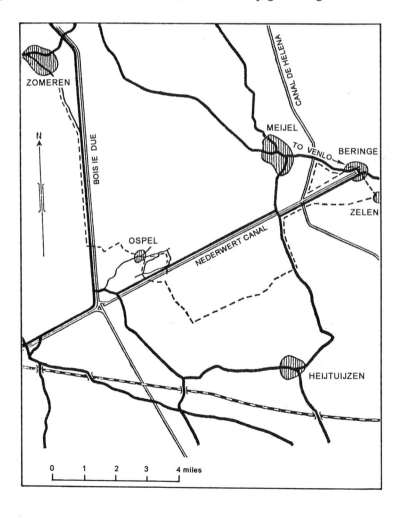

which we had not heard since St. Honorine; but in spite of the noise it was possible to realise that it was a still evening, that a few miles away the smoke from cottage chimneys must be climbing straight into the sky. Then in the heart of the greyest grey, where the smoke hung among the trees along the bank, great orange arcs of flame went curving through the air. Soon the bushes were alight, and the half-sunk barges. The jets of flame still sailed through the smoke.

Things were happening down there in the smoke which had not appeared in the plan. True, the buffaloes were all they claimed to be and more: they crossed the canal without a hitch and decanted "C" Company on the far side in record time. But "A" had not been so fortunate. Some of the tow-ropes attached to the sledges had broken, and in the smoke and confusion other sledges had been dropped in the wrong places, so that only one-third of their boats arrived on the bank. The boats had to make many extra trips and the crossing took longer than had been expected. "B" Company were also having a difficult passage. They arrived at the canal according to plan, only to find that the enemy had blown a lock-gate somewhere and lowered the level of the water. Where they had expected to float, they found yards of thick black mud. Men who tried to wade sank in to their waists and stuck so hopelessly that they had to be pulled out with ropes. However, some fast and accurate work was done, and inside ten minutes a bridge of boats had been made from bank to bank, across which the company scrambled. Then some of the tanks arrived late and began firing blindly through the smoke, scattering our men and wounding some. Fortunately they were soon stopped; and, as the enemy had fled, there were no more casualties for the moment. The Boche had been so overwhelmed by the artillery and the crocs that we hardly fired a shot, and all the assault companies were on their objectives a thousand yards south of the canal by 1800 hours. "D" Company had been waiting in reserve on our left flank, and they now crossed. "A" were mortared while they were exploiting and had a few casualties; and some shells from 153 Brigade, attacking on our right across the Bois le Duc, shook "B". Apart from that it was an uneventful evening. We took thirty-five prisoners. Our casualties were one killed and fifteen wounded, including O.C. "B" Company, who was slightly burned but managed to carry on. The chief lesson we learned was that buffaloes were ideal for an assault crossing, that carrier-borne boats were adequate if buffaloes were not available, and that sledges, despite successful tests we had carried out beforehand, could not be relied upon under battle conditions.

Next morning we wheeled left and advanced unopposed for two days towards the Uitwaterings Canal; and there the Germans seemed disposed to make another stand. We shall remember that canal with singular lack of affection. The local people called it the Zig, though it was Uitwaterings on the map. Whatever its name it was a filthy little ditch and it lay in deplorable country. We had advanced towards it with the growing hope that the Germans had pulled out for good; but when we crossed the main road a mile short of the Uitwaterings and emerged from the woods on the far side, Spandau Pete opened up and we had to halt. We established ourselves along the line of the road three kilometres south of the Nederwert, pushed "D" Company forward to the fringe of the woods to keep an eye on the Boche, and waited for a Brigade attack to be jacked up. While we waited, the rain came down.

We had arrived on the evening of November 16. On the 17th the Camerons, who were on our left where the Uitwaterings and the Nederwert canals intersected, crossed and made a bridgehead. They had a very bad time. The Germans seemed to have plenty of artillery, and between bouts of heavy shelling they put in several counter-attacks supported by self-propelled guns. The Camerons held on.

The weather grew steadily worse as the day advanced, but we still had sufficient judgment left to hope that we should attack. The canal was the last barrier before Venlo. By this time the 49th Division, full of martial zeal and as yet taking no part in the proceedings, were breathing down our necks and flourishing a four-page operation order for the crossing; and we knew what that meant. They would cross the canal, advance for a day or two, and then say they were tired. The only people they could possibly say it to would be ourselves, and we had no desire to tackle Venlo after a two-day rest. How much better, we reasoned, to go out on this utterly bloody night, cross the canal, and then say with truth that we were exhausted. Forty-nine Division would then have to take Venlo. This was possibly not a very charitable outlook, but then it was not very charitable weather, and we had been leading for three days.

By night, the weather was appalling and we began to modify this argument. We were still anxious to attack, but we felt that the best time for it would be on the following day when perhaps the rain should have eased a little. "D" Company in the woods were being shelled and were unable to leave slit-trenches which were knee-deep in water. They had been there since dawn and were soaked through and through; and, as if that were not enough, they ran into heavy mortaring when they withdrew at dusk. A night's rest would do them no harm, and the remainder of us were not eager to leave the houses where we had sheltered during the day. The rain was pouring down and the wind was rising. We cheered up when a warning order for a dawn attack arrived, but close on its heels came the counter-order. 153 Brigade were going to make an assault crossing of the canal to the south of us that night, and we and the 2nd Seaforth were to pass through the Camerons and enlarge their bridgehead. We would start at midnight.

This crossing differed from our previous ones in every way. First, it was to be silent, without artillery preparation. Second, our objective (the Zelen area) was two-and-a-half miles beyond the canal in a straight line, and the course we were going to follow was by no means a straight line. Third, we knew nothing whatsoever about the enemy beyond the fact that the counter-attacks on the Camerons had stopped.

The 2nd Seaforth were to precede us and take up positions on our left, close to the Nederwert. It was hoped that we should not so much fight for ground as steal it, slip through the enemy in the dark, dig, and by dawn be in position miles beyond anywhere we had the least right to be. It would be an expensive plan if we bumped into the enemy in force, but it had a good chance of success.

The route which was chosen after long study of the air photographs (the map was hopelessly inaccurate) ran to the canal up a track the Camerons had made and then struck out across open fields for a thousand yards until another track was reached which would take us to our objective; and as six hundred men marching in the dark will inevitably wander to the four points of the compass if their route is not clearly marked, the Intelligence Section led the column across the middle section weighed down under drums of white tape. However, that is getting a little ahead of the story. The Cameron track comes first.

Our start-line was on the main Heijthuijzen/Meijel road one kilometre south of the Nederwert. We crossed it at 0020 hours on November 18 and continued north up the road until we reached the track, which began fifty yards south of the Nederwert and ran parallel to it. "Track" is a courtesy title. On the previous day it had been a green and rather boggy field. Since then it had been traversed by many tanks and self-propelled guns, bren carriers, trucks, and men; and throughout its length of nearly a mile it was a continuous quagmire which reached half-way to the knee. The mud had been whipped to the consistency of cream. The ruts were invisible beneath it, because it flowed back after each vehicle had passed and covered all clues to their whereabouts. Through this morass we floundered, speechless, wondering what state we should be in if we were shelled and had to lie down. We were so intent on this that few of us noticed that the rain had almost stopped.

We came to a bridge which had been erected during the afternoon and crossed the canal. It was little more than a big drain. Ahead of us was darkness. We took out our compasses and set off, the whole Battalion in one long straggling file. No one had shot at us so far, there had been no shelling, and the rain had definitely stopped. We began to feel more cheerful.

The white tape was wound on to cable-drums, and a carrying harness had been devised which allowed a man to strap four hundred yards to his back and unreel it without having to use his hands. Refills were carried by other members of the taping party. Twelve hundred yards of tape had been laid and an evil-smelling bog crossed before we reached the second track, which ran due east and gradually diverged from the Nederwert. So far we had met nothing. The wind had dropped and it was now a still, gloomy night disturbed only by the shells which the 15th Scottish Division, doubtless with the best intentions, were dropping perilously close to us from the other side of the Nederwert. A few isolated farms lay along our track before we reached Zelen, and the Battalion halted while 9 Platoon (Lieutenant Roy Jones) went forward to investigate. It would be more accurate to say that the Battalion, less Corporal Galleitch, halted; because Galleitch, having laid all his tape and having nothing to do but wander along with the leading section, was dreaming happily of his native Thurso when the order to halt was passed down the line. He walked straight on unnoticed while Roy Jones was issuing orders to his platoon.

'I was at the front and never noticed the others stopping,' he said. 'After a while I was passing a house, and somebody at the side of the road said something – but, och, I paid no attention. You know how it is when you have been on the go for a long time. I was half asleep. Then the voice said something again, much louder, and it was talking in German, and it was talking to me. I looked round, and there was no Battalion at my back. Well, I'll tell you what I did. There was a big heap of turnips at the roadside, and I just took a running dive into the middle of them. Then the shooting started, and I couldn't shoot back because I could hear our own fellows joining in and I couldn't see where they were. So I just lay in my turnips until the show was over. It was quite interesting.'

There were thirteen Germans in the farm, and we wounded one and captured five. We had no further trouble, and were digging in around Zelen by 0500 hours. Our sudden advance had taken the enemy completely by surprise, and the sixteen prisoners taken by our patrols later in the morning were nearly all asleep, unaware that we had arrived. One hour after first light, however, information did get back to the German artillery, and for the rest of the day the whole of our area and that of the 2nd Seaforth on our left was persistently shelled. We had two men killed. Still, it had been a cheap advance. We had gained all our objectives, and the Germans had been so alarmed at finding a brigade on their doorstep when daylight came that their infantry pulled out as fast as they could, hastened on their way by Humphrey's Boys and our carriers, which advanced and shot them up as they made off.

This relatively unexciting night's work has always struck me as being significant. It could not have happened in any other war. Each platoon set off that night knowing exactly where it was going to dig in at the end of the journey; and this was only possible because we had good air photographs. Any commander knows the danger of choosing positions from the map – dawn is apt to disclose a very different landscape from the one imagined – but this danger is greatly reduced by good air cover. Both the 2nd Seaforth and ourselves followed an extremely tortuous route to positions which were invisible in the darkness and deep in enemy territory, yet we were able to do so knowing that when dawn came we should not be at a disadvantage. We could never have done it from the map.

153 Brigade had also crossed successfully during the night, and in the afternoon 154 Brigade passed through us in kangaroos. The battle faded away in the distance. We prepared for our long-promised rest, but we had still one small job to do – the clearing of the triangle of ground bounded by the Beringe/Meijel road and the Helena and Nederwert canals. "B" and "C" Companies under Major Blair were loaded into kangaroos (a great improvement on marching, they said), did a grand tour of the area without meeting opposition, and pronounced it clear by noon. By 1600 hours we were driving west for Leveroij, out for a rest. 49 Division was last seen heading despondently for Venlo.

II

As we were not called upon to take any further part in the offensive, which ended successfully a few days later, this should by rights be the end of the chapter. However, there followed a period of our history which is not long enough to warrant a chapter of its own, but which lingers so pleasantly in our memories that it must be recorded.

Until November 24 we stayed at Leveroij, a place of mud, discomfort, and incessant rain; and then moved north to relieve the American 101 Airborne Division in the Nijmegen Salient. There was widespread despondency when we heard of this: we had seen Nijmegen in far too many headlines on the front pages of newspapers, and "Salient," moreover, had an ominously businesslike sound about it. Nor was the gloom much mitigated by a movement order which announced an 0330 hours reveille on the 24th.

The morning was black, the mud deep, and the language much as might be expected. The journey was uneventful except for the satisfaction of being "over de Maas" at last after our various fighting approaches to it; and by 1400 hours we had reached Nijmegen, in which reputed hell-hole women were trundling perambulators round the shops and behaving as if it were an ordinary Dutch town, as indeed it was. It was seldom shelled, they said. We debussed, and marched over the big bridge to our new area at Heteren, twelve miles away across the island which lay between the Leck and the Waal. We were still unhindered by the Boche. We decided, however, that our forebodings had not been entirely groundless, because a rumour now filtered round that our area was overlooked by the enemy so completely that no movement was possible during daylight. We arrived long after dark and asked the Americans how many casualties they had had so far. They said five in the past six weeks. Grudgingly, for we dearly loved our little grouse, we began to admit that perhaps this was not such a bad place after all.

We saw our billets, and by midnight the word 'cushy' was being freely bandied about.

To appreciate fully why the island was the Soldier's Dream of Home, one must know the things which normally made a soldier's life a burden to him. They were (a) sleeping in doovers in mid-winter; (b) rations; (c) parades; (d) being shot at; and (e) the narrow-minded belief, obstinately held by civilians, that if a man owned a hen he also owned the eggs.

Examining these in turn, we find that (a) every platoon had a furnished house; (b) the Americans, after the unaccountable manner of Americans, had left vast quantities of rations behind them, including even chocolate; (c) as the Boche could see all we did during the day, few parades could be held; (d) shelling was negligible; and (e) the civilians had gone but their hens remained.

Of course there was a catch in it. The rivers were in flood and the island was below their level: the Boche were liable at any time to blow the dyke and flood us out, for the salient stretched across the middle of the island and both extremities were in German hands. However, they had failed to do this for at least six weeks and there seemed no reason to suppose they should do it during the period of our stay, which was to be a month. It even relieved our consciences in the matter of hens as distinct from eggs: a roast chicken would swim no more badly than a live one, and some day the dyke must go.

The Germans were only a thousand yards away across the Leck, but both sides seemed to realise that little could be done until the floods abated, and only a few shells landed in our area each day. The sentries stood their stag on the big Leck dyke while the others sat in armchairs, put their feet up on the stove, and saw that the American coffee kept warm. There were such things as toast, and the odd egg; and surprising numbers of pigs and fowls flung themselves to their deaths beneath the tracks of passing carriers. We grew sleek; and the odour of rich cooked meats was heavy on the air. From time to time we balanced great zinc tubs on the stoves and brewed ourselves baths. The gin ration arrived.

There were minor difficulties, though none sufficiently serious to disturb us. The Carrier Platoon had occasionally to go out at night and make tracks in the open fields where the Germans would see them – part of a plan to delude them into thinking a big assault was being built up. One fairly heavy mortar stonk came down on "B" Company. An N.C.O.'s training cadre (surely the first ever to be held within two kilometres of the enemy) was started, and a little training was expected of the rest of us. Then there was the Great Egg Crisis, when every hen in the Battalion H.Q. and "S" Company areas disappeared. At first it was thought that, in revolt at being prodded off their nests every five minutes by rapacious soldiers seeking eggs, they had migrated to a more peaceful place where a hen might lay in decency and comfort. However, it was discovered that the snipers had captured the lot, locked them in a bedroom, and were fattening them up for Christmas on a diet of corn and hot potatoes.

But on the whole our life was well ordered and without friction. The water rose in the ditches and the fields were heavy with it, for there were no pumps to lead it to the river. It was a dead land, flat and deserted; a shallow pan between the two rivers, slowly filling as the rain fell but as yet with the rim intact. It would take a month, we calculated, a whole beautiful month for the rain water to reach the level of the roads, and two for it to cover them. Beyond the rim the Leck and the Waal were in full spate and five feet above the level of the island.

Sometime in the early hours of December 2 the Germans blew the dyke some miles east of us. By 0200 hours the 49th Division on our right were evacuating.

We had all read the details of Operation Noah, which came into force when the dykes were breached. We knew that escape routes had been recced and that ferries were waiting to carry us over the Waal. We knew the water was not due to reach us for many hours. Yet it seemed strange, when dawn came, to find the same flat fields around us unaltered: we had expected something much more Hollywood. We packed the trucks and waited. The morning wore on. The water in the ditches rose a few inches and flooded the road between us and "B" Echelon. We had tiffin and a last mug of coffee. Still nothing happened. At last, at 1400 hours, the vehicles were ordered to move. The troops marched out without so much as wetting their feet, congregated on the Waal dyke on the south edge of the island, and were ferried across to safety in a fleet of motor assault boats. The transport crossed the Nijmegen Bridge. Some battalions came out waist-deep, but they were the ones farther east. We had no difficulty.

There was a mystery connected with our escape from the island which has never been satisfactorily solved. All our "F" Echelon vehicles had to move in convoy for two miles in full view of the Germans perched on the high ground beyond the Leck, and at the time it seemed to us inconceivable that we should not be shelled. We were right under their noses, and we knew they had guns and mortars. The Nijmegen Bridge, too, was an obvious bottle-neck, and their guns were known to have it ranged.

We formed up behind some houses and set off one hundred yards apart at a steady ten miles an hour. We trailed slowly across the Boche front, turned south, and reached cover. Not a shell came over.

Ten miles south we hit the Waal dyke and followed the road along its crest, past the ferries which were already filling up with infantry. It was a damp, grey afternoon. The river was a mile wide, with factories sticking out of the flood water, and seemed much more than five feet above the island level. The current was running fast. Upstream a heavy smokescreen lay over the bridge to protect it from dive-bombers. We drew close, turned on to the main road, and crossed the bridge. It was as easy as that. There were no shells. By night we were billeted near 's Hertogenbosch.

Next day Mary of Arnhem was on the radio, telling us how the brave Germans had wiped out the British on the island. Those who were not drowned, she said, had been slaughtered by shellfire as they struggled across the bridge. Her story could easily have been true. Why it was not true we shall probably never know.

THE ARDENNES

(previous page)   British troops, wearing special winter clothing, take positions during the counter-offensive in the Ardennes. This is a publicity picture which depicts the conditions well. In practice, few of the soldiers were lucky enough to be dressed like this as camoflaged clothing could not be rushed to them in time. The Seaforths' khaki looked black against the snow.

(below   The Dutch stove or kachel. Some enterprising Jocks carried their own private kachels from place to place throughout the winter. (Note: In this official photograph the soldier's hat badge has been blanked out by the censor.)

CHAPTER SEVENTEEN

The Ardennes

I

EVERYTHING WAS prepared for Christmas, and our plans had been laid in the knowledge that little could happen to interfere with them. No army in history had ever mounted a major offensive in Holland in mid-winter, and all the minor tidying up had been completed. We could look forward to a simple job of line holding until the spring, while the supplies poured in through the newly opened port of Antwerp in readiness for the big push which would end the war. Instead of being hustled from one minor offensive to another, sleeping when we could and never knowing what the next hour would bring, we should get down to an orderly system of reliefs, with so many days in the line and so many days out of it. And for Christmas and Hogmanay we should be out. We had been promised that.

We had been lying back at Vught since we left the island, billeted in a large and ugly seminary, refitting and re-organising, showing off the pipes, drums, and Pipe-Major Asher's beard, and holding company dances at Tilburg. Then we had been warned that the floods had abated a little, and that we should be going back to the island. The Germans had crossed the Leck and were now in our old positions: we should be crossing to the south side of the island in the Andelst area, with "B" Echelon and "S" Company on the home bank of the river in or near Diest. As soon as this news came through a double reconnaissance was made, one half to Andelst and the other to fix up Christmas billets in a little village called Mill, near Grave, so that everything would be ready for us when we came out of the line. We moved up to Andelst on December 19 with all our arrangements made.

We relieved the 7th Black Watch at 1300 hours, and exactly one hour later (both the C.O. and the Brigadier having gone home on leave) a warning order arrived. We were to leave the island. Next morning we were to go to Mill, and we were not going there to eat turkeys. Our Christmas dinner was *kaput*. The Germans had launched a vast new offensive in the Ardennes.

The Ardennes breakthrough was no local irritant like the German push towards Eindhoven at the beginning of November, but a full-scale attempt to cut our lines of communication, capture Liége, Brussels, and Antwerp, and force us to evacuate the Low Countries. If it had succeeded, it would have wrecked our plans for the spring offensive and prolonged the war by many months. It had been planned with great skill, the troops and supplies moving up into position under cover of the winter fogs, and when the blow fell it tore a sixty-mile gap in the American line. The panzer columns struck seventy miles into Belgium, and within a few days over a hundred thousand Americans were dead, wounded, or taken prisoner. Then they were held. The first rush was over, but the German reserves (including a whole panzer corps) had not yet been committed and it was touch and go whether sufficient Allied divisions could be rushed into position to hold the shoulders of the bulge before the second phase of the offensive started.

There followed a long period of juggling with divisions, our Higher Command

197

constantly moving us about as the situation altered from day to day; and as this type of move (frequently carried out far away from the fighting) never makes any sense at all to the troops involved, the finer shades of meaning implied by our pilgrimage were lost on us. All we knew was that we were one of the few units in Army Reserve, and that in succession we had three main tasks. First we went to defend the Meuse crossings near Maastricht. Next we went to defend Liége. And last we went in to cut the Ardennes Salient in two and help in the final defeat of the offensive. If these three tasks are kept in mind, our wanderings may have just a grain of meaning in them.

On the 20th we set off. Colonel Walford had been recalled while passing through Brussels, and was on his way to join us. We left at 2150 hours, headed south, snatched a few hours' sleep at a place called Hechdel, and carried on to Kortruk-Dutsael, near Louvain in Belgium. We arrived there at 0115 hours on the 22nd and were told we should be there for some days; but recce parties were dug out of their beds six hours later and packed off towards Maastricht. They were given an area north-east of the town, in Aalbeek, and were joined there by the Battalion next day. The general situation at this time was that the enemy's main thrust had been checked well to the south of us; but it was expected that an attempt would be made to enlarge the original gap in the American line by pushing northwest towards Liége, the first stage being the seizing of the Meuse crossings. We were now on the German side of the river, prepared to defend the approaches to the crossings.

We arrived in Aalbeek on the 23rd and were still there on Christmas morning, hoping against hope for our Christmas dinner. An order to move was liable to arrive at any time, but the cooks were told to carry on. The Padre held a church service at 1030 hours, and dinner was due for 1230. At 1145 the advance party was ordered to move immediately. They gulped their roast pork, roast potatoes, and Christmas pudding in ten minutes flat, grabbed their bottles of beer, and fled to the trucks. By noon they were on their way again, and at 1500 hours the rest of the Battalion followed. By evening we were established in les Cours, south of Liége.

We were now in reserve under command of the 1st United States Army, with a number of possible tasks to perform if the Germans should break through. As none of these tasks ever had to be carried out, there is no point in going into details. On the 29th the plan was changed, and we went down into Liége to form a protective screen forward of the many bridges there, leaving "B" Echelon and "S" Company at les Cours. We remained there until January 5, 1945, and returned then to les Cours, where we remained until the 8th.

The two outstanding features of this period were Hogmanay and flying bombs. Most Hogmanays are memorable and this one was no exception; but on the whole I think the bombs will linger longer in our memories.

The flying bomb, as anyone knows who lived in the south of England during this period, was one of the more objectionable weapons of the war. In Holland it was the flieger, in France and Belgium the robot, in England the buzz-bomb, V1, or a word more descriptive but less printable. In any language it was a small radio-controlled aeroplane with a ton of high explosive in its nose and a crude-oil power unit on its tail. It was jet-propelled, made a vulgar noise, and the blast when it landed was shattering. Its most maddening characteristic was its inaccuracy. Any form of bombing is beastly, but even of the worst saturation raids it could be said that a military objective lay in the centre of the area. These bombs quite often could not hit a target the size of London. Liége was much closer to the launching-platforms and therefore more accuracy was possible; but there was still no suggestion of being able to hit any specific part of the town or even of being able to hit the town at all. It was a criminally indiscriminate weapon. More than any other its victims were women and children. So far as I know, not one of the many hundreds which landed in or around the town did any military damage whatever or delayed our preparations for a second, yet every day scores of civilians were maimed or killed. The harsh, vibrating roar would grow and grow until the window panes rattled; the ugly, stub-winged thing would come in sight; silence would fall abruptly as the engine cut out; and it would dive vertically into the earth. Then would come the explosion, red flame, and smoke; and more Belgians would be dead. Our positions were close to the bridges which must have been among the targets, yet our only casualty was one man with a broken ankle. The bomb which injured him hit a tram-car with twenty people in it, and demolished two houses as well. There was nothing to be done for the people in the tram – they just disappeared – but for the others the civilians dug. I remember passing the place next morning. They were still digging in a heap of rubble, scraping away the stones and mortar from something which hung from the tightly pressed mass. It was a woman's arm, with a ring on the third finger.

On December 28 snow fell and continued to fall at intervals, never entirely clearing, until February 2. The sun shone over a brilliant landscape, and though the nights were cold most of the men were in good billets, grouped round that excellent European institution, the *kachel*. ('Kachel' – pronounced 'kahul' – is Dutch for a stove, and throughout the winter we used no other word for it). New Year's Eve was clear and starry, a night of iron frost, much handshaking, and discordant song; and perhaps an adequate way of describing it is simply to say that we enjoyed ourselves as we might have been expected to enjoy ourselves, and that we were sorry in the morning. What happened in the town I know only from hearsay: I was up at les Cours, where various officers from Battalion H.Q., "B" Echelon, and "S" Company were making merry in the Burgomaster's house. I remember slipping away about 2 a.m., and seeing the village street ice-covered in the starlight, with the strains of "Loch Lomond" rising and falling in three different keys in the distance. Two red pin-points grew in the sky, a rumble became a roar, and two flying bombs passed overhead. No one paid any attention. I waited. Two orange flashes lit the sky above Liége, and after a pause the sound of the explosions came across the snow. The New Year was in. I went to bed.

Next day we had our big dinner. Rations throughout the Army had been so augmented that a special meal could be served both on Christmas and New Year's days, with battalions left the choice of the day for their main celebration. We, naturally, had plumped for Hogmanay; and we sat down to tinned turkey, Christmas pudding, and an excellent selection of sweets, nuts, chocolate, beer, and cigars. The R.A.S.C. and the P.R.I. between them had certainly done us proud. Colonel Walford visited the companies, made his speech, and was cheered on his way accompanied by the Regimental Sergeant Major and the Pipie. The companies were widely spread, and all were very hospitable. Only the Colonel and the Pipie lasted the course.

As has been said, the Battalion re-congregated at les Cours on the 5th. On the 6th the Colonel went on his long-promised leave. On the 8th we set off in troop-carrying vehicles for Hotton in the Ardennes.

II

It was a very terrible journey. Since the beginning of the war we had accomplished many which scarcely conformed to peace-time standards of comfort, but this was the all-time worst. From the beginning it was miserable. The day broke as a thorough-going snowstorm was getting into its stride. We started at 0800 hours in a world that was grey, and windy, and hopeless. There was a foot of new snow on the road, covering the ice of the previous week. The wind was whipping the frozen particles into the air and driving them through every crack and crevice of the trucks, so that the men in them were blue with cold before they had so much as started and already they were stamping in unison to keep their feet warm. The carrier crews sat with shoulders hunched, white from head to foot.

The country south from Liége to the Ardennes is cut up into a series of parallel ridges and valleys, all very steep, and our road ran against the grain, so that we were perpetually either climbing hills or sliding down them. Even for a single vehicle it would have been bad enough, but the whole Brigade was on the move. The road was hammered ice after the first five minutes; and, just to make things more difficult, the carriers were moving tactically and were distributed in little packets all along the Brigade column. A bren carrier on ice had rather less grip than a curling-stone. They skidded downhill and stuck on the way up; and as soon as one stuck at least a dozen vehicles travelling behind were forced to stop as well. On the steeper hills some were unable to start again, and in many cases had to be pushed into the ditch and abandoned. As the day wore on, traffic discipline became worse and worse until, at 1900 hours, the road was one solid traffic block for eight miles. There were tanks in the block, and guns. There were weasels, and bulldozers, and seven-ton trucks. Nearly every type of military vehicle was there, jammed tight in the dark. Every hour or so we would move a hundred yards and then stop again. Once we could not move at all for three hours. As night came on, it grew colder. We reached Hotton at 0430 hours on January 9, after covering fifty-four miles in twenty-and-a-half hours.

The German offensive had been held by this time, and our armies had started to nibble into the sides of the huge salient which jutted into Belgium. Our 'planes had shot the Luftwaffe out of the sky and were roaming unchallenged over the long, vulnerable lines of communication, making the task of supplying the troops in the tip of the salient almost impossible. The first surprise was a surprise no longer. Every day brought more of our troops and tanks to complete the task of nipping off the salient at its base. There was nothing left for the enemy to do but withdraw with as little loss as possible.

We were midway along the north side of the salient, attacking south. Opposite us a big American force was attacking north from Bastogne, twenty miles away. With any luck we should meet before the Germans had had time to escape. 153 Brigade advanced on the 9th and took Cheux, Hodister and Warizy without much difficulty, thus closing the gap by five miles; and on the 10th our Battalion took Genes, another two thousand yards on the road south, without opposition. Our only difficulty was mines. Huge snowdrifts, some of them six feet deep, covered the road, and the distance was too great for our mine-detectors to penetrate; but fortunately such mines as there were were buried near the surface. Two armoured cars of the Derby Yeomanry went through before our pioneers cleared the road: both were blown up.

When we were firm, the other two battalions went through, 2nd Seaforth to Halleux and 5th Camerons to Ronchamps, making the Brigade advance for the day three miles. We could hear the Camerons and the 2nd being shelled, but we were left in peace for the night. It was not until next day, the 10th, that the Ardennes counter-offensive, so far as we were concerned, really began. On that day we were ordered to advance through the Camerons and capture Mierchamps.

The Battalion was commanded by our new second-in-command, Major J.C.Powell, who was in the difficult position of being flung into a battle before he so much as knew the names of half the officers he commanded. Major Fleming had been invalided home some weeks before while we were at Venlo. Major Jim Powell had arrived just in time to take part in the celebrated arctic journey to Hotton, which was scarcely a social occasion, and since then we had been either planning or on the move. Now he was faced with Mierchamps.

There were three parallel ridges. Between the first and second was a wide, gently-sloping valley. Between the second and third was a valley more deeply cut, narrow and very steep. We were on the first ridge. The Camerons were on the second, astride the crossroads at Ronchamps. The Germans were on the third. Beyond the third, out of sight behind the crest, was Mierchamps.

It was a crisp white-and-blue morning, with the sun sparkling on the snow, and the air wonderfully clear. It was the kind of day set aside by Providence for the waxing of skis and the building of snow-men, and war seemed even more of a nonsense than usual. The sky was eggshell blue, and there was blue in the shadows of the drifts, and the snowfields stretched silver as far as we could see as we marched down into the first valley. The whole countryside was at peace except for one small angry spot half a mile ahead, where the Germans were pasting the living daylights out of Ronchamps. We were going to Ronchamps. The shell-bursts were black against the snow. Nobody was particularly chatty as we trudged up the hill towards them.

We stopped a little short of the crossroads, and waited. The Boche, said the Camerons, were still on the third ridge, so this was not going to be another route-march. There were recces, and an "O" Group, and a lot of shells much too close, and then it was 1400 hours and we were attacking.

As this turned out to be the most peculiar attack we were ever involved in, the plan and the situation on which it was based must be gone into in some detail. We did not have a great deal to go on. The Boche were known to be pulling back, but no one knew how quickly they were doing it. They were shelling Ronchamps crossroads with great zest. This might mean they were covering a withdrawal, but on the other hand it might mean nothing of the sort. A few Boche had been seen earlier in the morning walking about on their own crest. A road sloped obliquely down to the right into the valley from the end of Ronchamps (the valley wall was too steep for the road to take it straight), crossed a small bridge on the valley floor, and crawled obliquely left up the far side. Down in the valley were thick pine-woods, but the upper slopes were bare. Early in the morning the bridge had not been blown, but there was no guarantee that it was still intact. There were mines on the road on our side of the bridge. That was all the information we had. Of the strength or dispositions of the enemy we knew nothing.

Major Powell decided to treat the whole business as an advance to contact rather than as a set-piece attack. "A" Company plus a troop of tanks and an armoured bulldozer was to be the advance-guard, followed by Tactical H.Q., followed by "C"

Company. The other two companies were to remain where they were, near Ronchamps crossroads; and in the event of something solid being hit by the advance-guard, "B" and "C" Companies were to put in a right-flanking attack on Mierchamps. "D" Company was to be in reserve for counter-attack.

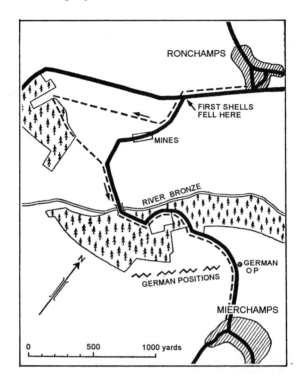

As there was no point in sending an advance-guard with tanks down a mined road, we were to follow a route which, for description's sake, may be divided into four stages. First, we were to march four hundred yards south-west along the main road from Ronchamps crossroads. Second, we were to turn down the minor road leading to Mierchamps from this point, and follow it for two hundred yards. Third, we were to leave the minor road there and make a long detour over the fields until we reached the edge of a wood seven hundred yards to the south-west. Fourth, we were to break a way through the wood, rejoin the road at the last bend short of the bridge, and follow it to Mierchamps. The critical point about all this was that although stages one and four could be followed under cover, stages two and three were in full view of the enemy – and stages two and three totalled nine hundred yards! The only possible order was given. The gunners were told to lay a barrage along the German ridge which would keep all heads down while we crossed the nine hundred yards.

So there we were, at 1405 hours, breaking cover at the end of stage one and praying that the Germans had neither courage nor periscopes. We were not reassured: the moment the first tank appeared, a crump came down all round it. There were seven shells, and they landed in a heap on the corner where we should have to turn on to the Mierchamps road. We kept moving along the ditch behind the tanks, noticing in the detached sort of way one does notice these things at such times how absurd and frog-like the men were in the orchard on our left. They were not in the advance, so they could duck if they wanted to. They had been sitting about in groups, but now they were scattering, and crouching behind trucks, and making jerky little dives for better 'oles. Fifty yards away, the explosions made straight dark columns in the air.

The fields we had to cross were bare, smooth, and unbroken, with the snow nicely crusted and little points of light glinting on the surface. Our khaki was black against the snow. The tanks were cockroaches on a white sheet and we were a long black caterpillar crawling after them. The caterpillar thickened slightly towards the head because we all tried to rush it at first, only to be pulled up by the snow. It was half-way to our knees. The German crest was only a thousand yards away, looking right down on us. I do not think that any of us had ever felt so naked in all our lives as we did in the middle of those smooth white fields.

The din was indescribable. There were mediums, and twenty-five-pounders, and mortars, and machine-guns, all firing over our heads; and the German ridge was spouting earth and snow. The snow was dotted with black craters, and more flickered on to it as we watched. There was no wind, so the gunners could not blind the ridge with smoke, but had to rely on high explosive. At first we could not understand why nothing came back at us, then decided that the Germans must be holding their fire until we were all out in the open. Still nothing came. We edged over to the firmer going in the tank tracks, and began to hope.

A single shell sailed out of the blue sky, landed in the middle of the column, and by chance wounded only one man. The column scarcely wavered, but plodded on, aiming for the woods and cover. No one was worrying about single shells: the sound all our bowels were waiting for was ten, twenty, fifty shells moaning over the ridge at us. The Boche would never have a better target.

Still the sound did not come. A spark of hope grew in the column, and we began to ask ourselves questions. Supposing, just supposing, the Boche could not see us. Supposing they were firing blind, from the map. Then the first crump had been a fluke: those seven shells would have fallen there whether the tanks had appeared or not. After all, shells had landed there before. The single shell? Another fluke. Maybe.

The bulldozer chugged past. No shells came. We had a hundred and fifty yards to go. Ahead were backs, nothing but backs in a long sluggish single line, hunched a little to make their owners small. Behind was a thin stem of footprints with a scarlet blossom where the single shell had fallen. A hundred yards. Fifty. The tanks were there, waiting while the bulldozer tunnelled into the brushwood. We had arrived. Most of us lit cigarettes and wondered why we were alive.

A slow rumble grew in the air and seven shells landed where the tanks had first appeared. "C" Company had the bad luck to be under them when they landed; but even so, we were reassured. The Germans did not know where we were. They were firing from the map.

III

That ended the first phase of the Mierchamps attack, because when we had penetrated the wood we found the bridge blown. It was an odd situation. We were only five or six hundred yards from the Germans, but owing to the steep sides of the valley we were invisible to them once we had reached the bottom of it. When news of the bridge reached Brigade we were ordered to stay where we were until dark, by which time a new bridge might be erected. Failing a new bridge, the attack would still go in, and we should have to hang on in Mierchamps until the tanks could follow us.

The latter turned out to be the case (the going in the wood was atrocious: the bridging truck bogged down), and so when we moved on at 1800 hours we were without benefit of either tanks or anti-tank guns – not too happy a state of affairs considering that Tiger tanks had been seen swanning about on the ridge during the previous afternoon. For the past two hours ''A'' Company had been forming a bridgehead, still out of sight below the crest, on the far side of the stream; and the rest of us had been sitting in the ditch growing colder and colder. It was brutally cold. According to the newspapers there were twenty-seven degrees of frost that night, and we saw no reason to disbelieve them. It was impossible to keep even moderately warm. We had no coats because it was impossible to fight in coats. All we had over our normal uniforms were hip-length leather jerkins. Furthermore, the Germans put down a dozen mortar bombs on the bridge every ten minutes or so from 1700 hours onwards, evidently thinking we were due to start repairing it; and after we had flopped down and stood up several times we were covered with snow from head to foot. It was a relief when darkness came and we were able to move off.

The whole Battalion was now in the valley. ''D'' Company was to be left to firm-base at the bridge. The first stage of the advance was for the other companies and Tactical H.Q. to cross the stream and join ''A'' Company, which had followed the road as it climbed obliquely leftwards out of the valley and were now astride it fifty yards below the crest. The crossing was not pleasant. The stream had to be jumped at a point where it narrowed a few yards left of the bridge; and as the men were encumbered by weapons, bunching was unavoidable. Three severe mortar stonks came down while we crossed, and somehow the orange-red flashes as the bombs exploded all round us seemed much more vicious in the grey snow-twilight than they normally did in the dark. The whole valley in that light looked unreal, like a half-tone illustration, and the sudden intrusion of colour seemed all wrong. We went skeltering up the far side of the valley, slithering and sliding where the ground was steep and foot-holds did not exist, and paused for breath on the comparative safety of the road above. In a little while the head of our column reached ''A'' Company. Soon we were ready for the final advance over the crest to Mierchamps.

It was now 1900 hours. If anyone had told me that exactly two hours later I should be sitting down in front of a stove to hard-boiled eggs, bread, fresh farm butter, and a pot of coffee, I should not only have disbelieved him but would have declared that the chances of our having so much as a roof over our heads that night were a hundred to one against. Even our gunner Forward Observation Officer, the celebrated Major H. J. Decker, was offering fifty to one and he was once a bookmaker. Yet that was how it ended. '' A '' Company captured two sentry-posts without a shot being fired, and we walked into the village. At first sight the place seemed to be deserted, but when the houses were ransacked seventy very surprised Germans were found. Some were sitting warming their hands at stoves. Others a little more *au fait* with the situation were hiding under beds or in cellars. Only six put up a fight, and that was settled with two bursts of bren and one hand grenade. There was nothing left to do but take over the village from the Germans, dig in, and hope that our tanks arrived before the Tigers did. Our tanks did arrive first, at 0430 hours, and that was that. Some of us even began to feel our toes again.

(left) Gordon Begg after four days with his platoon in ice-lined trenches guarding the bridge at Mierchamps. (above) A wrecked German half-track abandoned at Mierchamps. We found nine others, all undamaged, abandoned for lack of petrol.

(below) The 5th Seaforth pipers, led by Pipe-Major Asher.

We captured two half-tracks when we took the village, and next day seven more were found in a wood close by. Half frozen Germans came in to give themselves up for the next two days, and our final total of prisoners was one hundred and eighty.

IV

Now how, one might reasonably ask, did all this come about?   The prisoners were Panzer Grenadiers, husky types not normally caught bending, and to capture a hundred and eighty of them for little cost was something new in our experience. The answer must be largely guesswork; and, indeed, if the story already told in this chapter is examined in light of what we subsequently found out, it will be discovered that some of the guesses are incorporated in the narrative. The account of the crossing of the open fields, for instance, is based on the assumption that the Germans did not see us. I believe they did not; but it must be pointed out that "C" Company, who suffered most from the shelling, still believe they were seen. All I can do is present the facts, offer a possible solution, and invite the reader to disagree with me.

We were able to look at the ground from the German positions next day, and so far as we could discover, none of the posts on the crest commanded the floor of the valley: the view of our fields on the far slopes was magnificent, but the floor was invisible. We also found the German observation post, which was inside a hollow potato-clamp on the forward slope. It did not command the floor either; and the interesting thing about it was that when our barrage had started, fifteen minutes before we were due to advance from Ronchamps, a man had been seen running from the potato-clamp back over the skyline.

I believe that the shells which landed round the tanks as they emerged from Ronchamps were routine shots, fired from the map. If they were not a fluke, they must have been whistled up uncommonly quickly, because no more than a few seconds elapsed between the appearance of the tanks and the arrival of the shells; and in any case the German observer had run away quarter of an hour before.

Our barrage put the forward posts to earth. When they bobbed up again we had reached the cover of the wood. Even if our tracks were seen in the snow, they were bearing away to the German left, and might have been thought to be aimed elsewhere.

From this it would follow that the mortaring of the bridge was also routine, laid on beforehand for a time when we might be expected to be repairing it. We were at the bridge for over an hour before any bombs fell.

Two boys aged fourteen and sixteen seem to have been the only Belgians in the village with their noses above ground, and they declared that when the barrage opened at 1400 hours the Germans thought an attack was brewing, but returned to their billets when nothing developed. They were very cold and miserable, and maintained only lightly-manned alarm posts in the open. In the late afternoon they were ordered to withdraw; and half an hour before we entered the village all the officers and about a hundred men did, in fact, leave. The remainder had not the slightest inkling that we had crossed the valley, and panicked when we suddenly appeared. In their house, said the boys, the Germans ran to the cellar and hid behind the civilians, convinced that their throats were about to be cut.

This is all very well and makes a satisfactory picture, but there are two other discoveries which have not been mentioned. The first, a telephone which was hanging on a tree within a few yards of the bridge, may be explained away by saying that the Boche who manned it ran off when the barrage started; but the second is not quite so simple. When "A" Company jumped the stream and went forward to form their bridgehead, they captured six Germans sitting in a little wood with a wireless set. The wood looked right down on the bridge, and they could not possibly have failed to see us. Was the wireless set out of action? Were the Germans afraid to send a man back over the skyline with a message? We shall never know. Only one thing is certain: if the Germans in Mierchamps had known we were coming, it would have been an expensive action. Perhaps we had better leave it at that.

Our casualties were two killed and nineteen wounded.

We remained in Mierchamps until January 18, sweeping the neighbouring woods and patrolling villages to the south, east, and west while the rest of the Division went forward. On the 12th, "B" Company sent a strong patrol and a troop of tanks south to investigate Erneuville, where the Boche were found in residence. There was a short but brisk fight, during which Lieutenant Bert Brocklehurst was wounded. We took three prisoners. On the 14th came the end. The Highland Division met the 84th U.S. Division, the Ardennes Salient was cut, and there was nothing further for us to do. A great sigh of relief arose from "D" Company down at the bridge, which they had been guarding for three days in conditions of extreme hardship, living in ice-lined trenches in the woods. Six of their men were frost-bitten. One notable sight was the arrival of Captain Gordon Begg to search for billets after this ordeal. Even the famous moustache drooped, and his output of epigrams had dwindled almost to nothing. He had a three-day growth on his chin ('Well, would *you* melt ruddy snow for shaving water, you oaf?'), a sheepskin rug or doormat he had won somewhere was draped about his shoulders and was only partly covered by his jerkin, and his feet were encased in straw-filled sandbags. He was sensitive to criticism of any kind, and for once was not singing "Aupres de ma Blonde" or the song about the brush. A fine sight.

The postscript to the Ardennes offensive is best given in the words of the two Belgian boys, because their description of what they saw during the fortnight of German occupation shows in miniature the whole course of the offensive – the sweeping advance, the first check, the cutting of the supply-lines by our 'planes, the massing of our forces, the final disillusionment.

'They came on Christmas Day,' they said. 'They made a feast, and the toast was "To Paris, Brussels, Antwerp." But they did not go forward. And when that happened, they knew. In five days, in five days only, the soldiers were saying von Rundsted was a traitor who had led the Wehrmacht into a trap. Then there was fine weather, and your 'planes came. By New Year's Day they were slaughtering our beasts because they had no food. Already they had used all our petrol – those vehicles you took, they could not drive them away because of that. They became very miserable. They said they were betrayed by their officers. They knew nothing of the battle. A shell would land, and one would say: "That is British." And another would say: "No. It is German." They knew nothing, except that the British were creeping in. They stayed in one place, but it was as if the country round them had moved. When you came, they were in great fear and ran to the cellars. They made the old people sit on their knees so that they would be protected by them. They said they would be murdered. One in our cellar wept. Paris, Brussels, Antwerp! Aaah, the bandits, the dirty bandits!'

THE REICHSWALD

(previous page and below)   Seaforth Highlanders in the Reichswald.

(left) One of the young German "Para Boys" who fought so stubbornly in the Reichswald.

CHAPTER EIGHTEEN

The Reichswald

I

IF AT THIS STAGE one casts one's mind back over the campaign from D-Day onwards, it will be seen that the Battalion had been extraordinarily lucky. We had taken part in every advance and had seen at least as much action as any other unit in the British Army outside our own division; yet we had never fought a really tough action. At the Triangle only half the Germans fought. At Tilly they surrendered. At Favières they withdrew. At le Havre the infantry surrendered and left only the artillery to fight the battle. At the three canal crossings there was no one to meet us on the far bank. Mierchamps was taken by surprise. For the most part, this was due to good planning and good intelligence: in nearly every case we had known exactly where the enemy were, and if we could not avoid them had taken care to smother them with shells, tanks, and flame-throwers before we advanced. We had gone for the flank and the soft spot.

But there comes a time when the best of plans and the best of luck will not dislodge the enemy before heavy casualties have been suffered. It comes when there is no way round, no soft spot where a determined thrust will break through easily, when the place attacked is vital to the enemy and he has seen to it that his best troops are manning it in force. Then a slogging match develops and there must be casualties. Our time came in the Reichswald, probably the most important action, including Alamein and the Rhine crossing, that the Battalion ever fought.

From the Ardennes we went north on January 19 to rest at Weelde and Poppel on the Belgian side of the Dutch frontier, and from there moved back to our old billets in the seminary at Vught on the 23rd. We remained in Vught until February 8, and then went to Beers, ready to attack next day.

Here there must be a long digression, because it was at this stage, while we were at Vught, that we lost Colonel Walford. The Reichswald will have to wait.

It is the custom in the Army for the commander of an infantry battalion to complete an active tour of duty of a limited period, the idea being that if he has been doing his job properly and by some happy chance still remains alive at the end of it, the strain will have been so great that a fresh man should succeed him. As Colonel Walford appeared to be made entirely of indiarubber and strong springs he had not been visibly affected by the rigours of leading the Battalion in every action from Alamein to Venlo; but his time was more than up, and he had to go. While he was on leave he was appointed to command the 9th Seaforth, stationed in Scotland; and now he had come back to hand over to Lieutenant-Colonel J.M.Sym and to say goodbye to us.

This is a history, and opinion should have no place in it. Nevertheless I am going to say my say about Jack Walford. I was his Intelligence Officer from D-Day onwards, and as I lived with him twenty-four hours a day I reckon I know a certain amount about him. He was tireless and he was thorough. His method of planning drove a long line of adjutants to despair, and consisted in worrying and worrying at the facts until he had them arranged to his liking – a process which, in the case of a set-piece attack, might last for days. Where a tidier mind might have reached a quick conclusion, he continued to chew away at the facts, arranging, rearranging, thinking aloud, and in the end arriving at perhaps a different conclusion – the correct one. His set-piece attacks were always watertight.

Throughout the two campaigns he seldom stopped work until 1 a.m., at which hour he almost always settled down happily to letter-writing, deaf to the pleas of his second-in-command that he should rest. He slept less than any man I ever knew – three or four hours a night, on the average.

His reconnaissances were notorious, and many tank majors are still dining out on the stories arising from them. The unhappiest hours of my life have been spent in crawling (or, worse still, walking) along ditches behind him. He worshipped the study of ground, and would never, unless circumstances made it absolutely impossible, launch the Battalion before he had seen the ground for himself, or, as sometimes happened, walked over it. Many times these recces took him beyond our forward troops. Usually they lasted for hours.

Towards the end most of us, I think, became superstitious about him. We believed that if we stuck close to him we would not be hit. He appeared not only to be without physical fear, but to have the ability to survive all the normal consequences of high explosive. At Tilly, standing in the open, he had one shell land within twelve yards of him and another within five: none of us who were with him was hurt. He had a habit of tripping over booby-traps, but no one was ever any the worse for it. He was always up with the forward companies; but to the end the two who accompanied him, Miller his batman, and Isbister his wireless operator, were unscathed. He exposed himself constantly in his determination to know everything and see everything, attracted large numbers of shells while so doing, and – went quietly home to the 9th Battalion in February, 1945.

The Jocks trusted him implicitly. They used to say: 'If Juicy says it's all right, then it's all right.'

My personal opinion – and it is shared by many other officers who served under him – is that his thoroughness and those unsparing reconnaissances not only got the Battalion on to its objective every time but saved us anything up to five hundred casualties.

Colonel John Sym, his successor, was of the same cut, conscientious, thorough, sparing himself nothing; but there the similarity ended. It was my impression that he worried more about a battle after it was over than he did while he was preparing for it. He had a precise mind. His preparations were meticulous, and when they were made and every doubt had been resolved in his own mind he had the ability to wait without further heart-searching for the event to prove or disprove his plan. In action he was the same, cool and lucid, wasting neither time nor emotion on unnecessary things. Yet after a battle – this is only an impression, but I have felt it strongly – he worried about the casualties, blaming each one on himself and wondering if, had the plan been contrived differently, perhaps this or that man might have been spared.

Before joining us he had twice escaped from the Germans in Italy, and was soon to escape for a third time. His manner was quiet. He spoke slowly and clearly, and he had a feeling for the sound of words. He was the only Regular officer I ever knew who could read the lesson well in church.

On the day before we left Vught for Beers he gathered the Battalion into one hall; and for two hours explained to us all, officers and men, the plan for the Reichswald.

This was to be the decisive battle of the war; and though fighting, much of it fierce, was to drag on for two months after it was over, the Germans were never to recover again. For some reason, which history may be able to elucidate, the Germans had decided to defend their country not from the natural barrier of the Rhine, but from the frontier. There they had the vast concrete defences of the Siegfried Line, and between the Line and the river was a slice of Germany which ran north and south for two hundred miles and more and had a maximum width of a hundred miles. The south, down by the Moselle, was the widest part. As one travelled northwards it gradually narrowed, and its northern tip was a stretch of only a few miles connecting the rivers Maas and Rhine where they most nearly approached each other. Away to the south, at Aachen, the Americans had fought bitterly throughout the winter to penetrate the Line, and in the end had succeeded. They were now building up to attack through the gap they had made and fan out towards the Rhine.

The big plan was, in one respect, the same as the one which had defeated the Germans in Normandy. Once again the British and the Canadians were to hammer at the defences until they had drawn the maximum possible number of German divisions northwards away from the Americans, so that when the Americans attacked there would be little to oppose them. Thanks to the Ardennes offensive and the huge losses suffered there, the Germans had few reserves left and could not be everywhere at once; and it was reckoned that one really determined offensive in the north would soon leave the south clear. We would break the Siegfried Line where it stretched between the Rhine and the Maas. When the German reserves had been lured up to meet us, the Americans near Aachen would strike for the Rhine and turn both north to meet us, and south to drive behind the defences beyond the Moselle. In this way it was hoped to fight the decisive battle west of the Rhine. If we succeeded, the remnants would never be able to form an effective line beyond the river; and the chief bogey of the campaign, the crossing of the Rhine against heavy resistance, would be scotched.

This plan won the war. However, the infantry has its own outlook on these matters, a rather more parochial outlook, and while the field-marshal may look with satisfaction at the great arrows sweeping across his map, the platoon-commander is apt to moan and niggle about some quite insignificant quirk of the ground which lies on his immediate front. We heard the plan, and it was good; but when we looked at our maps and photographs we did not greatly like what we saw there. There was, for instance, this place called the Reichswald.

When the Germans conquered Holland in 1940 they extended the Siegfried Line northwards from the French frontier, but this sector was never made so strong as the original Line. The huge concrete pillboxes were there, but they lacked the depth of the southern fortifications. When we arrived in Holland there was much frantic digging to improve this state of affairs; but little new concrete was added, and the Germans contented themselves with fairly extensive earthworks arranged in depth along their side of the Maas. Even so, these defences were formidable, and on our side steps had to be taken to shorten the odds. The problem was to find a flank somewhere. If the Line could be attacked on a flank, and pierced, the attackers would then be able to take the rest of the Line from the rear, all the pillboxes would face the wrong way, and the defenders would be pinned against the Maas instead of having it in front of them. This possibility had, naturally, occurred to the Germans too; but one glance at their maps had told them that there was only one flank, and that it was secure. Our commanders looked at the same flank, and came to a different conclusion. They decided it could be pierced.

This critical sector of the Line was the part which bridged the gap between the Rhine and the Maas. It faced roughly north-west, and was thirteen miles long. Nearly half the gap was filled by the Reichswald Cleve, a dense forest; and most of the rest of it was low-lying ground or bog. The bog could easily be flooded by the Germans, who considered our prospects there so hopeless that the artificial defences were not nearly so closely knit as they were elsewhere The main defences lay along the south side of the forest, facing the Maas. Once through the Reichswald we could take them all in rear.

Once through the Reichswald....

The attack had already begun when we reached Beers on the evening of February 8. During the day, elements of three divisions had gone in, the 15th Scottish through the gap between the Rhine and the Reichswald, the 53rd through the north edge of the forest, and our own 153 Brigade into the south half of the forest, attacking from north-west to south-east. 153 had penetrated the defences along the forest edge and were now five hundred yards beyond them, digging in among the trees. We were to go through them.

The 9th dawned wet and miserable, but we had been up long before then. Reveille was at 0430, and for more than two hours we had been creeping about in the dark, packing trucks, checking weapons, swearing, shivering, stumbling into puddles, and trying not to think too much about what the day might bring. From long experience most of us had learned that it did not pay to worry before a battle, that things turned out much the same whether one had the wind up for five minutes or five days; and the one advantage of an early start was that nearly all of us were far too surly to see farther than the fact that we were cold, and hungry, and sleepy. Bad temper was a useful anaesthetic. We squeezed into barns and ate our breakfast standing and in silence. Then it was seven o'clock, and we were off.

It was raining hard by this time. We moved down to the Maas in troop-carrying vehicles, crossed at Mook by the Baillie bridge, and left our vehicles in the woods south-west of Groesbeek – the woods which had been the start-line for the previous day's attack. We had been told that we had twelve hundred guns to support us, and now we began to see what twelve hundred guns meant. A carpet of high explosive had been unrolled in front of 153 Brigade. The whole countryside was flattened. As we plodded through the mud down the Herwendaalsche Straat and the Breedeweg Straat we saw not ruin but utter devastation on a scale which made Fontaine la Mallet seem tidy. At Fontaine there had at least been a few houses left standing. Here there was hardly anything which was recognisable as a house. We had seen walls with holes in them before, but here there were not even walls: the roofs lay flat on piles of rubble. Through the wreckage of Breedeweg village the way – it could not be called a road – was marked by pickets and tape, dingy from the night's rain and splashed by the mud of passing vehicles. Into the mud, bulldozers were shovelling what had once been houses, but they worked all day before they made a firm bottom. In a garden, beside a dead calf and a German corpse, a heavy iron gate lay on its side. We had crossed the German frontier.

We entered the Reichswald by the ride which began a hundred yards north of the Breedeweg Straat, halted among the trees, and remained there for five and a half hours. The 5th Camerons were ahead of us, and were making slow progress.

Most of our efforts to abstain from thought were weakening by this time. We had been built up to go straight through the Camerons and attack, and the interruption jolted our minds from the rut into which they had been so painfully schooled. It was cold, too, and showery; and every half-hour a batch of shells landed amongst us. We stood shivering among the shattered trees where the ground was littered with German dead, and prayed that the advance would come soon. It came at 1600 hours, and in an unexpected direction. The Camerons were having trouble along their ride, the winter daylight would soon be fading, and our objective was the Hekkens/Kranenburg road, which ran north and south through the middle of the forest all of six thousand yards ahead. If we could not pass through the Camerons, some other way would have to be found. In the end we advanced along a parallel ride half a mile to the north, where 154 Brigade had reached a point only a thousand yards short of the road. This would take us to our objective just as quickly, and it was hoped that later we should be able to turn south down the Hekkens road and rejoin our original axis. It was late by the time we had gathered all the information we could from the forward troops of 154 Brigade and moved the Battalion up into their area; and when we moved off into the unknown we had only one hour of daylight in hand.

The Reichswald was planted on strictly Teutonic lines, with the trees evenly spaced and dressed smartly by the left. The trunks of the more mature ones were trimmed for the first few feet, so that when we moved off the ride we found ourselves among endless pillars with a solid ceiling of branches overhead. In other places, a patch of young trees thickly planted made movement except on the ride impossible; and in others again the monotonous pines gave way to more open stretches of free-planted oak and beech. The ride itself was so boggy in parts that except for tanks the only vehicles which could get through were half-tracks and weasels, the recently-introduced light, broadtracked runabouts we were using to evacuate casualties.

One result of this was important: we could take with us no supporting arms, no mortars, no anti-tank guns, no machine-guns. Our link with the rear was one slender channel of mud. We had only the weapons we carried in our hands, plus artillery support from outside the forest; and, worse still, we had no tanks. The Argylls, the battalion through which we were passing, had a troop, but it had no orders to accompany us; and it looked as if we should have to advance with no close support whatever until the personal element made its appearance in the paper plan and Colonel Sym discovered that the tank commander's father had been a Seaforth. The Colonel, praising the tradition of the county regiments, found himself the temporary owner of three Churchills.

The ground rose ahead of us as we began to shepherd them along the ride. There was no wind, and in the silence of the forest they seemed to make a tremendous noise. ''B'' Company led, and cleared a big quarry on the right of the track. The forest closed in again, and we began to drop down into the valley which lay between us and the Hekkens road.

It is almost impossible to describe the atmosphere of the Reichswald. One might say that it was an evil place, that it stank of danger, that it was one long natural ambush, and yet give little clue to the impression it made upon us. Still, putting oneself in the boots of a man in the leading platoon, something of the quality of the place may be appreciated. Such a man walked slowly forward through the trees near the edge of the ride knowing all the time that a German with a machine-gun could be hidden within fifty yards of him. Behind him were the tanks, roaring like tractors in an empty church. He felt sure the Germans must hear the tanks. He felt sure the Germans must know they could not move off the ride and that he, the man, must be close to them. Somewhere in the next half-mile the Boche would be waiting. All he could do was move quietly forward over the carpet of pine-needles, keep his head, and watch for the flicker of a cheek dropping to the stock of a spandau. Under the trees, dusk was already beginning to gather.

Five hundred yards from the Hekkens road, where the ride was only a slit through dense forest, there was a sudden rushing sound. Two immense sheets of flame and trails of red stars covered the leading tank as panzerfausts, the German infantry anti-tank weapon, struck it.

Here, we thought, was the ambush. It had been inevitable, and it had happened. Yet we were wrong. As we we were soon to discover, the Germans had evidently decided that the Argylls represented the limit of our advance for the day, and while we had been prodding our way forward along the final thousand yards, they had been busy organising a counter-attack. Just to complicate matters, their axis of advance was our ride, and their start-line our objective, the Hekkens road. The two attacks met head on.

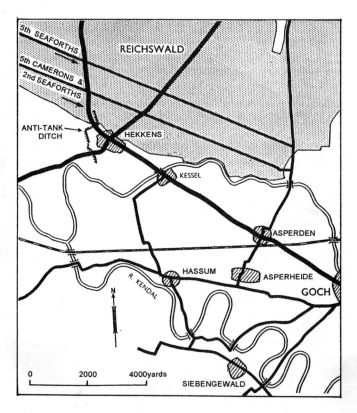

"B" Company (Captain Russell Ferguson) had two platoons beating the forest to the right of the ride, and one to the left. The tanks were undamaged but stopped, so that as the company attacked it drew away from them. Spandaus opened up at fifty yards' range, brens replied, and the forest was filled with muzzle-flashes and streams of tracer. Neither side could see much, but we had the advantage in that we were in battle order and expecting trouble, whereas most of the Germans were still forming up on the Hekkens road and only their advance guard had started to move down our axis. Still, it was a sticky ten minutes. Only the leading company was in a position to fight. The rest of us lay behind trees, peering into the shadows and watching the tracer tearing through the branches. In the lulls there was total silence. Then would come the crump of a grenade, and the shooting would flare up again. Russell Ferguson and Pat Grant went forward to investigate and were caught by a burst of spandau bullets. Russell was killed and Pat seriously wounded. The wireless died, and a runner had to be sent for the tanks. We heard them rumble forward, the sound of their heavy besas cutting clear above the rattle of the other machine-guns. The Germans stood only two or three bursts, and then fled. "C" Company (Major Hamish Paterson) went through with the tanks, caught the counter-attack still trying frantically to form up on the road, and scattered it. Once again there was silence. We were left in peace to dig in astride our ride by the edge of the road, a thousand yards farther into the Reichswald than any other unit in our part of the forest.

Peace continued throughout the night, but it was an uneasy vigil we kept. The whole Battalion was inside a two hundred yards' square, peering outwards through the darkness to front, flanks, and rear. Doubtless the Germans were no happier. They had a continuous line of trenches dug parallel to the Hekkens road and two hundred yards beyond it, so they were within hailing distance of us, and they too must have been straining eyes and ears into the night for moving shadows or the snapping of a twig. The forest was absolutely still. There was no wind. Every now and then we heard the distant rumble of our guns, then silence, then the growing wail as the shells passed overhead and crashed down behind the German lines. Then silence again. German 'planes passed over, flying low, seeking out our gun-lines. We saw the sky behind us light up as the flares dropped, and heard the crump of the bombs. The 'planes flew home. We settled down to watch and listen again.

As the first light of dawn began to creep up the sky behind the German lines a little breeze came sighing through the forest. It was uncanny. First there was a slight rustle of branches that made us cock our ears, then a more pronounced rustle, then scores of staccato cracks: the trees damaged by shellfire during the night were unable to bear this slight additional strain, and were breaking and falling down all over the forest. As the breeze passed on its way we could hear the crackling fade into the distance; and once again there was silence.

We could not move until the rest of our Brigade, still struggling along the ride to the south of us, had drawn level; and so we spent the day where we had spent the night, lying in our trenches and listening to the noise of battle creeping forward as the Camerons and 2nd Seaforth made ground along their ride. We could not make contact with them, but patrols we sent out reached the 53rd Division to the north. They were level with us, so we knew we were reasonably safe from attack from that direction. At 0900 hours the Germans discovered where we were, and for the rest of the morning they shelled us heavily every thirty minutes. In the afternoon they stepped up the pace and shelled us every fifteen minutes. Hundreds of shells and mortar bombs fell in or around the Battalion area; and, as many of them burst in the trees overhead, we had casualties. At one time during the morning one of our tanks ditched itself and made a great deal of noise revving up its engine to climb out again. The Germans, thinking we were about to attack, loosed off bank after bank of rocket-bombs which they had dug in in readiness for our final assault – a good thing, possibly, as once fired they were irreplaceable and we were all underground when they landed; but there were at least a hundred and fifty of them, huge things a couple of feet long and as heavy as a man could carry, many burst in the trees, and they were accurate. Single bombs blew full-grown pine trees out bodily by the roots. We heard the squeal as each bank was fired; then the moan, multiplying itself as the flight approached; then the crashes all round us as they burst; then silence, and the doleful cry of 'stretcher-bearer, stretcher-bearer.' Farquhar Macrae could find no cover at the crossing of the ride and the road where most of the casualties occurred. He lay in the open, binding up the wounded while the salvos were still coming over; and the stretcher-bearers, too, worked in the open to bring more to him.

The half-tracks with the wireless sets on board, parked by the edge of the ride, were particularly vulnerable: they were armoured, but had no roofs. Both the gunner half-tracks were hit. Of the eleven men who manned them and directed our artillery fire, only four were left by mid-afternoon. Our own halftrack escaped, but its turn was to come.

As early as 1300 hours we thought that the time had come to turn south and rejoin our original axis, because we could hear the Camerons fighting level with us, where their ride crossed the road. But time after time the fighting flared up again. For ten minutes there would be silence, then the *pup-turrr, pup-turrr* of the spandaus would begin again, the crump of mortarbombs and grenades would come through the trees, and a fresh salvo of shells would crashdown. At 1600 hours we saw heavy mushrooms of smoke floating above the trees, sure signs of a flame-thrower, and thought that now, at last, it must be over; but after a short interval the mingled rattle of spandau and bren broke out once more. That made us think. No one had ever stood up to a crocodile before.

The Germans who fought so well that day and who were to cause us so much trouble before the battle was over were what Major-General Rennie used to call 'those bloody little Para-boys' – the hand-picked parachute troops, mostly very young, who were as good as anything the German Army had. We never fought the S.S. and so have no accurate standard of comparison, but it is difficult to believe that even they could have been better than the Para-boys. They were tough and obstinate, and they fought like fiends. When the flame-throwers were finished that day they were still shouting: 'Come and get us, you English bastards,' through the trees at the Camerons. We did not like the Para-boys, but we respected them. They were good fighters.

However, they were pushed back at last beyond the Hekkens road. At 1800 hours we were ordered to turn south down the road, run the gauntlet of the German defences, and join the Camerons. Later we were to continue south and capture Hekkens itself.

The tanks left before we did, recalled for some other task. It was dark by this time. We heard them rumble off. Then there were explosions, and verey lights, and we could hear the tanks firing. The sound of their tracks on the tarmac died in the distance. An hour and a half later we followed on foot. The companies moved quietly along the grass verge, making no sound. The pioneer jeep, the half-track, and Farquhar's three weasels, the only vehicles we had, crept along the road itself at walking-pace. It was very dark. The searchlights were up; but they were a long way off and the trees soaked up the light. Dead horses and broken branches lay on the road. From time to time shells came over, but we were not seen: we were just a darker line in the darkness, trudging along the verge. Hidden in the darkness on the far side of the road were two of our three tanks with their tracks blown off by mines; but we could not see them, and somehow their warning had failed to get back to us before we started. The jeep and the half-track were among the mines before they knew they were there, and both caused explosions: the crews escaped by a miracle, but men on the verge who trod on mines were not so lucky. One body was recovered later from the treetops.

We took the wireless set from the half-track so that it could be carried on a stretcher, but all the valves were smashed and it was useless. Ahead of us the verey lights were arching over the Cameron ride and there seemed to be a fight going on. Possibly it distracted the Germans from their task of watching the road. In any case, we slipped past without further misadventure, though one verey light in the proper place would have given the game away.

It was now 1900 hours on the night of February 10. We moved a little way back along the Cameron ride, had the hot meal (our first for forty hours) which had been brought up by Donnie Munro, the adjutant, and planned our next advance.

If we had continued south down the Hekkens road when we reached the Camerons, we would have found that eight hundred yards farther on it turned slightly towards the left, or south-east. Five hundred yards farther on still, an anti-tank ditch cut the road; and six hundred yards beyond the ditch were the Hekkens crossroads, our objective. The road emerged from the Reichswald at the ditch.

At 0100 hours on February 11, "C" Company led off cautiously down the road, with "D" and "A" following, and a heavy barrage sweeping the ground ahead of them; and as far as the bend in the road they met nothing. Heavy rain was falling. Progress was slow and there were many halts, but nevertheless we were advancing and our hopes began to rise. After half an hour the leading section approached the anti-tank ditch, and as they went forward to investigate it all hell broke. Spandaus opened up all along the front, straight lines of tracer were striking the trees and flying off in all directions, grenades burst. They went to ground in a ditch by the roadside, with the Germans still firing at point-blank range. There was a hurried consultation, carried on in whispers in case the Germans would hear it, and a section was sent to work round the flank and discover the enemy strength; but before they had gone far, four more spandaus opened up and pinned them. There were more consultations, more expeditions; and always there were more spandaus. The Germans were in the ditch in strength, and try as we might we could not get to grips with them.

Here it is necessary to look into the mind of Colonel Sym, squatting in the ditch with his company commanders fifty yards from the enemy. A situation had arisen which had not been foreseen, for the plan had envisaged the main defence on the Hekkens crossroads, nearly half a mile farther on. Also, the defence was much stronger than had been expected. Next, he had only three companies to play with:

the fourth had been used to reinforce the others after the casualties of the previous day. And finally, there was the question of support.

This last was the real crux of the matter. The plan had been for our pioneers to sweep the road for mines behind the Battalion so that tanks and anti-tank guns could follow us and deal with any armour we might meet in the open country round Hekkens. With fixed-line spandaus firing down the road from the anti-tank ditch it was utterly impossible for this to be done. Even if we managed to outflank the ditch and advance on Hekkens, daylight would find us defenceless in good tank country with enemy and a mined road behind us.

There was only one chance. "D" and "C" Companies were both fully occupied. Launching "A" would leave us without reserves, but it would have to be risked. If we could not clear the ditch and sweep the road, we could not go on.

"A" tried to work round the right flank, and made good progress at first. Spandaus fired here and there, but the answering brens drew gradually away from us as the company advanced, and we began to hope. Shouts of 'Kamerad! Kamarad!' came through the darkness; and then, just as "A" Company seemed to be breaking through, a murderous burst of defensive shelling and mortaring came down on top of them and pinned them. They could go no further. All along the line the spandaus broke out again, worse than ever.

The Colonel – he had already been wounded in the neck, but refused to do anything about it – made his mind up. He tried our reserve wireless set, but there was heavy interference and he could not make himself understood. He went back to tell Brigadier Cassels that we could not reach Hekkens without tanks.

The Brigadier promised us tanks in the morning, and a scissors bridge to get them over the ditch.

The Colonel returned and found little improvement. It was an abominable place. "C" Company and Battalion H.Q. were so close to the Germans that they could hear the N.C.O.'s giving their fire-orders; and the leading men were inside grenading range. The ditch was deep, but not deep enough to stand in. There was so little room that at one time men were lying on top of each other three-deep to keep under cover. Outside, the fixed lines of the spandaus were firing tracer at stomach-height; and the only safe way forward was to crawl along the ditch, over all the bodies. In places the piles of humanity were so deep that even this method left the crawler exposed. The stretcher-bearers, unable to stoop and carry simultaneously, did magnificent work in carrying the wounded back through the hail of bullets in the open, but many of them were hit. Leslie Forshaw-Wilson, who took over command when Colonel Sym went to Brigade, had been wounded before he could issue any orders. Hector Mackenzie took over and continued to explore the enemy flanks. The Colonel resumed command, and gradually the congestion in the ditch was sorted out. Bodies were only one deep now. The firing slackened. By dawn only a few snipers were active, and after the alarms of the night there was relative peace.

Then began a long and anxious day. The lull did not last. Shortly after daylight the Germans concentrated every weapon they had, and for hours on end we were shelled and mortared and grenaded. The spandaus were firing almost continuously, now so deadly that it was impossible to move in the forward positions. Shells were bursting in the trees, not in ones or twos, but by the score, throwing great splinters of steel and wood at the men lying prone in the ditch. We heard the *pop-pause-pop-*

pause-pop of the mortars, flattened ourselves and counted twenty; and down they came all round us, bursting in the treetops, on the road, everywhere. There was a nasty little yellow rifle grenade, too (it was one of these which had wounded the Colonel) which we had not met before and did not want to meet again. Casualties were mounting, and still the storm of high explosive continued.

The tanks arrived in time to scupper a counter-attack coming in at us from the right; but neither they nor the bulldozer which accompanied them could linger, for an eighty-eight had come to life and was cracking armour-piercing shells straight down the road. They withdrew. We felt very lonely. Between the bursts of firing we could hear the rain dripping from the branches of the trees. Our ammunition began to run low, and men risked their lives to carry fresh supplies up the ditch. All the time the stretcher-bearers were carrying casualties back. Food arrived, but it could not be issued.

Late in the morning the Colonel, who should have been in hospital hours before, passed out cold ('I can't think why,' he said afterwards) and his place was taken by Major Powell. At mid-day we were ordered to withdraw. Donnie Munro was killed carrying the message to the forward companies.

The tanks returned a little later and kept the German heads down while we drew back into the forest. And that was the end. Our job, though we only then realised it, was done. We had not taken the Hekkens crossroads, but we had pinned down every German capable of defending them and another brigade had been able to walk in behind the backs of the defence.

It met hardly any opposition: every reserve the Germans possessed had by this time been drawn up to our ditch. When the Para-boys found they were almost surrounded they melted away, and the Hekkens/Kranenburg road was clear from end to end.

Our two nights in the Reichswald had cost us nineteen killed and sixty-five wounded.

II

The slogging-match continued. All along the line British and Canadian divisions hammered away at the Germans, giving them no respite and drawing more and more reserves north, away from the Americans. The Germans were in a dilemma which had no solution: they appreciated the danger of an American breakthrough, but they knew that if our advance were left unchecked it would develop into a breakthrough every bit as serious. They had to stop us. Playing for time, they blew the Roer dams, flooded the river opposite the Americans, and sent eight divisions north. In a week or ten days, they knew, the floods would subside; but by then a miracle might have happened. Perhaps they would have the British and Canadians licked and be able to switch their precious divisions back again. Perhaps the Americans would not attack. Perhaps anything, however improbable. But February was not a month of miracles, and when the dams were empty and the floods had receded the Germans were still bitterly engaged in the north. The Americans crossed the Roer in tremendous force, and found only one division waiting for them on the other side. They broke through. Within a week they were on the Rhine bank on a hundred-mile front, Cologne was in their hands, and General Patton's tanks were advancing fifty miles a day south of the Moselle.

However, that was still in the future. We had only reached mid-February and the slogging-match, as I have said, continued. Colonel Sym refused to go to hospital. We spent the next four days in reserve, tidying up the Reichswald and making a little ground to the east. On the 16th we moved off to attack Asperden, the key to the Siegfried defences covering Goch.

Living in the open in midwinter is unpleasant even in peacetime, and we had now spent a week without so much as a tent over our heads, being rained upon incessantly, trying to make a home in a muddy gas-cape, fighting for part of the time and being shelled for the rest. We had had little leisure and no comfort while in reserve, and we were very tired. Asperden, we hoped, would be our last throw.

It was a night attack. In the afternoon the Typhoons had come over and sent their rockets down into Asperden, and the artillery bombardment which preceded us completed the devastation. Every available gun was turned on the place, and just before we moved off down the Hekkens/Asperden road at 2240 hours several mattresses of rockets went over. Mattresses were a new and deadly invention. Rockets, weight for weight, were superior to shells because they accelerated gradually and did not have to be built to withstand the shock of sudden discharge. A rocket weighing ten pounds carried as much explosive as a shell weighing fifty; and furthermore it did not need a heavy gun to fire it. All that was required was a thin plywood tube. Several dozen of these tubes were mounted on a tank, a trailer, a jeep, or any vehicle which could be adapted to carry them. Nine or ten vehicles would then be directed on a single target, the signal would be given, and a "mattress" of over three hundred rockets would crash down on one small area. Each rocket was equivalent to a 5.5 inch shell.

Asperden had had three mattresses before we reached it. They made a sound like rushing water as they passed overhead.

The searchlights were up to help us, but they were pale beside the fires which raged. Half the village seemed to be in flames, and the church blazed like a torch in the middle of it. A single spandau was firing somewhere on the left, and from it an almost continuous stream of tracer bullets cut the road, chest-high. The whole Battalion crossed it. We went down the road as fast as we could, in what Colonel Sym afterwards called a midnight steeplechase, because we had learned long since that it paid to keep close to the barrage and catch the enemy before he had had a chance to recover. The road was blocked with rubble and fallen trees, dead horses, farm carts, so that no vehicles could go forward; but the Pioneer Platoon worked manfully behind the rifle companies and cleared it in record time. The companies pushed on, entered the village almost unopposed, and were on their objectives by midnight. Three hours later all stray Germans had been winkled out of cellars, we had dug in, and were firm.

The Germans had no intention of giving up Goch, their biggest town in the area, without a struggle; and a glance at the map was sufficient to tell them that the obvious route to it was through Asperden. So they shelled Asperden. However, we also had been glancing at the map and were prepared for it. We dug deep, lay low, and for two days watched that already shattered village being reduced to utter ruin around us. It was not pleasant; but we drew solace from the fact that at least the Germans were pounding German houses instead of Dutch ones. It was good to see a wall with *'Ein Volk, ein Reich, ein Führer'* written on it being slowly knocked to pieces, and to know that after all these years and after coming so far we were fighting on German soil. We had hundreds of shells and mortar bombs thrown at us, but had few casualties. Slit trenches were surprisingly effective even in the heaviest bombardment so long as we did not have to leave them; and at Asperden we had nothing to do but hang on. The climax came on the night of February 18 when another brigade, ignoring the obvious approach, came in on Goch from the left flank. The Germans could not tell in the darkness where the main attack was brewing, chose the likeliest direction, and put down nearly the whole of their defensive fire on top of us. Once again we were distracting the enemy's attention while others advanced; but this time the cost was not so great. We had hardly any casualties.

The next day was spent in mopping up two Siegfried Line pillboxes which still held out to the south and south-east of us. It was not an altogether easy job; but when one considers the awe in which these masses of concrete were held in 1940 and the legend of impregnability which surrounded them, it seems fantastic that a company of infantry, with proper support, could mop up two in a morning. "D" Company did the job under command of Captain Jock Gardiner, who had joined the Battalion in the Reichswald. It was not so very difficult. Thanks to the Reichswald plan we could take them from the rear, so that all long-range defence had to be conducted from trenches dug outside and the actual firing-slits of the pillbox could only be used to stave off the final frontal assault.

Other battalions had found that frontal assault was unavoidable. The pillboxes, which were about sixty feet square and heaped over with earth, were enormously thick, and experience had shown that it was practically impossible to blow a hole through the roof or walls. (Near Aachen, American engineers had spent nearly two days at their leisure on the roof of one of them, trying to blast a way through. After using more than a hundredweight of explosive they had got down only four feet and the Germans inside did not even have a headache.) The infantry's job was to shepherd the special supporting arms forward and deal with the trenches outside. Then the drill was to go for the casemate in front. Seventeen-pounder anti-tank shells were tried first, but they simply bounced off; so the final technique was to employ A.V.R.E.'s (Armoured Vehicle Royal Engineers) which had been specially designed for the job. One type of A.V.R.E. was a Churchill tank with a flying dustbin in front. The dustbin was a forty-pound charge thrown by a petard, and three or four of them blew the steel shutters out of the casemate and enlarged the casemate itself. If the garrison still did not feel like surrendering, a crocodile came up, squirted unignited fuel through the casemate for half a minute, and then fired one ignited squirt after the rest. The garrison died instantly and horribly.

At neither of the pillboxes "D" Company tackled was the full programme necessary: news of what to expect had travelled fast among the Germans, and they realised that their one-time 'impregnable' Siegfried Line had become a death-trap. They were afraid to enter the pillboxes. Beside all these tons of concrete, erected with so much labour and presented to the German nation in such a blaze of propaganda a few years before, they had dug ordinary infantry trenches. Even these were empty at the first pillbox, but they put up a short fight for the second, a massive affair so well camouflaged as a barn that "D" Company had captured it before they realised what it 'was. The Germans abandoned it when our tanks arrived, and pulled back to their main positions a short distance to the south. Battalion H.Q., praising the workmanship of the Hun, then moved into the first pillbox; and the rest of the Battalion covered Asperheide and its approaches, hanging on in close contact with the enemy and expecting to continue pillbox operations almost indefinitely. However, we were relieved on the 22nd and moved back to Asper for a rest. We had had as much as we could stand. Another four men had been killed and fifteen wounded; and we had had no respite for fourteen days. The men were out on their feet, utterly exhausted. A regiment of medium guns fired all night from our doorsteps at Asper, shaking the plaster from the ceilings and blowing in the windows; but we slept like children.

III

There was one more task to be performed before we could say that the Reichswald push was over. Two thousand yards south of our old positions at Asperheide was the village of Siebengewald, held in strength by the Germans and protected by the small River Kendel; and until it was captured the road from Gennep to Goch could not be considered safe for our supply columns. Our Brigade was given the task of capturing it on the night 26-27 February.

The Guards' Armoured Brigade was holding the river line, and laid a kapok bridge across it for us. We were to go over behind the 2nd Seaforth, pass through them when their objectives were taken, and enter Siebengewald.

It was a curious attack, and an interesting one. Not the least curious feature of it was the ground. The Kendel meandered across the landscape in a series of loops, and at the point where we crossed was the sharpest loop of all. It enclosed a narrow isthmus of ground which projected northwards into our lines like a thumb. We crossed at the tip of the thumb, and the two objectives of the 2nd Seaforth were the farms of Terporten and Blumenthalshof, one on each side of the base, beside the river. They could not capture either of them. Our old friends the Para-boys had dug themselves in, fortified the farms, and continued to blaze away happily down the isthmus despite anything the artillery or the 2nd could do. It was a bad night for morale. We had crossed the kapok bridge immediately behind the 2nd, expecting to advance in an hour or so; instead of which we lay until long after midnight, hearing nothing but sounds of strife from the base of the isthmus, alarming rumours, and the groans of 2nd Seaforth wounded as they were carried back over the bridge. There were a great many wounded. Every now and then the fighting flared up, spandaus and brens rattled, flashes dotted the distance, and stray bullets whipped overhead. Then came the sound of feet shuffling in the grass, and more stretchers passed dimly over the bridge. There were voices in the darkness at these times, asking the question which has been asked on battlefields since wars began:

'Hey, Mac! Mac! What's it like up the front?'

The stretcher-bearers all said it was adjectival awful and passed on their way, leaving us with nothing to do but think for another two hours and pretend we were shivering because we were cold.

By 0230 hours the situation was as follows. "A" Company 2nd Seaforth had twice tried to take Blumenthalshof and had failed both times with heavy casualties: one platoon of their "B" Company had been sent forward to reinforce them. "C" Company 2nd Seaforth had failed to take Terporten, and had withdrawn to a belt of trees eight hundred yards to the north. As the 2nd, like ourselves, were reduced to three companies after their experiences in the Reichswald, this left them only two platoons in reserve, not nearly enough to make much difference if the other two companies should try again.

The Brigadier decided that part of our Battalion should help the 2nd in an all-out attempt to capture Terporten. Colonel Sym went forward with his "O" Group, met Colonel Andrews of the 2nd, and retired to the nearest ditch to hatch a plot. The upshot was that "C" Company 2nd Seaforth plus their two reserve platoons were to attack frontally as before, while our "C" Company (Major Hugh Robertson, M.C.) tried to work round the left flank and take the farm of Jenkenshof two hundred yards behind the Germans.

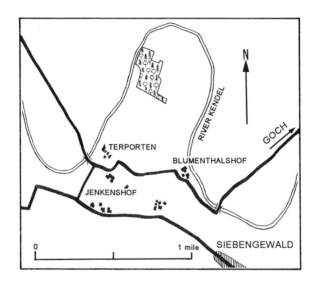

This plan was successful. The 2nd withdrew while a heavy artillery concentration was put down on Terporten, and at 0330 hours the two "C" Companies set off side by side. They were shelled on the start-line but had no casualties. One of our platoons (14 Platoon) worked round on the left under fairly heavy machine-gun fire until it was astride the Blumenthalshof/Terporten road, where it halted and covered 15 Platoon as it went forward to Jenkenshof. There were no Germans in the place, and at 0530 hours 15 Platoon was digging in on the far side. 13 Platoon moved up to cover the only exit from Terporten, 14 Platoon protected the rear of Jenkenshof; and there they sat until daylight, wondering what the reactions in Terporten would be when the Germans discovered they were surrounded. The reactions were highly satisfactory. The Para-boys took one look at Jenkenshof and came out with their hands up at 0740 hours. About the same time their friends in Blumenthalshof decided that they, too, had had enough; and we were able to walk into Siebengewald without further opposition. When "C" Company called the roll, they found that this successful night's work had been accomplished for the loss of only three wounded.

We were relieved that night and returned to Asper. Next day we were off for a week in Nijmegen, where the houses had roofs and windows and there were such things as theatres, and cinemas, and baths. The baths were best of all.

THE RHINE CROSSING

(previous page) On the west bank of the Rhine at dawn

(below) Two of the leaders in the battles to capture Groin – Hugh Robertson (right) who led the first assault and Jock Gardner (left) who directed the all-out attack on Hollands Hof.

CHAPTER NINETEEN

The Rhine Crossing

I

SINCE THE AUTUMN of 1944, when the Germans had stabilised their line after the Normandy breakthrough, the Rhine had been a symbol of the war's end. On the near side were battles, on the far side victory. It was the last barrier between our armour and the North German Plain, and we knew that once we were across it in force nothing the Germans could do would stop us. For months we had expected that the last and bloodiest battle would be fought there.

Thanks to the events set forth in the previous chapter, our forecast was not quite accurate; hard though the battle of the Rhine was, the edge of the defence had been blunted in the fighting west of the river, and the crossing was by no means so difficult as it would have been if the Germans had elected to withdraw behind it while they had the chance and had made their last stand there. In the south, they had met disaster. Patton had driven along the Rhine bank while the Germans were still manning the Siegfried Line nearly a hundred miles to the west. They were encircled, and a huge stretch of the river was left with no defence at all. Farther north, at Remagen, a bridge had been left intact and an American bridgehead was growing on the east bank. Only the sector north of Cologne was held in any strength, and even here the Germans did not have sufficient men to hold the river continuously.

Half the survivors from the Ardennes offensive, the precious reserves which alone could prevent a major Allied bridgehead being established, were on their way east to face the Russians, now only thirty miles from Berlin. There were many places at which we might cross, and German strength at one point could only mean weakness at another. They did the only thing they possibly could do: they defended the river with a light screen only, and held the bulk of their forces back, ready to be switched to any point which might be threatened.

The details of the Allied plan need not concern us here. The obvious answer to such a state of affairs was to launch several attacks on a broad front simultaneously, thus confusing the defence and splitting the reserves. In addition an airborne corps, the biggest air armada in history, was to be dropped in the rear to prevent the reserves moving up to the threatened areas. In this way we hoped to have our main force over the river before any effective counter-blow could be organised.

But even though the main battle was already won and, as Mr. Churchill said, one good heave together would push the Germans over, the Rhine still worked powerfully on our imaginations. We had thought about it too long. Germany west of the Rhine did not seem to count. In our mind's eye was fixed this river, immensely broad and hostile, and to us it was the real frontier of Germany. It made this battle different from any other.

We crossed it at dawn on March 24. The battle had started on the previous night when, at 2100 hours, the other brigades of the Highland Division had climbed into their buffaloes and led the assault. There were three main crossings made that night, one north and two south of Rees; and a big number of divisions, Canadian, British, and American, were taking part. Our two brigades were the first over. They were not heavily opposed on the actual crossing though they ran into plenty of trouble later, and were now fighting for their objectives (Rees was one of them) on the far bank. Our brigade was in reserve, ready to cross and keep the momentum of the attack going, with the village of Groin as the Battalion's probable first objective.

We had moved up near the Rhine on the previous night, had a mug apiece of tea well laced with rum, and waited.

It was a cold night after a day of sunshine, and a damp mist hung over the big flood-dyke, condensing on our clothes and chilling us slowly to the bone as the night wore on. Even when a little light came into the sky we could not see the river. It lay beyond the dyke. We could only wait, and imagine it, and listen to the hurricane of shelling going on in the mist across the water. The noise had been growing all night, and now it sounded like an almost continuous barrage. The dyke made a high straight line across our front. Occasionally one of the Sappers who were working the storm-boats appeared on top of it in silhouette, and sometimes a shell burst there; but that was all we could see. We lay and shivered.

The sun was just coming up when our turn came. As each little group was called forward we swarmed over the dyke and down into the storm-boats on the far side. The boats had outboard motors, and to start them a coiled cord had to be jerked, on the same principle as a child spinning a top. Some were difficult to start. The Sappers sweated as they jerked and jerked at the cords, visibly keeping a hold on their tempers. The engines roared, and we were off.

It looked like one of those paintings of a naval engagement. The river was broad, and smooth, and grey, with some dredgers rising gauntly out of the mist and a few dim farms in the background; and round the scores of little black boats scurrying to and fro rose plumes of water. It was grotesquely unreal. Everything was indistinct except the boats, and the firm outlines of the waterspouts, and the hunched shoulders of the man in front. The mortar bombs made little fat plumes, and the shells tall ones. A farm on the far bank grew and darkened, and leading to it from the water's edge we could make out a trail of discarded lifebelts, white like the droppings of seabirds. Dead Jocks lay sprawled among them. Shells were dropping all along the track. We grounded and jumped ashore.

The last company across was "D". This is how it struck the commander, Jock Gardiner:

'We were all pretty jittery,' he said. 'There was something about the Rhine that had us all worked up, even though there were two brigades across ahead of us. The waiting during the night hadn't helped much either. You know how it is when you wait. You want to get started, to be doing something; and instead you're lying in a hole, being shelled. When our time came, the Sapper officer in charge of our boats shouted to the man on top of the dyke: "All O.K.?" and the man shouted back: "Like hell it's O.K. There's only two boats left." There should have been ten. The rest were sunk: fifty Sappers were killed or drowned that night. Each boat took only ten men, and we had to lie about for another long while with the boats ferrying the Company across in penny numbers. By the grace of God we hit a lull in the shelling and not much was coming over when we crossed; but I can tell you I was never so relieved in my life as I was when I stepped out on the far side. I felt we were secure once we were over. Of course it was illogical: with half the Boche army trying to throw us back into the river we were a lot less secure. But that was how we all felt. There was just something about the Rhine....'

Most of us were struck chiefly by the discrepancy between the Rhine as we had imagined it and the Rhine we saw. I think most of us had memories of the Firth of Forth lurking at the backs of our minds: at any rate we were surprised to find the river much narrower than we had expected. It was four hundred and fifty yards in width where we crossed, quite wide enough, but by no means the tremendous obstacle we had imagined. We lost no men in the crossing.

The far bank was a level, featureless place, with most of the landscape still obscured by mist and the smoke of shell-bursts. Here we were met by Sergeant Mackenzie of the snipers, who told us that Lieutenant Donnie McLeod, D.C.M., had been killed while collecting his men by the bank of the river. That was a bad start to the day. Big Donnie was known to everyone, a grand man in a fight. He had gone forward with the 2nd Seaforth (who crossed ahead of us) to gather advanced information for the Groin attack.

There followed thirty-six hours which called for every ounce of stamina and determination the Battalion possessed; and if the sense of strain which built up in us during this period is to be appreciated fully, two things must be understood. First, the Germans had hundreds of guns; and second, the battle in our bridgehead ran behind its time-table, so that, although it was in reality going well, we suspected that it was not. It was a time of uncertainty and terrible shellfire; and in the end, after hours of almost continuous hammering which left us exhausted, we had to fight one of the toughest battles of the campaign.

First we went to a position south of Esserden, where we were shelled and mortared and shot at all morning. Then we were ordered to move up, still with no orders to attack, to the factory area north of Rees which the 2nd had captured early in the morning; but before we reached it we bumped the tail of the Cameron column. A bridge had been blown, and the enemy were holding the crossing in strength. The Camerons could make no progress towards their objective north of the factory, and three of their tanks had been knocked out. We were still being shelled, and everyone was becoming jumpy and bad-tempered. Once again we lay in ditches for hours, trying to scrape some sort of cover for ourselves in the damp earth. The Colonel was called to Brigade.

'I went with Derek Lang of the Camerons,' he said. 'The shelling was awful, and we got caught in a stonk on the way. We grovelled in some tank tracks until it was over. They were only eight inches deep, but I'm sure we'd have been killed without them. When we reached Brigade we found the Brigadier hit but carrying on. He said: "The General's dead. But you mustn't tell anyone yet, not until this business is over." Then he told me to take Groin from the north-west after dark. Derek was to let me know when the Camerons were on their objective, and then we were to start.'

The Colonel returned; and while he was passing on the orders to the company commanders, the house in which the "O" Group was being held had a direct hit from a shell, the ceiling collapsed about their ears, and everyone emerged covered with plaster. It was not a pleasant day. We had stood a great deal and had nothing as yet to show for it. No one was sorry when, at last, the Cameron success signal came through and we could get to grips with Groin.

It was a small village of no peacetime importance set in flat, featureless country; but it covered a main exit from Rees, and it was essential that no enemy reinforcements should reach Rees. Also, our bridgehead had to be expanded. We had to have it. Snugly tucked away in the village were our old playmates the Para-boys, prepared, as usual, to be bloody-minded. The Battalion moved from its cramped position in the ditches at 0015 hours on March 25 after seventeen hours on the east bank of the Rhine. A burning building in the factory which the 2nd Seaforth had captured acted as a beacon, and Groin too was on fire; but, even so, the route was difficult to follow, so tortuous was it and in places so blocked with rubble and trees. The main road was being heavily shelled by long-range guns, and we had casualties. The noise was so deafening that we could hardly hear the mattresses destined for Groin passing overhead. All round the horizon houses burned, and everywhere shells were bursting. We passed through the Camerons at 0100 hours, and advanced on the village.

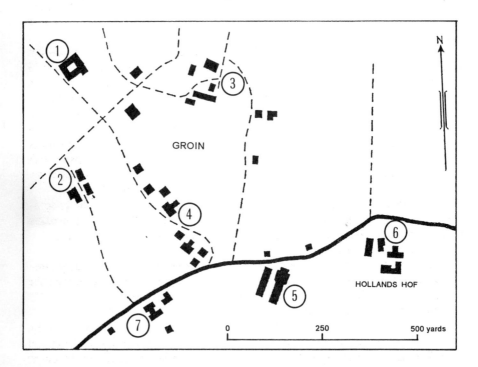

The complications of this battle by firelight were many, despite the fact that the village consisted mainly of a few farms and outbuildings; and it would probably be simplest to describe only the company objectives and the times at which they were reached. Yet Groin was the hardest village fight the Battalion ever fought, and I am loathe to let it go so cheaply. The action took place in an extremely restricted area, and the village fell house by house; but if the diagram is studied in conjunction with the story, the various moves and counter-moves can be followed.

Let us consider first the situation of Hugh Robertson, O.C. "C" Company. Hugh, with "A" Company ahead of him, was trudging down the road which approached Groin from the north, being heavily shelled and mortared. Three hundred yards short of the village he bumped the tail of "A" whose first objective was a farm on the outskirts (No. 1 on the diagram). The men lay waiting by the roadside while George Lisle and his platoon fought it out at the farm, and all Hugh could see were spandau flashes from the front and occasional figures running across the background of flames. His orders were to advance as soon as "A" was in the farm, so he halted his company and waited, worried by the fact that the time was 0230 hours, with little more than three hours of darkness left.

Colonel Sym arrived, and ordered "C" to advance immediately and take the right-hand group of houses (2). Hugh sent 13 Platoon under Peter Stone. When they were a hundred and fifty yards from the first house three spandaus opened up; but they managed to close, and the first house was cleared. While they were working their way down to the second one they walked into an extremely ugly concentration of spandaus and grenades, and were so badly knocked about that when Peter fell back on the first house he found he had only eight men left. There he met Hugh, who had heard the shooting and followed to find out what was happening.

'It didn't look too good,' he said. 'There we were, squatting in the back garden with one hell of a din going on, trying to get some sense out of Peter's men. They'd been badly shot up, and all I could make of it was that there were plenty Boche damn close, but no one knew quite where. I'd just decided to go back and send in 15 Platoon on a right hook, when a tattie-masher landed three yards from me and there seemed to be Boche firing from the hip all over the landscape. You know how it is when something like that happens. Time seems to stop for a bit. I remember looking up and seeing men coming full belt at us about thirty yards away with muzzle-flashes coming from their middles. It all seemed to take quite a long time. They were shouting something that sounded like: "Komm! Komm!"'

'Well, we didn't Komm. We went. I remember struggling through the hedge – we'd a man killed there – and then scattering back across the fields with the others to our firm base. The Boche swung too far right in the dark, and missed us....'

First round to the Boche.

Hugh sent 15 Platoon on a right hook under Lieutenant Rhodes, but they fared no better. After a time they withdrew, minus Rhodes, who was shot through the elbow and lost in the dark. He came in later under his own steam.

Second round to the Boche.

The third round went to us, for "A" Company reached its objectives in the houses on the left (3); and the fourth was ours also. At the same time as Peter had set off on his ill-fated expedition, Hugh had sent his last platoon, No. 14 under Sergeant Goldney, straight through the centre of the village to (4); and into this platoon blundered the Germans who had been chasing Peter's remnants across the fields. Goldney was ready for them; and they fled after losing three killed, one wounded, and one prisoner. Hugh, having launched everything he had, went into the village to see how Goldney was getting on.

'It was terrible,' he said. 'All the buildings were on fire. Roofs were caving in, and sparks were flying all over the place. Cattle were trapped inside. The stench sickened me. In the firelight I could see both the Boche and my own lads dodging about; and when I went down I found that Goldney had stopped short. After that he went through and beyond the buildings, and that was the last I saw of him alive. There was a lot of loose shooting, both bren and spandau, and when I got down he was lying dead on the road. They say he was shot by a German officer at close range. The rest of the boys carried on, cleared all the buildings, and took up a position astride the main road.'

Hugh had shot his bolt. He collected the survivors of the other two platoons and sent them down to reinforce Goldney's men at (4). And that was that.

Now, if this somewhat complicated narrative has been followed, it will be evident that by this time we held the left of the village and the far end of it, but as yet had been unable to do anything about the first group of buildings at (2) where Peter Stone had been shot up. The original plan had been for "D" Company to take the buildings on the far left of the village as we looked at it (5 and 6); but now this did not look too promising. Colonel Sym left the choice to Jock Gardiner, the company commander.

'He gave me the choice of two plans,' said Jock. 'I could carry on as laid down originally, or I could go for the buildings where Hugh and Peter had had all the trouble. I decided on Hugh's buildings. It just wasn't on to go stravaiging away into the dark with a place like that still holding out behind us. And there was another thing. Whatever we did, we'd have to make it pretty quick and blitzy, because there was only an hour of darkness left.'

So "D" Company proceeded to do something pretty quick and blitzy about the building at (2), starting from Hugh's firm base at (4).

It was not a straightforward task. If the diagram is consulted again, it will be seen that (2), the strongest position yet found in the village, covered the western approaches. What more likely, reasoned Jock, than that the only other buildings facing west should also be strongly held? Before sticking his neck out in the direction of (2), he would obviously have to investigate the buildings at (7).

Sure enough, as "D" was forming up at (4), such heavy machine-gun fire began to pour from these buildings that it was only with the greatest difficulty that Jock could get his men organised. Bullets were streaming down the road, buildings were blazing and cattle groaning all around; and as dawn was already breaking, the prospect of mopping up the whole village before full daylight was becoming increasingly remote. At last 16 Platoon went forward, and the "D" Company blitz began.

The Platoon was pinned almost immediately.

'I went forward to see what was happening,' said Jock. 'Bill Manson was in terrific form in spite of the pasting he and his men were getting, but I could see there was no future in it unless we could do something else as well. The centre house was a fort, there were trenches behind it and to the flanks, and there were spandaus all over the place. Bill had had six casualties already, and it was absolutely certain that an approach from either flank was impossible. I told him to give the centre house everything he had – bren, piat, everything – while I sent 17 Platoon to work round the rear and get at the trench behind.'

Then followed something which must be described in detail, the extraordinary performance of Corporal Purchase and Gray. Lance-Corporal Green tells the story.

'We were all in No. 5 Section,' he said. 'There was Corporal Purchase, and Gray was the bren gunner, and there was Hayes, and Hay, and Hanson, and myself. We'd been together a long time – right through everything – and we were all good mates. Captain Gardiner came up and called for volunteers, and Corporal Purchase says: "We'll go." Captain Gardiner says: "It's important. The place must be got." And the Corporal says: "We'll do the job properly if I have to do it myself."

'We got 16 Platoon to put down mortar smoke and high explosive in front of us, and set off down the road. The house and the trench were on the left of the road, and that was the side where Mr. Manson was held up, so when the smoke cleared a bit and we were fired on we dived into the ditch on the right. It was a good ditch, and we were able to work along it fairly fast until we hit the drain. That was the start of the business. The drain cut the ditch and the road at right angles, and a wee bridge carried the road over it; so of course that meant we couldn't crawl any farther. It meant we would have to nip out of the ditch, run across the bridge, and get back into the ditch on the far side. The Boche were only seventy yards away. They weren't fast enough to catch Purchase and Gray when they made a dive for it; but of course they were just waiting for us, and whenever we showed ourselves we got a burst through our hair.

'We thought the pair of them would wait for us and give us covering fire to help us over the gap: but nothing happened. I stood up beside a telegraph pole, and before a burst put me back into the ditch again I'd just time to see three spandaus and a hell of a lot of Boche in a big trench, and Purchase and Gray disappearing round the end of a house about forty yards away from them.

'The bullets were going through the grass a foot above our heads. We heard a bren firing, and then a sten, and we heard them shouting: "Give up, you bastards! The Seaforths are here!" That must have been when they charged. There were a few bursts of spandau, and then silence.

'We knew what that meant. They were our mates, and we were all boiled up.

' "To hell with this," I said. "Come on."

'We ran over the bridge, and into the ditch again, then across the road to the cover of a house, and then round to the Boche side. Purchase was lying about twenty yards from the trench, and Gray was almost inside it. There wasn't a scrap of cover for the last forty yards. The two of them had gone at it baldheaded, and there were three spandaus and forty-six men in the trench. Of course they were hit. They were hit all over. But they'd made the Boche look their way, and 16 Platoon had been able to get into the big house while the panic was on.

'We were mad when we saw them lying there. We didn't know what we were doing. We stood in the open, not even shooting, and called the Boche for all the names in creation, and yelled at them to come out. And so help me, they did. A wee white flag came over the edge, and then an officer, and then two or three, and then the whole issue. Forty-six of them. The officer was one of those right clever baskets – big smiles all over his face....

'Purchase was the best section leader ever we had.'

He died. Gray, though he had a burst clean through him, lived to receive the Distinguished Conduct Medal and survive the war. His bren was found actually inside the German trench.

It was now daylight, and Hugh Robertson's houses at (3) were still holding out;

but Bill Flynn and 18 Platoon went in, hit them hard, and cleared them in half an hour. In the cellars they found Peter Stone's wounded, and a number of Germans. The whole village was clear by 0730.

There was a short breathing-space while the companies dug in; but there still remained Hollands Hof, and the farm at (6), which in the original plan had been allotted to "D" Company and had been shelved temporarily while the fighting described on the previous few pages had been taking place. In it the Para-boys, obstinate as ever, still lingered.

The Brigadier gave Colonel Sym a free hand to take it either by day or by night. It was a difficult decision to make.

'Normally I should have chosen to take it at night,' the Colonel said. 'There was little cover, and the approach would have been much easier in darkness. But there was another consideration. The Germans knew that no bridges could have been erected across the Rhine in so short a time, and that we should therefore have no tanks. Yet we *did* have tanks. The D.D. type, equipped with canvas floats, had swum the river under their own power, and three of them had just reached us. They would be of little use at night, and in any case I reckoned that their appearance at this stage, when the German soldiers must have been told by their officers that they had nothing to fear from that direction, would have a profound effect on morale. So I decided to send "D" Company in during the afternoon. I have regretted it ever since.'

The only reasonable explanation of "D" Company's behaviour that day is that they were in a white fury at their losses of the morning. A company of infantry tended to be almost a family affair, everyone knowing everyone else; and the death or wounding of twelve men earlier in the day meant that nearly every man in the Company had lost at least one friend and was determined to make someone pay for it. They were brilliantly led and their past training must have told; but there was more to it than that. There was a tenacity and a recklessness in that attack which I do not think existed to quite the same degree in any other the Company fought.

The day was grey and raw, and Groin was mostly smouldering piles of rubble and blackened rafters. The Rees/Haldern road ran through it, open and bare as it emerged from the village, but with an orchard or two and a few skimpy woods farther on where Hollands Hof commanded it and stood guard over the anti-tank ditch which cut it farther on still. From Groin to the ditch was six hundred yards. In the early afternoon three tanks began to waddle along this road with "D" Company working up the ditches on both sides of them, and Jock Gardiner walking on the road itself, behind the leading tank, talking to its commander through the telephone attached to its tail.

One of the tanks peeled off from the column, swung away right, and lay waiting on the flank like a sheep-dog while Bill Manson and 16 Platoon attacked the first houses (5). They were empty. 17 Platoon went through and continued, a row of bobbing heads in the ditches, alongside the road to Hollands Hof. Jock and his tank travelled between the two leading sections.

Hollands Hof was an old and solid place with many outbuildings, and nobody had much faith in the silence which prevailed there for the moment. Houses, especially solid houses which covered anti-tank ditches, were not, in our experience, much inclined to hospitality; and it seemed to us only a matter of time before the windows staring blindly on to the road would be empty no longer. Yet "D" Company was very close, not more than fifty yards. If the Boche were there, they had nerve to hold their fire so long. Perhaps ... but that was too much to hope. Every window in Hollands Hof suddenly came to life, and bullets swept down the road at almost point-blank range. Simultaneously the German artillery and mortars opened up. Within seconds, 17 Platoon's two leading sections were wiped out.

Private Hayes says: 'I was in the section on the left of the road. We'd had a bad bashing before we started, and there were only six of us. The Boche opened up with spandaus when we were about fifty yards from the farm, and we dived for the ditch. Then Sullivan says: "Come on. Let's make a dash for it." We all got up and waded right into a burst of spandau before we were even out of the ditch. Sullivan was the first hit, but he carried on. Then he got another burst.

'I could hear Mr. Evans shouting: "Get smoke down! Get smoke down!" but there was nobody left to do it: all the boys ahead of me were hit. The tanks were firing almost on top of us, going slam, slam, slam at the house; and people were yelling and moaning. Foster, the bren gunner, was right behind me, firing bursts into the windows; but a spandau broke his gun in his hands and wounded him too. I ran back to Mr. Evans and told him there was no section left.'

Lance-Corporal Green: 'The section in the right-hand ditch got within fifteen yards, and then the Boche threw a phosphorous grenade into the middle of them and opened up with a spandau. Lowe and Betts were the only ones unwounded. One man was lying hit with his clothes covered with burning phosphorous. I could hear him yelling: "Get me out of this, get me out of this," and bullets were flying all around. Betts dragged him out and got his hands badly burned doing it. And that left only Lowe. But Mr. Evans shouts: "No one goes back till we get the wounded in." So Platoon H.Q. kept on shooting, and the stretcher-bearers went forward. There were twelve men in the two leading sections, and ten of them were lying wounded or dead in the ditches. And you should have seen the stuff that was coming out of the farm – there was a gun in every window.'

While this was going on, Jock Gardiner sent 18 Platoon under Bill Flynn to work through an orchard on the right, with the idea of turning the flank; but Bill was killed as he led them in, and his platoon was pinned by fire from a big hospital two hundred yards to the right. There were casualties; and 16 Platoon, which was in the rear, was being badly knocked about by mortaring.

Then Bill Manson was wounded. That left Jock with only one officer – Evans – and a desperate situation on his hands. The mortar, artillery, and spandau fire by this time was intense, not more than half the Company was left, the Germans were still on the top of their form, and the tanks said their ammunition was running out. It was in this situation, standing on the road with the crack of the tank guns (probably the most shattering noise of the war) going on within a few feet of him and his company in ruins, that Jock Gardiner made the decision which, in the long run, won the battle. No one could have blamed him for retreating. Instead he decided to collect the remnants and make one last effort.

One tank was out of radio touch with the others, and was useless. He ordered the other two to advance up the road with him and for five minutes give Hollands Hof everything they had at point-blank range while Evans gathered the men. This was done. As the shelling stopped, Evans went in with 17 Platoon H.Q. and bits and pieces of the other two platoons, and with a supreme effort stormed the house. They fought in the rooms and the cellars; and when the last German had been killed only Evans, two N.C.O.'s and thirteen men of the Company were left on their feet.

Without a pause he collected them and made for the last centre of resistance, a big barn at the end of the farmyard. Again the spandaus opened up; and, although Evans reached the barn, he could not find the entrance. Bullets were pouring from loopholes in the walls.

'Blow them an entrance. Knock the wall down,' Jock yelled into his telephone. The tank turrets swung round to the gable, the guns fired, and the walls collapsed. Evans gathered his gallant few and made for the hole.

And then several things began to happen.

As the dust cleared away, Jock looked over the front of his tank and found himself face to face with five Para-boys, two with bazookas on their shoulders and the others with spandaus. They stood staring at each other, less than ten yards apart; and as they stood, there was a tremendous explosion and the tank burst into flames. The second tank, knowing that another bazooka must be due at any moment, began to turn and run; but Jock ran after it and, failing to find its external telephone, pounded on the hatch with a shovel until the commander opened up and talked business. He was told we still had fifteen wounded to get out, not to mention his own mates in the burning tank, and that he would stay until the Company had brought them back, bazookas or no bazookas.

Lance-Corporal Green says: 'It was terrific. The tank turned its gun, and began blazing away over my head. I saw Captain Gardiner running back up the road to the fire. Hall, the wireless operator, heaved his 38 set into the ditch, and climbed up on top of the burning tank, and began hauling the crew out through the hatch. He was standing right up on top, and the tank was burning from end to end. Corporal Stevenson was there too. One of the tankies had a foot off, but they all got clear. Then the tank behind me got excited, and put a shell through the telegraph pole I was lying against, and damned nearly crowned me.'

Evans had been ordered to withdraw. He retired behind the first house; and, when all the wounded had been evacuated, the Company pulled right back to Groin. They had lost four men killed and twenty-three wounded, a tremendous sacrifice for so small a body of men but one which, as events proved, had not been made in vain: when "A" Company went to Hollands Hof after dark they found it deserted. The Para-boys had run, and the whole objective was in our hands.

For his work that day, Jock Gardiner was awarded the Military Cross.

The next day, the 26th, was spent in patrolling outwards from the Battalion area and in mopping up. A threatened counter-attack was broken up by our artillery. The bridge over the anti-tank ditch was found intact, so "A" Company went forward to hold it.

Next day we were relieved, and on the 28th prepared for yet another attack.

II

We had been promised ten days of hard slogging, and it certainly looked as if we were going to have them. The crossings had been successful. The Allies were firmly established across the Rhine, and already bridges were replacing the multitude of boats, buffaloes, and ferries which had carried the initial assault across and kept it supplied. But, although the enemy had been forced back ten or fifteen kilometres from the river they still retained their cohesion, and the grinding process would have to be continued for some time yet before the final collapse came and our armour could pour out into the North German Plain. Our divisions were now reorganising on narrow fronts, much as they had done in Normandy during the previous autumn, and were hammering their way along the main roads which were to feed our future advance. The Germans, foreseeing this, were holding all towns and crossings along these roads. One such town was Isselburg.

Isselburg was expected to be strongly held, and the whole of our Brigade was put in against it on the night of the 28th. However, much to everyone's surprise, the leading battalion captured it almost unopposed. We had been disillusioned too often in the past to take this at its face value immediately; but it was difficult to arrive at any conclusion other than that the Boche, at long last, was cracking. Hitherto every yard of our advance had been stubbornly contested; but this was something new. There was a hurried alteration of plan, and at 1945 hours we moved off to seize the crossings of the River Astrang, a small stream north of Isselburg and immediately west of Dinxperlo.

'I did not like the look of the operation,' said Colonel Sym. 'The Division was already miles ahead of everyone else. We were going farther forward still into territory where the enemy was active, and in doing so we were going to cut the road between Dinxperlo and Anholt, two towns still in German hands. Now, Dinxperlo was north of the river, and Anholt south of it. When we captured the Astrang bridges we should be sitting between them, equally in the path of a counter-attack from Dinxperlo or a mass retreat from Anholt; and we had only three companies.

'Still, I had the consolation of knowing that, for the first time since taking over command of the Battalion, I should be advancing with all my supporting arms complete. A bridge was being built in Isselburg, so this time there would be no difficulty about tanks, or anti-tank guns, or carriers.'

Alas for the frailty of human hopes. Isselburg was well alight, and the Germans were pouring shells into it at such a rate that the Sappers could not complete the bridge there. After a last-minute change of plan, Colonel Sym found himself advancing yet again into what he called 'a bare hands battle', stripped of tanks or any other form of close support. All he had was one company of Camerons to protect our rear, and a promise that by 0400 hours next morning there would be a bridge. The tanks would positively reach him before first light.

We scrambled forward between burning buildings, through the ruins of a factory, and across the Issel where a wall had collapsed into the river and made it just passable to infantry. It was difficult to see on the far bank after the brightness of the flames; but as our eyes became used to the darkness we picked our way along a railway line torn and twisted by bombing, and so to the open fields. From there onwards it was a case of companies leapfrogging through each other in the dark. We seized the crossings of the Muhlen Bach, a little stream half way to our objectives, and left the Cameron company to guard them. Little groups of prisoners began to drift back down the line, coming out of the darkness with their hands silhouetted against the sky.

About midnight, "C" Company was closing in on the positions covering the main Astrang bridge, and "A" was preparing for the big gamble of the night – a dash to capture the bridges before they could be blown. There were two of them, for the river ran in a double course at this point. The bigger was the first. "C" made firm, and "A" began to creep quietly up the road, led by Lieutenant Morgan of 9 Platoon.

'I was commanding 8 Platoon,' said Sergeant Elliott. 'Just short of the first bridge a spandau opened up and Mr. Morgan was hit. We were behind him. I could hear him shouting to his men to carry on, and then there were boots clattering on the road as the Jerries who'd fired ran back over the bridge to their own side of the river. I thought it would go up then for sure; but 9 Platoon went right in and got it before the Jerries could blow the charges. Then my lot went through. I was worried, crossing the first bridge. It was a funny thing, but I'd forgotten the second one might go up in my face. I kept thinking that if a section of Boche had been on this side and had run back, then there would probably be a platoon waiting for us on the other side. My one idea was to get across before the shooting started. The second bridge was about fifty yards away. There was a terrific explosion and a bit of a flash – not a very big one – and a wave of blast; and whether I was blown down or fell down I don't know, but I was lying on my face in the middle of the road with all sorts of stuff coming down round me – stones, and earth, and bits of iron. It seemed to fall for a long time – minutes it seemed like, though I suppose it was only seconds. It was coming through the trees and bouncing off the road, and my mouth was full of dirt....

'I got two of the boys, and we crawled up the ditch to see what had happened. The bridge had been blown all right, but they hadn't made much of a job of it. Only the left-hand side was down: the pavement on the right was still O.K., so the whole lot of us (there were fifteen in the Platoon then) were able to run across. We met a couple of Jerries, but we bumped them off. Then we dug in, and after a bit "C" and "D" Companies came through.'

The Battalion consolidated; and if any reader of this book would care for mental exercise he is invited to study the diagram and consider how he would have disposed his force. The problem is simply stated, but not so simply solved. First, we were liable to attack either from Anholt or Dinxperlo. Second, an attack from Anholt would threaten the little bridge over the Muhlen Bach, to our rear, and prevent the tanks reaching us. Third, the Cameron company guarding this bridge had been withdrawn by Brigade and was no longer under our command. Fourth, we had only three companies of our own. Fifth, infantry could cross the Astrang bridges, but tanks could not. Sixth, the tanks were due before first light. Colonel Sym's reasoning followed these lines. The Muhlen Bach had to be guarded, and the road had to be guarded both north and south of the Astrang bridges. Tanks could not cross the bridges, but could approach them. Therefore two companies, "C" and "D", would go where the tanks could not go – north of the Astrang – and "A" would be responsible for everything south of the river until dawn, after which they would have the tanks to help them. That left only two carrier sections, which had advanced on foot, leaving their carriers in Isselburg to come up with the tanks. One of these dug in beside the first bridge in case the Germans tried to approach it under cover of the banks; and the other, the only reserve left, was used to protect Battalion H.Q. Add to this lay-out a few tanks beside the road, half a dozen mortars beside Battalion H.Q., and the platoon of "A" Company relieved of its task on the

Muhlen Bach bridge as soon as the tanks had crossed; and it will be seen that we could look the future squarely in the face.

But it all depended on the tanks – and the tanks did not come.

Meanwhile, life was becoming very difficult for the Germans in Anholt; and during the night the commander there decided to pull out under cover of darkness and seek some healthier spot for holding up the British advance. The Astrang bridges, it seemed to him, were just the sort of place he was looking for. Two hundred Germans lined up in threes and set off smartly along the road. So there was the position at dawn – the Germans marching north in peacetime formation, unaware that we were there before them; and we with our main force on the wrong side of the river, not a tank in sight, and nothing between Battalion H.Q. and the oncoming Germans except one under-strength platoon of ''A'' Company and a dismounted section of carriers.

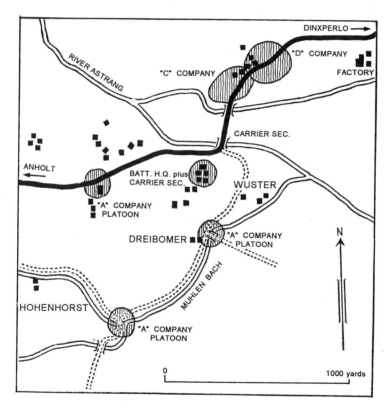

The ''A'' Company platoon was swamped. Sergeant McAllen of the Signal Platoon is credited with the first shot from Battalion H.Q. He looked up, saw the two hundred marching blithely along the crown of the road almost on top of him, and let fly with his sten. The Germans scattered and began to flood into our area. Battalion H.Q., almost without support, suddenly found themselves with a first-class battle on their hands.

They were established in and around two rows of houses a little way to the south of the road. The houses were modern, two-storeyed, semi-detached, well built and with deep cellars. Signallers, runners, clerks, snipers, and pioneers were now manning the lower windows and the trenches outside; and the Command Post was in a cellar. More and more Germans came swarming off the road, and hand-to-hand fighting developed. A house went up in flames.

'I got the wireless sets in, and then went upstairs to see how Sergeant McLeod was getting on with the lay-out of Battalion H.Q.,' said Jack Latta, the Signal Officer. 'Just as I reached the top of the stairs, shooting started all over the place. Hughie McLeod was firing a sten round the edge of the front door; and when I got to the hall window there were Germans within a hundred yards, dodging about among the buildings. I started shooting too. Then the hall was full of grey smoke with sparks all through it, and the door came flying off its hinges, and I was lying against the wall. Hughie was groaning at the door. It's funny, but I don't remember a bang at all – just the smoke and the sparks. It was a bazooka. Hughie was dying, but I didn't know that. I dragged him downstairs. There were four other wounded there too. I turned back, and at the top was a German pointing a gun at me and shouting down into the cellar.

'Well ... what could we do? We could hear more Boche outside, scraping away at the earth and sandbags over the cellar windows. We were helpless, and one grenade would have been the end of us. So we put our hands up.'

The Colonel and the part of Battalion H.Q. that most mattered were marched off to a house a short distance away.

In the other houses the situation was chaotic. Germans were still flooding into the area. Ammunition on both sides was running short. We were firing captured spandaus and some Germans were using brens. Both sides were taking prisoners. Eventually the area was swamped; and the carrier section and the pioneers, realising that the situation was hopeless, collected all their prisoners, their wounded, and some civilians, and hid in two cellars.

Meanwhile, "C" and "D" Companies were busy turning themselves about on the far side of the river to meet this new threat. Their H.Q.'s were in adjoining cellars of the same building, a hundred yards north of the bridges, so they were able to fight their battle together.

'The first we knew about it,' said Hugh Robertson, 'was when spandaus opened up from Battalion H.Q. behind us. The odd bren replied. We could see the Boche coming in left and right towards the first bridge and swanning about among the Battalion H.Q. houses. Just to complicate things, a message came through from Evans that enemy were forming up beside a factory five hundred yards to the north-east of us – that is, on our side of the river. It looked as if we were being attacked from front and rear simultaneously. Then Battalion H.Q. came on the air: "We are being overrun. We are being overrun."

'Jock Gardiner and I decided that if the Boche were after anything they were after the bridges. They were cut off from their pals to the north, and to get away they would have to come through us; so we decided to make a strongpoint of our joint H.Q. That seemed the best thing, because it overlooked the bridges and by this time the platoons out in the open hadn't a hope of altering their positions. The country was dead flat, and there was no cover. We sand-bagged and bricked up a first-storey window facing directly on to the bridge, and did the same for a bren position on the ground floor covering the same area. Sentries were posted at all available windows looking in all possible directions; and, at the same time, an Order of the Day went out to both companies: "They shall not pass!"

'Morale was terrific. The boys really were right on their toes. Then the carriers came on the air, and Major Powell (he'd come up to take over when the Colonel was put in the bag) asked us if we were firm. We said we couldn't be firmer – or happier. A Gunner had been with us for about half an hour, and he was fretting because the Battalion H.Q. wireless was *kaput* and he couldn't tell his guns to plaster the Boche at the factory. (They were still milling about, but not causing us much trouble.) However, a gunner set had come up with the Second-in-Command, and that made the mannie happy. He got cracking on the air, and whenever Jerry showed his nose after that a stonk came over. That was a comfort. Our own three-inch mortars had come up too and joined the party. They pasted the Battalion H.Q. area and the river bank west of the first bridge. It shook the Boche considerably – and our own fellows by the bridge as well.

'We knew better than anyone where the enemy were, and we didn't want to be left out, so we decided to concentrate our two-inch mortars and put down a really good stonk. Jock collected three and all the H.E bombs "D" Company had, and gave them to Donnie Sutherland, the Company Sergeant-Major. Donnie put the whole lot down on the first bridge. The Boche scattered.

'One of Bert Brocklehurst's sections was sited facing north-west, lying in the open and unable to bring fire to bear on the Boche. This section he managed to move under cover of mortar smoke, and linked them up with his other two sections on the river bank. At this stage four or five Huns tried to get over the first bridge, but Sergeant Haggarty's two sections opened up on them and they went back in a hell of a hurry. At least two of them were killed. Kavanagh was the life and soul of that party. Not content with firing from his slit trench, he dashed out firing from the hip and forced the enemy to withdraw back down the river bed. He went back to his trench, but when the Hun tried a second time he emerged again and gave an encore. His gun jammed. They got him through the head. But they had learned a lesson, and they didn't try crossing the bridge again. They began to lick their sores, and the spandau fire eased off until there was only the odd single shot every five minutes or so.

'Round about 0900 hours I saw British tanks in the distance, the best sight I'd seen for many a long day. White flags began to pop up all along the bank on both sides of the first bridge and from the buildings beyond. It was all over. We took a hundred and six prisoners in one batch, and later two more lots of fifty each came in. The last of them gave themselves up about 1000 hours. We buried thirty-seven Boche in our area alone, and goodness knows how many more were in the river or back at Battalion H.Q. Forty were wounded.

'Jock Gardiner produced his last half-bottle of whisky....'

The Battalion's casualties were fourteen killed and forty wounded. We recovered all our prisoners. Colonel Sym walked in under his own power, after escaping for the third time in two years: when our mortars stonked the area and the Germans fled to the cellars, he had hidden behind a stove and escaped in the confusion.

Early next day our armour was pouring over the bridges. The Germans had cracked, and the hunt was up.

THE LAST SWAN

(previous page and below) The 5th Seaforths clearing snipers from houses in Bremervörde, their last action of the war.

CHAPTER TWENTY

The Last Swan

I

THE GERMAN COLLAPSE was almost complete. The Ruhr was encircled, the Americans had run amok in central Germany, and a million prisoners were already streaming into our cages. In the centre of the great line which ran from Switzerland to the sea there was no front at all: American armour was advancing fifty miles a day with little to stop it except difficulties of supply. The rest of the story was to be a quick link-up with the Russians, and unconditional surrender.

But still the Germans fought where they could. The main breakthrough was in the centre, and as it progressed the two flanks were pushed inwards until they faced each other. In the north, where we were, the enemy still held north Holland and, using it as a hinge, were swinging back like a door slowly opening. Their line – not so solid as it once had been, but still a line – now faced south; and its back was to the North Sea. The British and Canadians swung north after it, aiming at Bremen and Hamburg.

From March 29 until April 6 we rested in the shattered houses beside the Dinxperlo bridges while the fighting passed far beyond us and we prepared for the travels we knew must lie ahead. We were glad of the rest. We were sorely depleted, and very tired. The rain came down and the buildings leaked, but we were content to be left alone.

On April 6 we went north over the frontier to Enschede, a clean, almost undamaged town where we were made very comfortable and enjoyed for the last time our old life round the *kachel* with the hospitable Dutch. "B" Company was reformed there. On the 9th we were back in Germany, holding Altlingen on the Dortmund/Ems Canal, a pleasant little village in the woods which contrasted strangely with the picture most of us had had of the Dortmund/Ems. For years we had heard it mentioned in the bombing reports, and most of us had imagined slag-heaps and factories. None of us could have foreseen that one day we should lie on its banks in the sun in perfect peace and tranquillity.

On April 12 Colonel Sym went on leave, Major Powell took over, and we were off once more to join in the chase.

First we drove west through fine rich farmland to a concentration area at Aacht, spent the day there waiting for orders, and drove off after dark to an assembly area a few kilometres south of Vechta. There were no searchlights up in the rear areas, and it was one of the blackest nights we had known. I remember leading the Battalion column with only a 1:100,000 map to help me, steering by faith and sense of smell, and realising with horrible certainty that two churches must have moved five hundred yards if I were still on the proper road. I told the driver to stop. Two Jocks approached.

'Is this the road to Vechta?' I shouted.

'You've had it, chum,' said they. 'There's naethin' doon there but a lot o' mines and an angry man with a spandau.'

Turning the column was difficult. There was a bottleneck, and at that precise spot a carrier had elected to chuck a track. I was not very popular.

We reached the assembly area, halted for a little and sat listening to occasional eighty-eights landing on the road ahead, and then moved on to Vechta itself, where we left the trucks and sat by the roadside until our time should come to go forward. It was peaceful there, and silent. We sat on the pavement with our backs propped against the walls of the houses, watched the stars, nibbled hard biscuits, and wondered what lay ahead of us. The war seemed far away. We sat there for three hours. Next day fighting broke out again in Vechta: I have often wondered if there were German soldiers in those houses we leaned against.

The plan was typical of the kind of thing which was happening all along the front. If the momentum of the advance were to be kept up, chances would have to be taken. When the front was static and limited objectives were the fashion, one could spend ample time on patrolling and the study of air photographs and intelligence reports, and in the end go into the attack knowing what to expect. When, on the other hand, the enemy was withdrawing at the rate of several miles a day, pressure had to be kept on him and there was no time for the finer points. One had to make big advances into totally unknown country, trusting for success to the disorganisation of the enemy. It was a risky policy, but it paid.

A few weeks earlier, our plan for the night would have been lunacy: even now it shook Major Powell, and I heard him having an earnest conversation over the blower with the Brigadier. Yes, that was the plan. Yes, the risk would have to be taken. We should start at 0300 hours.

Our *first* objective was the village of Goldenstedt, seven miles east along the road. The Camerons were firming up three-and-a-half miles ahead. We were to march through them, cross a blown bridge and a crater in the road, and carry on without even a three-inch mortar in support. When the road was repaired (a long job, because no bulldozer could reach the crater until the new bridge was erected) our supporting arms would come up, and we should go·on again.

It would be light by 0630 hours, and no one had any illusions about what would happen if we were caught short of the objective by then: the road was devoid of cover and there were many big woods overlooking it. The crossing of the bridge and the crater both involved delay. The final marching speed necessary to take us to the objective in time was over three miles an hour, more than normal infantry marching pace under peace-time conditions.

There was no question of clearing anything as we went along. We simply marched as fast as we possibly could along the crown of the road and kept our fingers crossed. The rear companies had to wait by the roadside while the leading ones crossed the crater; and it was at this stage that the only excitement of the expedition took place. With two companies across and two waiting, one small Opel car rattled down the road from the German side and stopped on the edge of the crater. As this small car contrived to sound exactly like a tank, there was a good deal of consternation in the Battalion H.Q. area and much shouting for piats; but before they could be brought to bear a burst of bren stopped the car and four Germans surrendered.

Chips Gelling, the Pioneer Officer, was probably more impressed by this incident than anyone else: he was inside the crater wondering whether to stay and have the ''tank'' fall on top of him, or climb out and be shot by our own brens,

There were no obstacles after that, and a marathon started in which those burdened with wireless sets or the heavier weapons could not possibly keep up with the others. As day began to break, the Battalion was revealed cracking along in a long, untidy string eastwards, while neat little bundles of German prisoners, very smart, marched in threes towards the west. I remember stopping to question some of the prisoners just after dawn, and suddenly finding that I had been left behind. As I trotted along to catch up with the others, the sheer impertinence of the plan struck me. It was a good joke. Here we were, streaming along the road past woods containing goodness only knew what towards a village about which we knew nothing. Our tanks could not join us for hours; and, most absurd of all, we were enjoying ourselves. The whole business was too crazy to be taken seriously. We had chanced our arm, and by golly we were getting away with it. It was exhilarating after all the months of creeping forward.

It was broad daylight by this time and Germans were surrendering all over the place. Their morale must have been low, but I do believe that many of them gave up out of sheer astonishment. Seeing our Sunday-school picnic, it must have seemed to them that a British army had passed in the night without their knowing it: anything less like an advance-guard than our column I have never seen. Some stepped out of the ditches to surrender. Some came from houses. Some even arrived on bicycles. Few shots were fired. At Goldenstedt they came out in shoals; and by 0700 hours we were on our objectives and had captured a hundred and eighty-five, including a lieutenant-colonel. They had not expected to be attacked for at least another day, and then from the east, where they had seen British armoured cars some time before. We had come in by the back door.

We dug in. A self-propelled gun was firing less than eight hundred yards away, but as the shells were landing six miles behind us the Germans had obviously no idea that we had arrived. "A" Company sent a patrol out to the east, and lost four men. The S.P. closed down in a hurry. A light anti-aircraft gun towed by a horse appeared over the horizon and was promptly shot up. For a while the Jocks loosed off at imaginary Germans in barns, but eventually retired to count their watches. It was a nice peaceful morning.

It was with relief that we saw the arrival of the tanks and full menagerie at 1230 hours, as the S.P. had opened up again, this time at us, and we were beginning to feel lonely. At 1300 hours Major Powell called in all our supporting arms and held an "O" Group for the second phase of our advance.

II

The programme was much the same as before, only longer. We had to advance seven miles due north, and this time there were no Camerons at the half-way mark. "B" and "D" Companies were to form mobile columns in kangaroos, with tanks and machine-guns in support, and move off to take the villages of Holzhausen and Barglay. "A" Company was to march, and "C" to remain in Goldenstedt until we could send back kangaroos to collect them next day. As a preliminary, "B" Company was to capture Ambergen, a village a mile to the north of Goldenstedt where the self-propelled gun was lurking.

Ambergen was taken unopposed, though the S.P. escaped. As "B" Company disappeared into the village, white flags began to appear from the windows of the outer houses and a few people came to their garden gates. Our preliminary bombardment had finished, but our shells were still landing beyond the village. As each salvo came over, the people ran to their houses, then re-emerged cautiously. Then round a corner came an enormous French flag followed by thirty cheering and gesticulating men, slave-workers kept by the German farmers.

Our advance continued according to plan for a few miles; but unfortunately we had not reckoned with the poor quality of the tracks which lay ahead. By 2300 hours practically all transport was bogged up to the axles and the companies were advancing on Holzhausen on foot. As this had not happened all at once or in the same place, there was some confusion. Vehicles were scattered in the darkness over many different fields. However, out of the tangle emerged the one important fact that some of our troops had reached the objective, though no one quite knew which troops. There was a rumour, subsequently confirmed, that there were no Germans there. Nothing was heard of Barglay, which was scarcely surprising as "B" Company were still bogged four miles short of it.

Throughout the night the Battalion continued to arrive (Battalion H.Q. in two instalments three hours apart) but by dawn all except "B" Company had come up, and the position was firm. "B" straggled in later and took Barglay without opposition. We had covered fifteen miles in less than twenty-four hours, nearly eleven of these miles through virgin territory.

There were still enemy in the woods north of our new positions, and for the next two days we sent out patrols, sometimes a company strong, to bring them in. They did not offer much resistance. However, those in Battalion H.Q. will remember Holzhausen for a different reason. They will remember it for the chaos which arose when the population realised that some one had arrived who might be able to answer the many questions which trouble a German who wakes up one morning and finds his village in enemy hands. Military Government was not due to arrive for several days; and, although we were very much in the line (there were still armed Germans within three hundred yards of us) someone had to deal with the civilians and released labourers. I had the misfortune to be landed with the job.

There were scores of callers every day, but the two principal thorns in my flesh were a minister evacuated from a nearby town, and the man with the brown loaf.

Their technique varied, but both were trying. The minister, a cadaverous, earnest soul, spoke English at twenty words a minute flat out, and could not be goaded into any sense of urgency either by the sounds of battle in the woods or by the multitude of Czechs, Russians, French, Poles, and Lithuanians who kept lining up to be told how to get home. He spoke for all the German villagers at the rate of about one complaint per half hour throughout the day, invariably tagging his own request on at the end: 'It is possible that I may have a permission for the town? I desire to visit my house. It is incended.'

By the end of the first day I was afraid to leave my office in case I should meet the minister. I had not slept for forty-eight hours, and I felt there was a limited number of times that I could hear about that incended house and still remain responsible for my actions. Nevertheless he still sought me out to plead the cases of old women who wanted to milk cows in No Man's Land, or nurses who wanted to return to their hospitals. He even produced a man who wanted to carry a pail of water a mile to our flank to prime a pump to pump water to water five pigs. (All at twenty words a minute, and he did not know the word for "prime"). He was a patient and persistent man, was the minister.

But the man with the brown loaf was altogether different. He was believed to be a baker seeking permission to distribute his wares, but he was so objectionable that he was always kicked out before he had time to explain. He was about fifty years old. His face was long, and pale, and expressionless; and his eyes were a washed-out blue. He had a Hitler moustache; but, as his hair was light brown, it was apt to pass unnoticed. The first time we saw him he walked into the office as if he owned it (as in fact he did: we were in his house), tossed up a Nazi salute, walked to a chair without a by your leave, and made himself at home. After looking us up and down he began to speak quickly in German, pointing to the brown loaf he carried under his arm. He was hustled out to see Sergeant Schlatts.

For the next two days he hung around, usually with the loaf under his arm, staring without change of expression at any officer who passed. Schlatts had disliked him on sight, and made it his business, while compiling a census of the foreign workers in the village, to ask questions about him. On the last morning he came back with two Russians who led him to a spot in the garden. They dug. They unearthed a pistol and a rifle, both well greased.

I do not know what happened to the baker after he was led away. He was shot, I suppose.

III

After two days in Holzhausen we were relieved and sent back a few miles to the village of Beckstedt for a rest. We lay there for another two days, and on April 18 moved up to a concentration area in a wood beyond Ippener, ready to take part in the next stage of the drive towards Bremen. Our Division was not attacking Bremen itself, but was paving the way towards it by taking the town of Delmenhorst, a biggish place to the west of the city. Our Brigade was to capture the outskirts, and one of the others was to make the final assault.

The Camerons were leading and we were not to go through until they were firm on a triangle of roads south-west of Adelheide, after which the 2nd Seaforth were to take Holzkamp and we were to fetch up in a wooded area on the main Delmenhorst/Wildeshausen road two kilometres south of the Holzkamp crossroads.

The battle, so far as we were concerned, took place mainly in our imaginations. We had practically no fighting to do; but the Camerons had a very sticky time of it, attacking again and again to reach their first objectives and even then hanging on to them only by the skin of their teeth. We lay in our wood all night and most of the next day listening to the racket and wondering what was going to happen when we went in. During the morning of the 19th, our "C" Company (Major Hamish Paterson) went down to help them, the 2nd went through, and at 1600 hours we followed in kangaroos. We had one casualty from shelling, and a few shots were exchanged in the woods; but our advance was otherwise uneventful. We were firm by 2200 hours.

Now, all this had simply been a preliminary to the main attack on Delmenhorst itself, and many of us felt that the General was being a trifle sanguine in imagining it would fall to one brigade. It was the biggest town we had yet seen in Germany, and we knew from experience that even the smallest village soaked up men like blotting-paper once street-fighting began. We had an uneasy feeling that we should be called upon again to help with the *coup de grace*. We were therefore both surprised and gratified next day when the Derby Yeomanry took their armoured cars in and reported that the whole place was undefended: a few plums had dropped into our lap lately, but this was by far the biggest and most difficult to believe. There was general rejoicing, and George Green was sent off ahead with the usual harbour parties to snatch the best billets.

However, George had been in the Army far too long to believe in miracles and was, moreover, of a naturally canny disposition; so when he saw "C" Company pulling out ahead of him he decided that this was the time for him to light his pipe and admire the scenery for a while. After all, a few jeep-loads of signs were not very heavy armoury if there should be trouble. So he waited, and tailed "C" at a safe distance.

It was as well, because only the centre of Delmenhorst was clear. However, after a few minor excitements the last of the Boche moved out and left us in possession of the town. We remained there for five days, "D" Company astride the main road south of Elmeloh living in something like the old Triangle conditions, for the enemy were not far off and there was occasional shelling. A light anti-aircraft gun ranged on their positions beside the cemetery was particularly objectionable. "C" sent out a patrol and had five casualties in an ambush. The rest of us lived in peace, and Battalion H.Q. (which had, thanks to the expert eye of Jack Latta, acquired an hotel) in luxury. Only one person was dissatisfied. Hector Macrae, most efficient of quarter-masters, complained loudly that two truckloads of Middlesex had descended on his "B" Echelon billet, the billet being a mere barracks capable of holding three thousand men. Hector, like all in his trade, was a great believer in the rights of property.

IV

Colonel Sym returned from leave, and on April 27 we crossed the Weser, heading north for the last battle of the war. The Guards Armoured were ahead of us, and we moved up by slow stages through Eversen and Vorwerk to Selsingen, which we reached on the 30th. We were now in the centre of the peninsula which lay between the estuaries of the Weser and the Elbe, with the remains of the German Army on our front huddling closer and closer to the North Sea. There was no escape for these Germans. The Elbe had been crossed and soon Denmark was to be cut off from Germany, so that even an evacuation across the estuary would not help them. They held two main towns, Bremerhaven and Cuxhaven, and we were within thirty miles of both. Nevertheless, they were in a strong defensive position. Meandering across the peninsula from south-west to north-east was the River Oste which, set as it was in a maze of canals, drains, and ditches, was a formidable barrier to our armour, for throughout its length any movement off the roads was impossible. The maze was miles wide, and in one place only did firm ground approach the river on both banks. This was at Bremervörde. The river ran in a double channel there; but if the two bridges could be crossed there was good going on the far side which would allow us to establish a bridgehead, fan out, and advance on Bremerhaven. Our Brigade was ordered to capture Bremervörde.

I believe this attack was the most miserable one we ever did. In the wars of the past, envoys seeking peace had carried out their missions in silence, leaving the ordinary soldier to carry on with the fighting undisturbed by the knowledge that some day soon the fighting was going to stop. In this war we had no such luck. The papers were full of rumours. Statesmen made cryptic announcements. Hitler was variously reported to be dead, alive, mad, and dying of a cerebral haemorrhage. Himmler had surrendered to us, but not to the Russians. Himmler had surrendered to everybody. Himmler had not surrendered at all. The war would end in a day, a week, a month. This was no doubt extremely entertaining to non-combatants in Britain and must have given intense pleasure to the circulation managers of newspapers, but it did the poor bloody infantry no good at all. With Bremervörde ahead of us, the only time for the end of the war that interested us was before H-hour. People who had fought in twenty actions, seeing their friends drop one by one, began to think that once more would be once too often; and there was no one to blame them. Not a man went in at Bremervörde without a sense of grievance. We did not object to the fighting: we knew that had to be done. But we were bitter at the people who made it difficult for us with too much talk.

I remember a subaltern – his name does not matter – being briefed for a patrol on the night of April 30. He had to go out to the woods beside the river and find a place where the buffaloes could cross. He would be within a hundred yards of the Germans. He sat gravely, nodding his head as the enemy dispositions were pointed out on the air photograph, occasionally asking questions about routes and the details of our plan. We were sitting round a table with an oil lamp on it, and his face stood out against the shadows beyond. In the middle of the briefing someone suddenly said: 'Nine o'clock. The News!'

We rushed to the wireless, but he remained at the table, the photograph still in his hand, his head raised, listening.

'Count Bernadotte,' said the announcer, 'has returned to Stockholm from Germany, but reports that he has been unable to make further contact with Himmler.'

We switched off the set. The hope which had grown on the subaltern's face died, and he suddenly looked very tired. He began to study the photograph carefully.

On the following night the 2nd Seaforth, who were entrenched near the bridges, sent out a patrol; and this patrol returned with strange news. Something very queer was happening. Although the bridges were right on the edge of the town and less than a hundred yards apart, no one was covering the nearest one. It was damaged, but they had crossed over and walked about freely on the far side without being challenged.

Our plan had been for two battalions to make an assault crossing of the Oste in buffaloes, form a bridgehead in Bremervörde. and hang on while the bridges were repaired behind us; but now anything seemed possible. If the Germans were crazy enough to leave their demolitions unguarded, perhaps we could rebuild the first bridge before we crossed. It was beginning to look (and this was probably the truth of the matter, though we were not able to verify it afterwards) as if the local garrison knew the war was ending and wanted us to cross without a fight. In any case there was a hurried consultation, and an alternative plan was prepared. The buffalo crossing had been timed for the night of the 2nd. During the night of the 1st, the Sappers would try to repair the nearest bridge. If they succeeded by dawn, an A.V.R.E. would cross and drop a scissors bridge over the next gap, which was a small one. 2nd Seaforth would then cross and form a small bridgehead, and we should go through and take the town. The whole business would be finished without fuss by mid-day on the 2nd, whereas the more elaborate plan could not be carried out in all its details before first light on the 3rd.

The Sappers worked all night without a shot being fired, and at 0715 hours on May 2 the A.V.R.E. crawled over and dropped its bridge. Two companies of 2nd Seaforth went across. All they found between the river and the outskirts of the town were a few Boche waiting to be taken prisoner.

While this was going on, we were waiting in and near some houses five hundred yards from the bridge, being shelled from time to time. Although only moderate in volume, the shelling was exceptionally accurate, and before long the Colonel's jeep and half-track had both been holed and a shell had gone clean through the house next door to Battalion H.Q. We lay in the ditches or in the houses watching slates clattering down from the roofs and branches falling in the gardens. "A" and "D" Companies led off at 0820 hours with their tanks and flame-throwers, and took up positions on the far side of the town without opposition. "C" Company followed at 0900 hours, and "B" and Battalion H.Q. at 0930. Except for one heavy machine-gun post which came to life in "B" Company's area some time later, there was no fighting. Within two hours of our arrival, the Camerons were bowling through in kangaroos to objectives far beyond the town; and by evening Bremervörde was a rear area.

However, it was not so simple as all that. On paper it may sound easy enough; but the combination of accurate shelling and the knowledge that the war was nearly over made it thoroughly unpleasant. The scissors bridge was the worst place. The street leading to it faced into the guns and was littered with broken glass, bricks, branches, and the usual dead horse. It turned left just before the bridge, and at that point there was cover in the lee of a warehouse. Wounded men had crawled there for safety. Beyond there was no cover at all, and a self-propelled gun was laying shells methodically round the bridge and the open space. Mud, turf, and stones rose in columns by the roadside, spattering the men as they scampered out from behind the warehouse and ran over the bridge to the comparative safety of the town. All but two were lucky. A shell landed on the tail of "B" Company as they cleared the bridge. A dozen men fell, but even through the smoke it was possible to tell which had fallen and which had been flung. Two went down as if jerked on a string. The others peered cautiously round, and struggled to their feet. The first of the casualties sat up on the road, rocking himself to and fro and holding his thigh. The other staggered to his feet, wounded in the head. Someone helped the first man (it was Lance-Sergeant Snow) back over the bridge to the warehouse, and the others ran on towards the town. Shells continued to fall only a few yards from the bridge, but no one else was hit.

Later the shelling spread to the town itself and continued until mid-afternoon, after which it tailed off. By evening it had stopped. Our total casualties by then were one killed and five wounded.

V

A period of uneasy calm followed. We were to make another advance as soon as 153 and 154 Brigades were firm, and we expected to move up on the night of May 3 . Demolitions delayed 154 Brigade, however, and the move was cancelled for twenty-four hours. On the 4th it was cancelled again. Meantime, peace rumours of all shapes and sizes were going the rounds, notably one which said we were in touch with the commander of the 15th Panzer Grenadier Division, the only formidable opposition left on our front. By 1700 hours this parley was said to have broken down, and we were certain that we should have to attack after all. Hope and despair alternated throughout the evening. According to the six o'clock News, our troops beyond the Elbe had linked up with the Russians and were roaming at will; but that did not seem to help us much. We knew the 15th P.G. of old. We had fought them in the desert, and knew they were stubborn. Italy might be finished, the Elbe might be finished, central Germany might be finished; but we were simply not interested. We wanted to know about the 15th P.G. The eight o'clock News brought peace no nearer. We began to study the maps of the road to Bremerhaven. Then, at 2040 hours, a special announcement was broadcast: the German armies in north-west Germany, Holland, Denmark and the islands had surrendered unconditionally. The cease fire would be at 0800 hours on May 5

We were having dinner at Battalion H.Q. We heard a car drive up the street with loudspeakers blaring in German, but thought it was only an ordinary curfew announcement by Military Government. Then there was cheering outside. George Green came in, grinning from ear to ear.

'I heard it myself,' he said 'It's true.'

Shooting began. I went outside. Men were milling about in the street, shaking hands and cheering. Shots were being fired into the air. Verey lights were going up. There was not much laughing, but everyone seemed to have a speechless grin on his face, as if the full meaning of the thing were only beginning to dawn. All along the battered street, with the tiles and the glass still littering the pavements, men were congratulating each other on being alive. From the outskirts of the town came a series of explosions: Sammy Hall's platoon was loosing off everything it had, including mortar and piat.

Bremervörde was well supplied with liquor. The celebrations became noisy and involved, and I do not believe that most of us really understood what the peace would mean to us as individuals. The mood was of tremendous excitement, but it did not go very deeply and little of it was personal. The Battalion was blowing off steam as a battalion, not as five hundred private lives.

Colonel Sym spoke to all the companies, one of the few comprehending voices raised that night. He told us what had happened and how much we had done; and he thanked us. He spoke more in thankfulness than in jubilation. He spoke very well. It was the right mood, but it was not for us that night. The cheering broke out again. The crowds divided and scattered to the billets to drink, and tell innumerable stories beginning: 'D'you mind the time when ....'

We remembered friends who were dead. It had been a long time. Sometimes we could not remember their names. We talked of drought in Africa and floods in Holland, and how the eighty-eights had come down on the olive grove at Sferro. We argued about which truck had sunk on Nan Beach, and whether or not there had been a rum ration after Francofonte. Others, not so reminiscent, thanked their gods that the Germans had never used gas, and that we had always had the luck to avoid schumines and flame-throwers. Perhaps, said these people, it hadn't been such a bad war, all things considered: last time they were always moaning about the General Staff, but we'd always gone in knowing that things were buttoned up.

There was that much to be said for it. Yes, and old Hector had always managed to get the grub up, no matter where we were. Good old Hector. Have another drink. Far into the morning we were still going strong.

It seemed strange in the following days to find the same drab landscape outside our windows. This, we felt, was not the way wars should end. We should feel suddenly different. Yet, apart from that one spontaneous and almost unthinking celebration, we never did have any keen personal realisation that for us nearly six years of abnormality were over. Perhaps we were too tired. Perhaps the abnormal had become too much our second nature. The war had just petered out and left us, disillusioned and weary, in a world where even peace had lost its savour. There was nothing left but anticlimax.

ENVOI

The last of the signs were stowed on board and the harbour party moved off. The road was like any front-line road, dusty, crowded, the trees on the verges scarred by shellfire and the road surface crumbling from a weight of traffic it had never been designed to carry. We moved along slowly at first behind a troop of tanks, but managed to squeeze past when the traffic thinned. There were not nearly so many vehicles now. Occasionally an ambulance went back down the line, and once we passed a bulldozer clanking forward; but we were beyond the supply companies and only infantry trucks had reason to operate so far forward. At last we came to a line of slit-trenches with some men sitting outside them, and after that there was nothing. The road stretched smooth and unmarked before us.

As we drove on we saw cows and horses in the fields, but no other sign of life. It might have been a Sunday morning in peacetime. The cows were all unwounded, too. Habit was strong in us, and it was difficult not to imagine spandaus firing down the long, straight ditches. Automatically we sized up arcs of fire and possible lines of approach. The peace was unnatural and made us uneasy.

After three miles we came upon another line of slit trenches, this time with Germans sitting outside them. They looked up curiously as we went by: we were the first British they had seen since the surrender. There were more in the houses beyond; and after that there were soldiers wherever we went, some washing their clothes outside their billets, others in work-parties, some parading. Their N.C.O.'s pulled them to attention, and saluted as we passed. In a wood, arms were being piled ready for destruction. There were great heaps of spandaus, and mortars, and steel helmets, and equipment; and work-parties were adding to the piles as we went by. In another place there was a gun-park, and in another an ammunition dump.

The men, in their attitudes and bearing, were oddly like our own. For years we had seen the Wehrmacht only in battle. We had forgotten that behind the lines they must live as we did.

Their military policemen signalled us on our way and we came to our village. There was much clicking of heels, and saluting. The staff-officer, a lean impassive man in jack-boots, produced a map for us. Here was the headquarters, and here a billet for fifty men. This barn was good: it would take another fifty. The signal office? Here, by the crossroads: the cables, of course, could be left or not, as we desired. We should arrive by noon tomorrow? Good. The billets would be cleared. Perhaps our officers would care to inspect the billets...?

My opposite number was a husky lieutenant with a limp, a square rugged face, and the East Front ribbon on his tunic. This, he said, was the first billet. He stood aside and bowed me in ahead of him. As he followed he shouted: 'Achtung!', and the men tumbled from their bunks and stood to attention. I said the billet was good. He clicked his heels in acknowledgment, and we went on to the next one.

I pointed to the brown band on his cuff.

'Afrika Korps?' I asked.

'Ja Herr Kapitan.'

He hesitated, then pointed to my ribbon and raised his eyebrows.

'Africa Star,' I said.

He clicked his heels and bowed. I bowed back. We went on to the next billet. Soon we had it all arranged; and Goodman, my driver, was erecting our Command Post sign by the roadside, closely watched by the Wehrmacht. The others returned, we formed up our little convoy, and drove off in a rattle of heelclicks.

Goodman had been greatly moved by the whole performance. He could not reconcile himself to the fact that all these Germans were wandering about, as he put it, loose. It was unreasonable. We had been shooting each other only three days before. He was very thoughtful on the way home. As we came in through our own lines again he shook his head, giving it up.

'Well, sir,' he said, 'I guess the war must be over.'

'Yes,' I said, 'I suppose it must.'

(below) The Battalion marches past in the Victory Parade in Bremerhaven.

A Highland Division Advanced Dressing Station during the Battle of El Alamein.

(below) Captain Farquhar Macrae, M.C., 5th Seaforth Medical Officer throughout the war, who worked in the middle of every action.

Roll of Honour

AGNEW	Captain P. A.	O.C.,	'B' Coy.	Sicily	14. 7.43
AGNEW	Pte. D.	14768872	'C' Coy.	Germany	29. 3.45
AITKEN	C.S.M. J., D.C.M.	2818488	'D' Coy.	Africa	23. 3.43
AKEHURST	Pte. K.	14650891	'D' Coy.	Germany	20. 4.45
ALEXANDER	Lieut. P. J.		'A' Coy.	Sicily	1. 8.43
ALLAN	Pte. A.	2822550	Signals	Africa	21. 1.43
ANDERSON	Pte. T.	14725406	'C' Coy.	Belgium	11. 1.45
ARMSTRONG	Sgt. J.	2821450	Pioneers	Holland	7.12.44
AUSTINE	Pte. S.	5345001	'C' Coy.	France	11. 9.44
BAILEY	Lieut. R. R.		'B' Coy.	Sicily	14. 7.43
BAILEY	Pte. D.	4535107	Pioneers	France	18. 7.44
BAMFORTH	Pte. H.	2824321	'B' Coy.	France	19. 8.44
BARTLETT	Cpl. J.	2822317	'B' Coy.	Africa	2.11.42
BARTON	Pte. D.	2823899	'B' Coy.	Africa	2.11.42
BASSAM	Pte. F.	10602041	'B' Coy.	France	26. 7.44
BATE	C.S.M. A.	2818378	'D' Coy.	Sicily	14. 7.43
BAWDEN	Pte. R.	3602089	Signals	Africa	7.11.42
BECKETT	Pte. A.	5777262	'A' Coy.	Africa	23. 3.43
BEECROFT	Pte. F.	14440750	'B' Coy.	Germany	11. 2.45
BELL	Cpl. D.	2821506	Carriers	France	13. 7.44
BENTLEY	Pte. J.	14791717	'D' Coy.	Germany	25. 3.45
BERWICK	Pte. H.	14750948	'D' Coy.	Germany	31. 3.45
BETHUNE	Sgt. D.	2822797	'D' Coy.	France	15. 8.44
BLACK	Cpl. J.	2824288	'B' Coy.	Africa	21. 1.43
BLINCO	Pte. A.	14556609	'A' Coy.	France	11. 9.44
BONAR	Pte. W.	14731886	'B' Coy.	Germany	9. 2.45
BORWICK	Lieut. W. S. F.			Sicily	14. 7.43
BOUCH	Pte. J.	14201323	'B' Coy.	Africa	6. 4.43
BOWMAN	Pte. R.	3195792	Anti-Tank	Africa	22. 3.43
BOYD	Pte. A.	2825766	'B' Coy.	Sicily	24. 8.43
BOYLE	Pte. F.	2935442	'B' Coy.	Sicily	14. 7.43
BRAWLEY	L./C. W.	3318426	'A' Coy.	France	21. 8.44
BREMNER	Pte. D.	2822015	Carriers	Sicily	2. 8.43
BREMNER	L./C. A.	2822888	'A' Coy.	Africa	6. 4.43
BREMNER	Pte. I.	2829074	'D' Coy.	Africa	22. 3.43
BROOKES	Pte. E.	4865287	Signals	Africa	21. 1.43
BROOKS	L./S. B.	4545771	'D' Coy.	France	8. 8.44
BROWN	Pte. J.	2820276	'B' Coy.	Africa	2.11.42
BROWN	Pte. P.	2823278	'D' Coy.	Africa	26.10.42
BROWN	Pte. A.	2825179	Anti-Tank	Africa	2.11.42
BROWN	L./C. W.	4980783	'D' Coy.	Africa	17. 3.43
BRUCE	Cpl. A.	2822347	'C' Coy.	France	15. 8.44
BUDDEN	Pte. A.	5511261	'A' Coy.	Africa	23. 3.43
BUDGE	Captain A. C.		Adjutant	Africa	21. 1.43
BUDGE	L./S. W.	2822890	'C' Coy.	England	.12.43
BURBERRY	Pte. G.	6206497	'D' Coy.	France	8. 8.44
BURNS	Pte. J.	14731891	'A' Coy.	Germany	11. 2.45
BURNS	Pte. R.	14792627	'C' Coy.	Germany	29. 3.45
BUSSEY	Pte. T.	14752054	'C' Coy.	Germany	24. 3.45
BUTLER	Captain J. L.	O.C.	Carriers	Africa	2.11.42
BUTLER	L./C. J.	6470919	'D' Coy.	Africa	6. 4.43
CAIRNS	Pte. V.	2829077	'A' Coy.	Sicily	14. 7.43
CALDER	Pte. J.	2820421	'B' Coy.	Africa	28. 9.42
CAMERON	L./C. J.	2818439	Carriers	Africa	2.11.42
CAMERON	Pte. W.	2819761	'C' Coy.	Belgium	21. 3.45
CAMERON	Pte. P.	14767930	'A' Coy.	Germany	11. 2.45
CARDWELL	Pte. D.	2823692	Mortars	France	16. 6.44
CASSIDY	Pte. B.	3195520	'A' Coy.	Germany	11. 2.45
CHAPPEL	L./C. J.	3321414	'B' Coy.	France	18. 7.44
CHURCHILL	Pte. E.	2824327	'A' Coy.	Africa	6. 4.43
CLARK	L./S. J.	2820384	Signals	Africa	21. 1.43
CLARK	Pte. A.	2825469	'A' Coy.	Africa	6. 4.43
CLARK	Pte. P.	2827281	'B' Coy.	France	18. 7.44
COCKBURN	Pte. M	1820115	'B' Coy.	France	18. 7.44
COCKBURN	Pte. O.	2940134	'B' Coy.	Africa	15. 4.43

COCKTON	Pte.R.	10602057	'C' Coy.	Holland	18.11.44
COGHILL	Sgt. W.	2820254	'B' Coy.	Africa	2.11.42
COLQUHOUN	Pte. D.	14209018	'B' Coy.	Sicily	14. 7.43
CONLIN	L./C. W.	3245847	'D' Coy.	Germany	27. 3.45
CONNOR	Pte. C.	14741858	'C' Coy.	Germany	29. 3.45
COOMBES	Pte. S.	5115566	'B' Coy.	Africa	21. 1.43
COWAN	Pte. W.	2822703	HQ. Coy.	Africa	6. 4.43
COWAN	Pte. W.	3251051	'D' Coy.	Germany	29. 3.45
CRABTREE	L./C. A.	2966858	'C' Coy.	France	18. 7.44
CRUICKSHANK	Cpl. J.	2824501	'C' Coy.	Africa	29. 3.43
CURTIS	Pte. H.	3597531	Anti-Tank	Africa	2.11.42
DALTON	Pte. T.	2933816	'A' Coy.	Africa	6. 4.43
DARGIE	Cpl. G.	2885671	Carriers	Sicily	14. 7.43
DAVIDSON	Major J. H., D.S.O.	O.C.	'D' Coy.	Sicily	4. 8.43
DAVIS	Sgt. D.	2828233	'B' Coy.	Africa	21. 1.43
DEACON	Pte. L.	14714138	'B' Coy.	France	11. 9.44
DENARD	Pte. R.	3194288	HQ'. Coy.	Sicily	14. 7.43
DENOON	L./C. P.	2820969	'B' Coy.	Sicily	14. 7.43
DENT	Lieut. J. H.		'B' Coy.	Sicily	3. 8.43
DEVINE	Cpl. D.	10662190	'A' Coy.	Germany	26. 3.45
DOCHERTY	Pte. G.	2823032	Mortars .	France	16. 6.44
DOUGLAS	Pte. D.	2823673	'D' Coy.	Sicily	14. 7.43
DOULL	C.S.M. A.	2822272	'D' Coy.	Holland	28.10.44
DOWNING	Pte. S.	2764070	'S' Coy.	Holland	16.12.44
DRUMMOND	Pte. W.	2828670	'B' Coy.	Africa	11.11.42
DUFFIELD	Pte. J.	14498080	'B' Coy.	Germany	26. 3.45
DUNBAR	Pte. R.	2820926	'C' Coy.	Africa	6. 4.43
DUNBAR	Pte. D.	2825796	HQ. Coy.	Africa	21. 1.43
DUNCAN	Lieut. J.		'B' Coy.	Africa	2.11.42
DUNCAN	Pte. A.	2822610	HQ. Coy.	Sicily	14. 7.43
DUNLOP	Sgt. A.	2823211	Carriers	France	29. 6.44
DURRAND	L./C. J.	2822255	'D' Coy.	Africa	6. 4.43
DYSON	Pte. J.	4544764	Carriers	France	29. 6.44
EASTWOOD	Pte. H.	4983955	'C' Coy.	Africa	2.11.42
ELDER	C.S.M. C.	2815873	'B' Coy.	Africa	21. 1.43
ELY	Pte. P.	2827997	Signals	Africa	2.11.42
ETHERINGTON	Pte. P.	2828959	S.B.	France	18. 7.44
EVANS	Pte. H.	3058590	Signals	France	11. 9.44
FALCONER	Pte. D.	2820753	'B' Coy.	Africa	23. 3.43
FERGUSON	Captain A. R.	O.C.	'B' Coy.	Germany	9. 2.45
FINDLAY SHIRRAS	Major C. I. D., M.C.		'C' Coy.	France	11. 9.44
FIRTH	Pte. L.	5690892	'B' Coy.	Sicily	1. 8.43
FITSIMMONS	L./C. H.	2823296	Carriers	Africa	6. 4.43
FLANAGAN	Pte. W.	3254762	'B' Coy.	Sicily	15. 7.43
FLETT	L./C. J.	2823644	'B' Coy.	France	18. 7.44
FLYNN	Lieut. W. T.		'D' Coy.	Germany	25. 3.45
FORBES	Cpl. A.	2820779	Carriers	Sicily	2. 8.43
FORBES	Pte. H.	2822642	'C' Coy.	Africa	2.11.42
FORDYCE	Pte. D.	2883801	'A' Coy.	France	11. 9.44
FORSYTH	Pte. A.	2825478	Signals	Africa	2.11.42
FOULDS	Pte. G.	4983971	'C' Coy.	Africa	4.12.42
FRASER	Cpl. J.	2822470	'B' Coy.	Africa	2.11.42
FRASER	Pte. M.	2824520	'B' Coy.	Africa	6. 4.43
GALBRAITH	Pte. S.	2823673	'A' Coy.	France	29. 6.44
GALLACHER	Pte. C.		Carriers	Africa	19. 9.42
GALLACHER	Pte. P.	2823017	S.B.	Africa	2.11.42
GAMMIE	Lieut. W. D. D.		'D' Coy.	Africa	22. 3.43
GARVIE	Cpl. D.	2822296	'B' Coy.	France	11. 9-44
GEORGE	L./C. W.	5392766	'D' Coy.	Germany	13. 2.45
GLOVER	Pte. N.	3602742		Africa	2.11.42
GODDARD	C.S.M. A.	3186297	'C' Coy.	Sicily	14. 7.43
GOLDNEY	Sgt. C.	5384491	'C' Coy.	Germany	24. 3.45
GORDON	Captain D. M.	O.C.	'C' Coy.	Africa	6. 4.43
GRANT	Pte. R.	2822097	'C' Coy.	Africa	2.11.42
GRANT	Pte. A.	2822197	'I' Section	France	18. 8.44
GRANT	Pte. J.	2823741	'C' Coy.	Africa	30.10.42
GRAVES	Pte. L.	2828748	'D' Coy.	Holland	6.10.44
GRAY	Lieut. W. J. D.	O.C.	Mortars	Africa	6. 4.43
GRAY	L./C. J.		Carriers	Africa	19. 9.42
GREGORY	Pte. S.	5050654	S.B.	France	11. 9.44
GUNN	Pte. J.	2820092	Carriers	France	29. 6.44
GUTTERIDGE	Pte. H.	14714156	'B' Coy.	France	11. 9.44
HALLAM	Pte. H.	4983334	'C' Coy.	France	16. 6.44
HANNA	L./C. A.	3196732	'S' Coy.	Sicily	14. 7.43
HARKIN	Pte. J.	4391101	'D' Coy.	Africa	2.11.42
HARRIS	Pte. J.	2822882	Carriers	Africa	2.11.42

HARRIS	Pte. S.	14362879	' A ' Coy.	Germany	9. 2.45
HARRISON	Pte. G.	2822292	A.A. Pl.	Africa	8.11.42
HARTWELL	Pte. H.	14377335	' A ' Coy.	Germany	11. 2.45
HAWKINS	Pte. W.	6018055	' S ' Coy.	Germany	29. 3.45
HECTOR	Lieut. A. F. J.		' A ' Coy.	France	15. 6.44
HEMPHILL	Pte. A.	14444914	' A ' Coy.	Germany	11. 2.45
HENDERSON	Pte. T.	2825724	Pioneers	France	18. 7.44
HENDERSON	Pte. W.	3050992	' B ' Coy.	Africa	21. 1.43
HENRY	Pte. P.	14775761	' A ' Coy.	Germany	11. 2.45
HILL	Pte. G.	1669457	' B ' Coy.	Africa	21. 1.43
HILL	Sgt. W.	5677781	' B ' Coy.	Germany	11. 2.45
HILLCOAT	Cpl. N.	2823400	Signals	Africa	6. 4.43
HOGG	Pte. J.	14209360	' A ' Coy.	Africa	6. 4.43
HOGG	Pte. M.	14442595	' B ' Coy.	Germany	29. 3.45
HOLMES	Pte. R.	3317932	' B ' Coy.	Africa	21. 1.43
HORN	Lieut. D. G.		' C ' Coy.	Africa	2.11.42
HUGHES	Pte. J.	2827822	' D ' Coy.	Africa	2.11.42
HUGHES	Pte. R.	3314375	' D ' Coy.	France	8. 8.44
INGRAM	Sgt. R.	2823264	Carriers	Africa	19. 9.42
INMAN	Pte. J.	14781590	' D ' Coy.	Germany	5. 4.45
IRVINE	Cpl. J.	2821271	HQ. Coy.	Africa	23. 3.43
JACK	Pte. E.	2829199	' B ' Coy.	France	16. 6.44
KANE	Pte. M.	14502862	' A ' Coy.	France	11. 9.44
KAVANAGH	Pte. W.	14422856	' C ' Coy.	Germany	29. 3.45
KEEFE	Cpl. J.	2824130	' A ' Coy.	Africa	6. 4.43
KENNEDY	L./C. W.	2824548	' C ' Coy.	Africa	2.11.42
KENNEDY	Pte. D.	14725503	' C ' Coy.	Holland	2.11.44
KERR	Pte. D.	2828678	' C ' Coy.	Belgium	11. 1.45
KIRKWOOD	Pte. J.	2825826	' A ' Coy.	Africa	6. 4.43
LAING	Pte. A.	3594077	' B ' Coy.	Africa	21. 1.43
LAMB	Pte. R.	1519785	' A ' Coy.	France	21. 8.44
LAMB	Pte. S.	14207688	' A ' Coy.	Sicily	14. 7.43
LISTER	Pte. J.	3986669	' B ' Coy.	Africa	21. 1.43
LITTLE	L./C. J.	3602669	' D ' Coy.	Germany	20. 2.45
LLOYD	Cpl. A., M.M.	3603393	' D ' Coy.	France	8. 8.44
LORKING	Pte. H.	2819637	' B ' Coy.	France	9. 7.44
LOY	Pte. G.	2827846	' B ' Coy.	Africa	21. 1.43
MADDEN	Pte. R.	2825870	HQ. Coy.	Africa	2.11.42
MAMMEN	Pte. R.	14445413	' D ' Coy.	Germany	11. 2.45
MANSON	Cpl. G.	2929541	' B ' Coy.	France	18. 7.44
MARSHALL	Pte. R.	3599916	' A ' Coy.	France	11. 9.44
MARTINDALE	Pte. R.	14793932	' C ' Coy.	Germany	29. 3.45
MASSON	Pte. G.	2820513	' C ' Coy.	Africa	6. 4.43
MATCHWICK	Cpl. S., M.M.	5339300	Sniper	Germany	25. 3.45
MATHESON	Pte. J.	2822815	HQ. Coy.	Africa	21. 1.43
MATTHEWS	Pte. J.	2820501	' C ' Coy.	Holland	18.11.44
MERCER	Pte. W.	2823513	' D ' Coy.	Africa	6. 4.43
MILLER	Pte. W.	2829114	' C ' Coy.	Africa	23. 3.43
MITCHELL	Pte. W.	2821229	' D ' Coy.	France	8. 8.44
MITCHELL	Sgt. J., M.M.	2823253	' C ' Coy.	Africa	26. 3.43
MITCHELL	Pte. S.	3254459	' C ' Coy.	Sicily	13. 7.43
MOFFAT	Pte. D.	3058408	' C ' Coy.	France	18. 7.44
MOORE	Pte. A.	2825882	' D ' Coy.	Africa	23. 3.43
MOORE	Pte. J.	2939873	' B ' Coy.	Africa	21. 1.43
MORE	L./C. F.	2829116	' A ' Coy.	Africa	23. 1.43
MORRISON	Sgt. W., M.M.	2820793	Mortars	Sicily	13. 7.43
MORRISON	Pte. D.	2823649		Sicily	14. 7.43
MORRISON	Cpl. J.	2825883	' A ' Coy.	Africa	2.11.42
MORRISON	Pte. W.	14742030	' B ' Coy.	Germany	11. 2.45
MUIR	Sgt. J.	2817075	Master Cook	Germany	13. 4.45
MULHOLLAND	L./C. J.	2825886	' C ' Coy.	Africa	6. 4.43
MULVERHILL	Pte. D.	14437753	' S ' Coy.	France	18. 7.44
MUNRO	Captain A. D.		Adjutant	Germany	11. 2.45
MUNRO	Cpl. G.	2825344	' A ' Coy.	France	21. 8.44
MURRAY	Captain A. G.	O.C.	' D ' Coy.	France	8. 8.44
MURRAY	Pte. J.	7362698	' C ' Coy.	France	11. 9.44
McAVOY	Pte. J.	2939851	' B ' Coy.	Africa	21. 1.43
McBEAN	Cpl. A.	2824596	' A ' Coy.	Africa	21. 1.43
McCARTHY	L./C. G.	3328697	' B ' Coy.	Sicily	14. 7.43
McCRACKEN	L./C. J.	3316028	' D ' Coy.	France	8. 8.44
McCULLOCH	Captain J. H.	O.C.	' A ' Coy.	Africa	2.11.42
MACDONALD	Sgt. J.	2815590	' D ' Coy.	Africa	2.11.42
MACDONALD	Pte. W.	2820927	Piper	Africa	21. 1.43
McDOUGALL	Pte. S.	2823106	Signals	Africa	2.11.42
McDOWALL	Sgt. J.	2823220	' A ' Coy.	Holland	23.10.44
McFARLANE	Pte. D.	2827852	' C ' Coy.	Africa	1.11.42
MACGAW	Pte. R.	2823923	' B ' Coy.	France	7. 7.44

McGILVRAY	Lieut. J.		'B' Coy.	Africa	6. 4.43
McGINIGLE	L./C. J.	2825304	Anti-Tank	Africa	17. 6.43
McGONIGLE	Pte. I.	2825306	'A' Coy.	Africa	26. 6.43
McGRATH	Pte. W.	2940006	'D' Coy.	Africa	6. 4.43
McINTOSH	Sgt. F.	2825845	'D' Coy.	Germany	13. 4.45
McINTOSH	Pte. D.	14995465	'C' Coy.	Germany	24. 3.45
McINTYRE	Pte. R.	3322088	'D' Coy.	France	8. 8.44
MACKAY	Pte. A.	2818726	'C' Coy.	Africa	27. 2.43
MACKAY	Sgt. D.	2820042	'D' Coy.	Africa	2.11.42
MACKAY	Pte. T.	2821959	'D' Coy.	France	11. 9.44
MACKAY	Pte. A.	2822337	HQ. Coy.	Africa	6. 4.43
MACKAY	Pte. A.	2824883	'D' Coy.	France	8. 8.44
McKENNA	Pte. P.	2840250	'C' Coy.	France	20. 7.44
MACKENZIE	Captain I. D.		'D' Coy.	Africa	6. 4.43
MACKENZIE	Pte. J.	2819960	'R' Coy.	Germany	25. 3.45
MACKENZIE	Pte. J.	2822068	'A' Coy.	Sicily	14. 7.43
McKENZIE	L./C. E.	3600810	'S' Coy.	France	11. 6.44
MACKIE	Pte. A.	2829129	HQ. Coy.	Africa	18. 3.43
MACKINTOSH	Captain W. L.		Adjutant	Africa	4.11.42
MACKINTOSH	Cpl. J.	2825855	'C' Coy.	Africa	6. 4.43
McKIRDY	L./S. J.	2824648	'I' Section	Africa	21. 1.43
McLACHLAN	Pte. G.	2829131	'B' Coy.	Africa	2.11.42
McLEOD	Lieut. D., D.C.M.	O.C.	Carriers	Germany	23. 3.45
MACLEOD	Lieut. A. B.		'C' Coy.	Africa	2.11.42
McLEOD	C.S.M. D.	2815755	'A' Coy.	France	21. 8.44
McLEOD	Cpl. D.	2818311	'D' Coy.	Germany	26. 3.45
MACLEOD	Pte. J.	2820661	'C' Coy.	Africa	27. 2.43
McLEOD	Sgt. D., M.M.	2820987	'I' Section	Germany	30. 3.45
MACLEOD	Cpl. A.	2821797	'A' Coy.	Africa	2.11.42
MACLEOD	Pte. A.	2822704	HQ. Coy.	Africa	2.11.42
McLEOD	Pte. J.	2829132	'C' Coy.	Germany	11. 2.45
McLEOD	Pte. R.	14214610	'D' Coy.	France	8. 8.44
McLELLAN	Pte. H.	2184912	'C' Coy.	Sicily	14. 7.43
McPHEE	Pte. D.	2827869	'C' Coy.	Africa	4.12.42
McPHERSON	Pte. W.	2822947	'C' Coy.	Africa	6. 4.43
McSHANE	Pte. R.	14444921	'D' Coy.	Germany	29. 3.45
McTAGUE	Pte. A.	3059365	'B' Coy.	Sicily	14. 7.43
NELSON	Pte. D.	2824485	'B' Coy.	France	23. 8.44
NESS	Pte. A.	2667604	'C' Coy.	Germany	21. 2.45
NEWNES	Pte. L.	2929293	HQ. Coy.	Sicily	13. 7.43
NEWTON	L./S. H.	2930669	'B' Coy.	Sicily	14. 7.43
NICHOL	Pte. J.	2940176	'B' Coy.	Africa	21. 1.43
NICHOLSON	Pte. B.	2718409	'B' Coy.	Africa	21. 1.43
O'BOYLE	Pte. J.	2938275	'D' Coy.	France	14. 8.44
OGG	Pte. R.	14212187	'A' Coy.	France	18. 8.44
OLIVER	Pte. J.	2829141	Anti-Tank	France	16. 6.44
O'NEILL	Pte. T.	2823672	Signals	France	11. 9.44
ORR	Pte. A.	14205401	'B' Coy.	Africa	6. 4.43
OWENS	Pte. F.	4865554	'B' Coy.	Sicily	14. 7.43
PATIENCE	Pte. A.	2822892	'D' Coy.	Germany	29. 3.45
PAWILONIS	Pte. J.	2822327	'D' Coy.	Holland	16.11.44
PHILPOTT	Pte. J.	5385280	Signals	Germany	29. 3.45
PICKERING	Cpl. F.	2824361	Carriers	Africa	2.11.42
POLSON	Sgt. J.	2814959	'D' Coy.	Africa	2.11.42
PRESTON	L./C. J.	3601645	'B' Coy.	Africa	2.11.42
PURCHASE	Cpl. J.	4916406	'D' Coy.	Germany	25. 3.45
PURGAVIE	Captain D. G., M.C.	O.C.	Carriers	France	19. 8.44
QUINN	Pte. J.	2819132	'B' Coy.	Africa	2.11.42
RAFFERTY	Pte. O.	2824631	'D' Coy.	France	11. 9.44
RAY	Pte. J.	3604735	'C' Coy.	Africa	3.11.42
REDDING	L./C. E.	2825708	'C' Coy.	Africa	2.11.42
REED	Lieut. G. B.		'B' Coy.	Africa	6. 4.43
REES	Pte. E.	2824364	'B' Coy.	Africa	6. 4.43
RIMMINGTON	Pte. J.	4865241	'A' Coy.	Africa	23. 3.43
ROBINSON	Pte. H.	4804589	'C' Coy.	France	17. 7.44
ROSE	C.S.M. G.	2818072	'B' Coy.	Sicily	14. 7.43
ROSS	L./S. C.	2824432	Carriers	Sicily	13. 7.43
ROSS	Pte. A.	2885116	'C' Coy.	France	13. 6.44
ROWLEY	Pte. R.	14431467	'S' Coy.	Germany	17. 2.45
ROYS	Pte. J.	1516033	'C' Coy.	France	15. 8.44
ROYSTON	Pte. R.	2824370	Signals	England	24. 4.44
RUSSELL	Pte. N.	5387789	'B' Coy.	Africa	2.11.42
SAUNDERS	Pte. W.	2816274	'B' Coy.	Africa	2.11.42
SCOTT	Pte. A.	2822823	Carriers	Africa	2.11.42
SELLEY	Pte. T.	15201529	'A' Coy.	Sicily	15. 7.43
SEWELL	L./C. C.	827902	'C' Coy.	Germany	26. 3.45

SHARP	L./C. M.	2823270	Carriers	Africa	2.11.42
SHAW	Pte. J.	2822538	'C' Coy.	Africa	2.11.42
SHAW	Pte. D.	2930425	'A' Coy.	Sicily	14. 7.43
SHEARER	L./C. E.	2822973	'I' Section	Africa	25. 5.43
SHELTON	L./C. J.	5831905	'A' Coy.	Germany	11. 2.45
SIM	L./S. J.	761581	'D' Coy.	Africa	13. 3.45
SINCLAIR	Pte. L.	2822811	'D' Coy.	Sicily	14. 7.43
SINCLAIR	Pte. C.	3196548	'C' Coy.	Africa	4.12.42
SINCLAIR	Pte. J.	14819256	'D' Coy.	Germany	25. 3.45
SINGER	Pte. F.	2934082	Signals	Sicily	14. 7.43
SMITH	Pte. P.	2822608	Carriers	Sicily	4. 8.43
SMITH	Pte. A.	2825366	'C' Coy.	Africa	8.11.42
SMITH	Pte. F.	2825367	'B' Coy.	Africa	2.11.42
SMITH	L./C. R.	2825369	Anti-Tank	Africa	28. 4.43
SMITH	Pte. D.	3315446	'C' Coy.	France	16. 6.44
SMITH	Pte. W.	6982666	'C' Coy.	Africa	6. 4.43
SPENCE	Pte. J.	3135346	'A' Coy.	France	11. 9.44
STEVENTON	Pte. R.	3249727	'B' Coy.	Holland	14.11.44
STEWART	Pte. W.	2823855	'B' Coy.	Africa	21. 1.43
STOCKDALE	Pte. J.	14423562	'A' Coy.	France	11. 9.44
STROWGER	L./C. G.	3195155	'D' Coy.	Africa	6. 4.43
STUART	Sgt. W.	2887013	'B' Coy.	France	11. 9.44
SUTHERLAND	Pte. J.	2815522	'C' Coy.	Africa	2.11.42
SUTHERLAND	L./C. H.	2822177	'A' Coy.	Africa	24. 1.43
SWANSON	Captain M. M.	O.C.	'C' Coy.	Africa	4.11.42
SWANSON	Pte. D.	2820257	'B' Coy.	Germany	26. 3.45
SWANSON	Pte. D.	2822898	'A' Coy.	Africa	2.11.42
TAIT	Pte. C.	3190847	S.B.	France	18. 7.44
TAYLOR	Pte. J.	1802483	'C' Coy.	Germany	8. 4.45
TAYLOR	L./C. G.	3318437	'A' Coy.	France	2. 7.44
TAYLOR	Pte. W.	14364414		Sicily	1. 8.43
TEECE	Pte. R.	14200691	'B' Coy.	France	16. 8.44
THIRD	Pte. D.	2824393	'D' Coy.	Africa	28.10.42
THOMAS	Pte. E.	2827073	'A' Coy.	France	11. 9.44
THOMPSON	Pte. E.	5506417		Africa	2.11.42
THOMSON	Cpl. A.	2939404	Signals	Germany	11. 2.45
THORNE	Pte. A.	5674439	'B' Coy.	France	11. 9.44
TOUGH	Pte. J.	2886655	HQ. Coy.	Sicily	10.10.43
TRAINER	Pte. J.	3196252	Anti-Tank	Africa	6. 3.43
TURNBULL	Pte. A.	2829373	'A' Coy.	France	18. 7.44
TURNBULL	Pte. G.	3605633		Africa	3.11.42
URQUHART	Pte. W.	6475694	'B' Coy.	Africa	6. 4.43
WAITES	Pte. V.	14781742	'D' Coy.	Germany	25. 3.45
WARDLAW	Sgt. R.	3058511	'B' Coy.	Africa	21. 1.43
WARDLE	Pte. J.	3058471	Signals	Germany	11. 2.45
WARES	L./C. C.	2820653	Post Cpl.	Africa	21. 1.43
WATSON	Pte. W.	2823658	'B' Coy.	Africa	7.11.42
WATSON	Pte. T.	3601772	'B' Coy.	Africa	2.11.42
WEAVING	Pte. K.	14730698	'S' Coy.	Germany	29. 3.45
WEIR	Pte. D.	2822607	'S' Coy.	Holland	16.12.44
WHALLEY	Pte. H.	2939953	'A' Coy.	Sicily	18. 7.43
WHEELER	Pte. H.	3600833	'C' Coy.	Africa	2.11.42
WHITE	Pte. D.	14742130	'A' Coy.	Holland	4.11.44
WILLEY	Pte. J.	10602159	'D' Coy.	France	29. 7.44
WILLIAMS	Pte. E.	14780325	'C' Coy.	Germany	16. 2.45
WILLIAMSON	Pte. W.	2939929	'D' Coy.	France	8. 8.44
WILLIAMSON	Pte. E.	14514112	'A' Coy.	Germany	25. 3.45
WILLOCK	Captain G. A., M.C.	O.C.	Mortars	Sicily	14. 7.43
WILSON	Pte. F.	4982697	'B' Coy.	France	19. 8.44
WILSON	L./C. D.	14405391	'D' Coy.	Germany	25. 3.45
WISE	Pte. W.	14496597	'B' Coy.	Germany	9. 2.45
WOODLEY	L./C. A.	5341679	'B' Coy.	Germany	2. 5.45
WORSLEY	Pte. G.	3861315	'S' Coy.	France	18. 7.44
WRAY	Cpl. A.	2817100	'A' Coy.	Africa	21. 1.43
WRIGHT	Pte. A.	1656485	'D' Coy.	Germany	25. 3.45
YATES	Pte. H.	1829130	'D' Coy.	France	11. 9.44
YOUNGER	R.S.M. J.	2814843	HQ. Coy.	Africa	21. 1.43

The following were still missing in November, 1945:

SMART	Lieut. R.			Lost on patrol	9. 7.44
SMITH	Pte. J.	908009		Lost on patrol	9. 7.44
DAVISON	Pte. A.	3064177		Lost on patrol	9. 7.44
DOBSON	Pte. A.	3190247		Missing	23. 4.45

SUMMARY		Officers	Other Ranks	Totals		
AFRICA	... ...	14	140			
SICILY	... ...	7	37			
NORTH-WEST EUROPE		8	153	Officers	Other Ranks
Killed in Accidents in England			2	30	335
Missing	... ...	1	3			

Honours and Awards

5th Battalion The Seaforth Highlanders

OFFICERS

OTHER RANKS

D.S.O. and Bar

Lt.Col. J.H.WALFORD

D.S.O.

Lt.Col. J.E.STIRLING
Major J.H.DAVIDSON
Lt.Col. J.M.SYM

M.C.

Capt. J.GASTON
Lieut. F.A.MACRAE (R.A.M.C.)
Lieut. J.H.DIMECH
Capt. G.A.WILLCOCK
Lieut. I.J.C.GRANT
Capt. C.I.D.FINDLAY-SHIRRAS
Lieut. P.D.NAIRNE
Lieut. H.S.ROBERTSON
Capt. D.G.PURGAVIE
Capt. H.G.P.MACRAE
Major R.E.FLEMING
Lieut. W.J.C.MAIR
Major D.A.BLAIR
Rev. I.SIMPSON (R.A.Ch.D.)
Lieut. P.H.GRANT.
Capt. J.H.GARDINER
Major H.A.C.MACKENZIE
Major G.H.GREEN
Lieut.G.LISLE

Mention in Despatches

Lt.Col. J.E.STIRLING
Capt. H.G.P.MACRAE
Capt. C.I.D.FINDLAY-SHIRRAS
Lt.Col. J.M.SYM
Major K.L.F.WILSON
Capt. Q.MACKENZIE
Capt. I.G.H.HOULDSWORTH
Lieut. R.B.GALLOWAY
Capt. J.H.LATTA
Major J.L.PATERSON

Croix de Guerre with Gilt Star

Major K.L.F.WILSON

Chevalier of the Order of Leopold II - Belgium Croix de Guerre, 1940, with Palm

Major J.C.POWELL

D.C.M.

L/Cpl. D.McBEATH   Pte. J.GRAY
CSM. J.AITKEN

M.M. and Bar

Pte. D.BRIDGES   Cpl. S.MATCHWICK

M.M.

Cpl. H.MACKAY	Cpl. A.FORBES
Pte. C.MUNRO	Pte. D.BREMNER
Pte. D.CRAWFORD	Pte. J.GRAHAM
Sgm. W.SUTHERLAND	Pte. J.CORMACK
Pte. G.ANDERSON	Pte. J.HODGSON
Sgt. W.MORRISON	Sgt. H.McLEOD
Sgt. J.MITCHELL	Pte. J.McLAUGHLIN
Sgt. W.McGACHIE	Pte. J.GRAHAM
Sgt. A.POLSON	L/Cpl. A.LLOYD
L./Sgt. D.KENNEDY	Pte. P.DAVIDSON
L/Cpl. S.WILCOCKSON	Sgt. D.SUTHERLAND
CSM. R.MILNE	Pte. H.BAILEY
Sgt. J.DAVIDSON	Sgt. J.MORE
Sgt. A.SINCLAIR	Cpl. R.McLEOD

Mention in Despatches

RQMS. H.PRATT	CSM. J.GEDDES
L/Cpl. J.MURRAY	Cpl. J.GEDDES
Pte. J.HEELEY	Cpl. J.YOUNIE
C/Sgt. A.MUNRO	Cpl. J.PURCHASE
CSM. R.MILNE	Pte. C.KAVANAGH
RSM. G.DURRAND	Sgt. A.MACKAY
CSM. J.DAVIDSON	Pte. R.WOODS
L/Cpl. N.GUNN	Sgt. W.McALLEN
Sgt. W.PRICE	Sgt. W.GALLEITCH
Sgt. R.MACKAY	Sgt. G.MACKENZIE
Cpl. R.McLEOD	CSM. A.LOCKIE
Pte. R.GILMOUR	L/Sgt. H.GUNN
L/Cpl. S.MATCHWICK	L/Cpl. L.SULLIVAN
Pte. E.FRASER	

C.-in-C.s Certificates:

Gallantry

Sgt. J.SUTHERLAND
CSM. A.DOULL
Pte. G.LUMSDEN
L/Sgt. L.STEWART
L./Cpl. A.PEACOCK
Pte. L.WEEKS
Pte. J.ROSS
L/Sgt. J.HARRISON
L/Cpl. R.WAYGOOD
Pte. F.MORGAN
Sgt. J.BUCHANAN
L/Cpl. T.GRIBBEN

Good Conduct

Sgt. A.STEWART
CSM. A.McLEOD
Pte. A.SUTHERLAND
CSM. J.MANSON
L/Cpl. P.KETCHEN

Croix de Guerre with Bronze Star

Pte. E.FRASER

Operation Guy Fawkes

THIS OPERATION order is reproduced exactly as it was run off from the duplicator at Battalion H.Q., with the single exception that a small appendix, containing a list of code-names no longer of any interest, has been omitted. The order, like most military documents, is peppered with map-references. Owing to the area covered by the battle, it has not been possible to print a map which includes more than the immediate Battalion front, but grid-lines have been drawn on the map on page 179, so that readers with a crossword turn of mind may be able to plot those references which have an immediate bearing on the story. Readers without crossword minds may be relieved to hear that the story can be followed perfectly well from the narrative on pages 178 to 181.

5 SEAFORTH OPERATION ORDER No. 9. TOP SECRET.
Operation 'GUY FAWKES' G/2/2

Ref Maps— 3rd Nov 44.
    HOLLAND 1/25000—10 SE, 10 NE.

INFORMATION

  1. Enemy

    (a) Little is known about the enemy but believed to be holding island bounded by R WAAL—'S HERTOGENBOSCH —AFWATERINGS CANAL with 6 Bns which consist of a mixed collection from various Divs we have been fighting stiffened by elements of SS.

    (b) Bridges over R MAAS still intact indicating ability to reinforce with SP Guns and the 'odd' Tank.

    (c) Plans have been captured indicating that the enemy has a withdrawal plan ready to put into effect if attacked in strength, therefore initial resistance is expected to be stiff.

  2. Own Tps

    (a) 153 Inf Bde is attacking at H+40 on Right flank of 152 Inf Bde to capture NEEUWKUIK 2346—VLIJMEN 2646 —HAARSTEEG 2448.

    (b) 131 Inf Bde and 154 Inf Bde are staging diversions in area of BAARDWIJK 1747 and 'S HERTOGENBOSCH.

    (c) An Armoured coln consisting of AVREs, Sqn of Tanks and Sqn of 2 Derby Yeo are forcing a route from 'S HERTOGEN-BOSCH along NORTH bank of Canal to open an early tank route.

  3. Additional Tps

    (a) Under comd 152 Inf Bde :—
        'D' Coy 1/7 Mx.
        2 Pls 'D' Coy 1/7 Mx.
        243 A/Tk Bty RA
        CCP 175 Fd Amb.
        Sec Div Pro Coy.
    In support
        East Riding Yeo
        Div Arty
        Two Tps 141 RAC (Crocodiles)
    (b) Under comd
        In support—5 Seaforth—Nil.

INTENTION

  4. 5 SEAFORTH

    (a) Will make an assault crossing over AFWATERINGS CANAL at 205444 and form an initial bridgehead.

    (b) Will capture area GROENWOUD 210462.

METHOD

  5. Gen

    (a) The attack will be carried out in Two Phases as under :
      Phase I Codeword—SPADES

    Assault Crossing and Formation of initial bridgehead.
Note :—5 CAMERONS will make a simultaneous assault crossing on Left of the Bn.

      Phase II Codeword—DIAMONDS

    Capture of area GROENWOUD 210462.
Note :—2 SEAFORTH will simultaneously attack and capture area X Rds DRUNEN 199463.

    (b) On completion of Phase I and Phase II 5 CAMERONS will pass through the Bn and capture area WOLFSHOEK 2147.

  6. Phase I

    (a) Tps—Right 'B' Coy, Left 'D' Coy.
        'A' Coy will carry out tasks allotted.
        'C' Coy will cross on order behind 'B' Coy.

    (b) Tasks
      (i) 'B' Coy—area dyke 207453. One Pl 'B' Coy will exploit to corner of dyke at 216453.
      (ii) 'D' Coy—area rd and dyke junc 198454.
      (iii) 'C' Coy—will cross on order and will pass through 'B' Coy and capture SEMPKE 2045.
      (iv) Two Pls of 'A' Coy will cross the Canal on the Right and Left of 'B' & 'D' Coys respectively at initial assault.
      One Pl 'A' Coy will supply ferrymen for the Bn. 'A' Coy will be responsible for the local protection of Class 40 bridge under construction at 208444.

    (c) Boundaries
      (i) Inter Bde Bdy.
      Between 153 Inf Bde and 152 Inf Bde—all incl 152 Bde :—Tract from ZANDKENT 220409—218442—SE edge of wood 217444—tk junc 218452—thence tk to 215460.
      (ii) Inter Bn Bdy.
      All incl 5 SEAFORTH X tks 189435—190444— rd crossing dyke 198453—X rds 199463. (Note :—after initial crossing 5 CAMERONS will be responsible for covering Class 9 bridge in area 198444)

    (d) Assembly Areas and FUPs
      (i) Coys will move by march route from present locn to assembly areas indicated on the ground at 1200 hrs.
      Route—X rds 220396—X tks 209411—GIERS-BERGEN 211430—KLINKKAERT 203437.
Order of March—'D' 'C' 'B' BnHQ.
Head of 'D' Coy will pass SP 220391 at 1230 hrs. Tail of BnHQ will pass SP at 1300 hrs.
      (ii) Coys will be in assembly areas by 1445 hrs.
      (iii) At 1530 hrs Coys will move to FUP as recced and will be in posn ready to assault at 1630 hrs.

    (e) Boating Equipment
      (i) 25 MkIII Assault Boats with decking have been allotted to the Bn.
      Boats are allotted as under :—
      'A' Coy—4 boats, 'B' Coy—7, 'D' Coy—7, Spare—7.
      (ii) Boats have been off-loaded in areas recced during night 3/4 Nov.
      (iii) 'A' Coy will detail one Pl, which will provide ferrymen for leading Coys as under :—
      'B' Coy—14 men
      'D' Coy—14 men
      Ferrymen will report to 'B' & 'D' Coys at 1500 hrs in Coy assembly areas. Os. C. 'B' & 'D' Coys will allot ferrymen to boats before moving to FUP. Ferrymen will stay with boats until 'tying up' on near bank after 2 SEAFORTH have crossed.

(f) Assault Boat Bridge

OC 6 Pl will be responsible for constructing a bridge with MkIII Assault Boats and decking as soon after initial assault as possible at 205444.

Two Med jeeps and two Jeeps towing A/Tk Guns will cross over this bridge.

(g) Bridge Construction

The following bridges are being constructed by RE under Div arrangement :—
(i) Class 9 bridge at 198444 by 275 Fd Coy RE—expected to be finished by 0500 hrs 5 Nov.
(ii) Class 40 bridge at 208444 by 280 Fd Coy RE—expected to be finished by 0800 hrs 5 Nov.

(h) Tpt

(i) The following vehs only will move with the Bn in the initial stages :—

Two Jeeps towing A/Tk guns
('B' &'D' Coy Jeeps)
Two Med Jeeps
Sig Handcart (22 Set)

These vehs will cross over assault boat bridge.

(ii) These vehs will move with BNHQ marching personnel to assembly area under OC 5 Pl, leaving present locn at 1200 hrs.

(i) Routes

152 Inf Bde have established two main routes.
AMBER—X tks 209411—GIERSBERGEN 211430—KLINKKAERT 203437—X tks 197437 to Class 9 bridge 198444.
GREEN—X rds 160441—tk junc 165444—tk junc 178436—tk junc 178437—tk 197437.

(j) Tanks

(i) Two Sqns ERY are lining Canal and engaging opposite side from H to H+10.
(ii) On completion of bridge Sqn ERY will move up in sp of the Bn.

(k) Crocodiles

One Tp Crocodiles will be established area bridge 197444 by 1635 hrs 4 Nov and will fire for ten minutes from H to H+10.

(l) H—Hour—1635 hrs—Time tanks fire across Canal.

H+10 1645 hrs—Time of assault crossing by Bn.

7. Phase II

(a) Tps—Right 'B' Coy Left 'C' Coy.

'D' Coy will move in axis of 'C' Coy.

(b) Tasks
(i) 'C' Coy—area rd and tk junc 210466
(ii) 'B' Coy—area rd and tk junc 214464
(iii) 'D' Coy—will not move until 2 SEAFORTH have passed through. Coy will then join BnHQ in area 208453 and will act as reserve Coy.
(iv) The Bn will exploit to rly crossing 211474.

(c) Inter Bn Bdy—all incl 5 SEAFORTH SEMPKE 2045 —rd and tk junc 205464.

(d) Axis of adv—tk and dyke junc 204452—tk junc 210453—X rds 209463.

(e) Action on capture of objective
(i) Exploitation as ordered to rly crossing 211474.
(ii) 'B' Coy will be responsible for contacting 1 GORDONS on the Right in area 221464.

(f) Start Line—as indicated on ground.

(g) Z Hour—To be given by Bde on completion of Phase I. It is not expected that 2 SEAFORTH will be in a position to attack before 1820 hrs.

(h) Rate of Advance—100 yards in two minutes.

8. Arty

(a) Arty Trace will be issued later.

(b) Smoke will be put down across Bde front along line of dyke from H to H+15 lifting from H+15 to H+35 to SOUTHERN outskirts of DRUNEN and GROENWOUD.

9. MMGs—One Pl in Bn area SOUTH of Canal—to protect Right flank of bridgehead.

10. Mortars

(a) 4.2 Mortars will be in position area 185438 and will fire in sp of the assault.
(b) 3 Pl will fire in sp of the attack as ordered verbally from area 204443.

11. RE

(a) 275 Fd Coy will issue block and tackle for manhandling A/Tk guns over dykes—to be with Bn by 1000 hrs 4 Nov.
(b) One NCO and two sappers will join the Bn to supervise use of block and tackle and will report to OC 5 Pl by 1030 hrs 4 Nov.

12. 4 Pl

Sec 4 Pl will carry out tasks as ordered at H Hour and will then report to BnHQ where crews will dismount and act in local protection role

13. Tp of 243 A/Tk Bty will provide Bren Guns to sp from Canal bank initial assault.

14. Pioneers will be under orders OC 6 Pl.

15. Snipers will move with BnHQ.

16. Veh Marshalling Area

(a) A VMA will be established under SC 152 Bde in area 1643 by 1500 hrs 4 Nov.
(b) Serials of vehs as shown in App 'A' will be formed up in VMA by OC 'S' Coy and called fwd by Bde Control Centre along GREEN route to Class 9 bridge.
(c) No vehs will move after initial conc without authy Bde HQ.

17. Marking of Routes

(a) On completion of bridge main axis will be marked by Bde Pro as under :—
GREEN route to bridge at 198444—rd junc 199463—rd junc 210463.
(b) I.O. will arrange to mark routes as under :—
(i) route from assembly areas to Coy FUPs.
(ii) route from Assault Boat Bridge to main Bde axis.
(iii) axis of 'B' Coy in Phase I. Thence axis of BnHQ in Phase II.

ADMIN

18. Tpt—See App 'A.'

19. Med—

(a) RAP will be established by 1530 hrs at FARM 207436.
(b) An Adv Post with two Med Jeeps will be established at 'B' Coy's crossing.
(c) Until RAP is established over Canal evacuation of cas will be through 'B' Coy's crossing.
(d) On completion of Phase II MO will arrange to establish Adv Jeep Post NORTH of Canal.
(e) One Stretcher Bearer sec will come under comd and will report to RAP by 1030 hrs 4 Nov.
(f) CCP will be established area SPRANGSCHE VAART 1543 by 1000 hrs.

20. Feeding

(a) A 'tiffin' meal will be eaten at 1115 hrs.
(b) Tea and dinners will be cooked during morning 4 Nov and issued to Coys in assembly areas at 1500 hrs.
(c) OC 'S' Coy will detail one empty carrier to report to 'B' 'C' 'D' & 'HQ' Coys by 1030 hrs 4 Nov to convey containers. These carriers will move at 1200 hrs with marching personnel of Coys.
(d) A hard haversack ration will be issued to each man at 'tiffin' meal at 1115 hrs.
(e) Coys will arrange to load Compo rations for 5 Nov on Coy Carriers.

21. Amn

(a) As much amn as possible will be carried on the man.
(b) A Bn reserve AP will be established by the RSM in locality 203437 by 1500 hrs as under :—
SAA—12000 rds, Sten—2 boxes, PIAT—36 bombs, 36 Grens—12 boxes, 2" Mortar—6 boxes HE, 3 boxes Smoke, 3" Mortar—10 boxes.

22. Weapons

(a) PIATs will be carried on the man.
(b) Lifebuoys may be carried on the man or on Coy Carriers.

23. Os C. Coys will ensure that all men carry four sandbags.

24. PW—PW will be evacuated through BnHQ to Bde HQ.

25. Wireless

(a) S.O. will issue Wireless diagram to Coy Sigs.

(b) 46 Set has been allotted to the Bn as an additional Rear Link.

(c) 22 Set on Handcart will move with BnHQ on foot. A second 22 Set will move with Serial 1 of Vehs.

26. Line

S.O. will arrange to continue Bde line fwd of BnHQ at 203437 as BnHQ moves up.

27. Success signals

Success signals if required are allotted to Coys as under and will be used throughout the operation.

Coy		2″ Mortar Flare
' A '	...	Multi Star
' B '	...	RED
' C '	...	WHITE
' D '	...	GREEN

28. Codewords—See App ' B '

29. BnHQ

(a) BnHQ will be established by 1500 hrs at KLINK-KAERT 203437.

(b) It is anticipated that BnHQ will cross over ' D ' Coy's crossing simultaneously with ' C ' Coy.

(c) At end of Phase I BnHQ will be established in area ' B ' Coy 208452.

(d) During Phase II BnHQ will move up main Bn axis to area 209463.

30. ACK.

P. D. NAIRNE,
Captain and Adjutant.

Appendix ' A '

Issued in conjunction with 5 Seaforth Op Order No. 9.

Organisation of Transport.

Vehicles with Assault

See para 6 (h) (i).
' B ' & ' D ' Coy Jeeps will report to OC 5 Pl by 1030 hrs 4 Nov.

2. ' F ' Echelon

' F ' Echelon vehs have been allocated to Serials as under and are shown in order of priority for crossing the canal. Vehs will assemble at BnHQ by 1200 hrs and will be formed up by OC ' S ' Coy.

(a) Serial 1

C.O's Carrier
S.O.'s Jeep
RA Bty Cdr's Carrier
RA Bty Cdr's H Track
ERY Sqn Scout Car
Four Coy Carriers
One Sec A/Tk Guns (5 Pl)
C.O's Jeep

(b) Serial 2

One Sec 4 Pl
One Sec Wasps
One Sec A/Tk Guns (5 Pl)
3 Pl

(c) Serial 3

Four Coy Carriers
Bde Rear Link
Bn H Track
Amb Car
RAP 15 cwt
HQ Coy Scout Car
I.O.'s 15 cwt and trailer

(d) Serials will move under OC ' S ' Coy by route UDEN-HOUT 2038—SCHOORSTRAAT 1839—LOON OP ZAND 1540—X rds 145437—rd junc 160441 to VMA in locality 1643.

(e) Head of coln will be past SP rd junc 212375 at 1315 hrs.

(f) OC ' S ' Coy will despatch a DR to report as guide to the SC at tk junc 163442 ten minutes ahead of coln.

3. ' A ' Echelon

' A ' Echelon, organised as under, will remain in present locality under Capt. L. Macgillivray and will NOT move except on orders of BTO.
Rifle Coys—2 X 15 cwts each
Amn—2 x 3 tonners & 1 × 1 × 15 cwt. 3 & 4 Pl Carriers (Taxis)
Sig Pl—1 x 15 cwt
' S ' Coy—1 x 15 cwt
6 Pl—1 x 15 cwt
Remainder of vehs will join ' B ' Echelon in present locn during afternoon 4 Nov. ' B ' Echelon will be Bded under BTO.

268

269